Jesus sound explosion

Jesus sound explosion

by Mark Curtis Anderson

The University of Georgia Press
Athens and London

Published by the University of Georgia Press
Athens, Georgia 30602

Designed by Mindy Basinger Hill
Set in New Caledonia by Stephen Johnson
Printed and bound by Maple-Vail
The paper in this book meets the guidelines for permanence and durability of the Committee on Production Guidelines for Book Longevity of the Council on Library Resources.

Printed in the United States of America
07 06 05 04 03 C 5 4 3 2 1

Library of Congress Cataloging-in-Publication Data
Anderson, Mark Curtis, 1961–
Jesus sound explosion / by Mark Curtis Anderson.
p. cm.
ISBN 0-8203-2554-6 (alk. paper)
1. Anderson, Mark Curtis, 1961– 2. Baptists—United States—Biography. 3. Popular music—Religious aspects—Baptists. I. Title.
BX6495.A64 A3 2003
286'.1'092—dc21 2003006541

British Library Cataloging-in-Publication Data available

winner of the
associated writing programs award
for creative nonfiction

for patricia

★in loving memory
of ron and carol eckert

contents

acknowledgments

Enormous thanks and love to Mom, Dad, Marna, and Marshall for putting up with me all of these years, letting me write about it, and loving me anyway. Thanks and love also to Betty, Jim, Evelyn, Arlen, and Ashly.

Grateful, heartfelt thanks to:

Sue William Silverman, Marc Sheehan, Stephen Barnett, the Associated Writing Programs, and the University of Georgia Press for making this publication happen.

Patricia Hampl, Julie Schumacher, and Charlie Sugnet for close reading and generous feedback at crucial points in this book's development.

Valerie Miner, Madelon Sprengnether, Michael Dennis Browne, Maria Fitzgerald, Diane Glancy, and all of the teachers and students in the creative writing program at the University of Minnesota who helped shape sections of this book.

Haddayr Copley-Woods, Julie Gard, Scott Muskin, Margie Newman, Susan Taylor, and Stacy Thieszen (the w/cheese writer's group) for reading the bulky beast and giving tremendous encouragement at Matt's.

Julie for reading and listening to me read the earliest stories and poems.

Debbie Blue, Jon Colburn and the folks at *Spout,* John Engman (R.I.P.), Cynthia Fogard, Kim Fortier, Jan Zita Grover, Joseph Hart,

Bill Hayes, Pete Hedberg, Jean Henze, Joel Hodgson, Kevin Kling, Dave Koenan, Jim Larson, Sara McDonnell, Russell Rathbun, Jerod Santek, Patricia Savanick, Mark Stenberg, and Barton Sutter for saying yes.

Everyone at The General College of the University of Minnesota, especially my current and former officemates, Barbara, Jan, and Patty, and all of the good people in the writing program.

Special Thanks to Bruce Springsteen, Jon Landau Management, Bruce G. Grossberg, and Howard L. Wattenberg for generous permission to reprint lyrics from the following songs:

"Born to Run" by Bruce Springsteen. Copyright 1975 Bruce Springsteen (ASCAP). Reprinted by permission. All rights reserved.

"Tenth Avenue Freeze-Out" by Bruce Springsteen. Copyright 1975 Bruce Springsteen (ASCAP). Reprinted by permission. All rights reserved.

"Badlands" by Bruce Springsteen. Copyright 1978 Bruce Springsteen (ASCAP). Reprinted by permission. All rights reserved.

"Something in the Night" by Bruce Springsteen. Copyright 1978 Bruce Springsteen (ASCAP). Reprinted by permission. All rights reserved.

"Racing in the Streets" by Bruce Springsteen. Copyright 1978 Bruce Springsteen (ASCAP) by Bruce Springsteen. Copyright 1978 Bruce Springsteen (ASCAP). Reprinted by permission. All rights reserved.

"Prove It All Night" by Bruce Springsteen. Copyright 1978 Bruce Springsteen (ASCAP). Reprinted by permission. All rights reserved.

"Darkness on the Edge of Town" by Bruce Springsteen. Copyright 1978 Bruce Springsteen (ASCAP). Reprinted by permission. All rights reserved.

"My God, I Love Thee (O Deus, ego amo te)" from *The New English Hymnal,* translated from Latin by Edward Caswell. Reprinted by permission of The Canterbury Press Norwich.

"Gladys Snow" appeared in the Fall 2001 issue of *Spout.*

a note to readers

The following names are fictitious: Jon Ackerman, Jerry Bergman, everyone named Ed, Dan Griffin, Uncle Howard, Ken, Dr. Graham Lewis, Nolan McCormack, everyone named Mike (except Mike the drummer), Jane Owens, Justin Owens, Gordon Rasmussen, Rick, Stan, Stephanie, Steve, the Thomas boy, Tim, Bob Williams, and Alex the jerk.

Jesus sound explosion

wally johnson rides by
an introduction

Seven years ago, before Julie and I divorced, I sat smoking a cigarette on the oak-shaded porch of our tan stucco house in St. Paul, relaxing before I bused to my one-to-nine shift at the Electric Fetus, a big independent record store in Minneapolis.

The smoke goes in, the smoke comes out. Life had become difficult and I needed additional evidence that I was still doing what I naturally did: breathe in breathe out breathe in breathe out breathe in breathe out breathe in breathe out … cigarette smoking sometimes seems more like a good breathing exercise than a bad habit.

Breathe in breathe out breathe in breathe out …

And there on Lafond Avenue in the late-morning sunshine, Wally Johnson, my sixth-grade Sunday school teacher, bicycled by. Wally was looking intent, looking old, whiter-haired and riding slow, paying careful attention to every pedal rotation. I was surprised to see him riding at all. How old was he? Must have been in his eighties. How startling to see slow-riding Wally so alive in that present, that past. He seemed old when I had him as a Sunday school teacher over twenty-five years earlier—as men who are in their sixties seem old to boys who aren't yet in their teens.

Well, I became a teen, we moved to California, I went to college, I got married, I tried adulthood, adulthood tried me, the divorce became inevitable, and before that morning on the Lafond porch (because the recent past felt distant and the distant past felt ancient), Wally was dead to me. As were all of the people at my dad's old Central Baptist Church, though the place was less than a half mile from where Julie and I were living.

I wanted to shout, "Wally! Hey Wally." Stop him and talk to him. Say, "Remember me? Mark Anderson. Pastor John Anderson's middle child. You taught my sixth-grade Sunday school class."

But that would have required me to step into a past that I didn't want to acknowledge at that moment. I was, after all, smoking a cigarette, something that, twenty-five years earlier, I never dreamed I'd do, good Baptist minister's son that I was. I would have to put the cigarette out to become the pastor's son Wally would surely remember. And I didn't want to startle Wally, disrupt his careful pedaling rhythm, cause him to fall.

There I was then, here I am now, and I don't know how to explain this. There I was then, here I am now, and now looks nothing like what I pictured. The straight and narrow way has been abandoned, the way to get home has been lost, but Wally Johnson, it seems, has been riding by all this time.

I want to say that Wally Johnson was the best Sunday school teacher I ever had—because I actually remember something he said that's worth remembering. He said it every Sunday: "It's good to be alive. Don't ever forget that it's good to be alive." Do I remember, really remember, anything else that a Sunday school teacher said? Besides the standard fare: the essential Jesus Christ as personal Lord and Savior, the Bible verse memorizations and interpretations, the Old and New Testament stories that got told and retold so many times that the telling became one collective voice. What gets told.

I remember "It's good to be alive" because it was so unlike anything else I heard in Sunday school. Everyone else told me that this life was mostly a vale of tears and grief that was good only for saving souls and preparing them for the next world, the much better world after this one. Responsible Sunday school teachers could maybe say, "It's good to be alive—if you are living in Christ." They could make us memorize Jesus' words in John 10:10: "I have come that you might have life, and might have it more abundantly." But that abundant life required a personal decision to accept the Jesus Christ who died for the sins of this world. Alone, without qualification, "It's good to be alive" is a denial of original sin, a denial that we are in need of salvation, in need of forgiveness, from the time we are born.

We were to be in the world but not of the world.

Wally was telling us something secret, something that he wasn't supposed to tell us, something that he thought without scriptural backing: that living in the here-and-now world was, quite simply, good. Of all the things he might have said every week, he chose to say that. By and for what authority? Who was he saying it for? God, perhaps. Certainly not Jesus Christ. Jesus might say, "I didn't die on the cross for it to be good to be alive."

Every year, on the first Saturday in December, Wally took his sixth-grade Sunday school class ice skating at Aldrich Arena in North St. Paul, where he and his wife, Alice, skated every Saturday.

Wally and Alice wore speed skates with blades twice as long as the ones on my hockey skates, as did most of the adults who skated in time, in pairs, to the Aldrich organ music. Their steps were long, slow, and synchronized, but they moved much faster than they looked like they should be moving. This made the pairs seem all the more graceful: they looked slow, as they stepped together in time, but they moved fast.

The rest of us—boys with black hockey skates, girls with white figure skates—got tired just watching them. Before long, we headed for the bleachers. Wally and Alice smiled each time they passed us, their audience of youngsters. They even waved the first time they noticed us watching.

Wally began a Central Baptist tradition that older siblings told younger siblings about, and we all came to expect it when we got into his class. After the annual skating outing, he brought his whole Sunday school class, ten or fifteen kids, to his corner grocery store after closing time. It was an old dusty store on St. Paul's Rice Street: creaky, graying, wooden floors in need of a good sand and varnish; shelves of shredded wheat, Tastee white bread, Fairway peanut butter, Old Dutch potato chips; walk-in coolers well stocked with whole milk, orange juice, RC and Diet Rite cola, Dad's Root Beer, and every flavor of Shasta.

The surrounding neighborhood housed plenty of people who were down on their luck, so Wally extended credit to anyone without enough money to pay. Behind the counter he kept a box of index cards to write purchases of the on-credit buyers. Before going to the store with my Sunday school class, Dad took me there one Saturday. I remember a woman standing at the counter, telling Wally that she needed only two loaves of bread, some peanut butter, and some milk—she knew that she was a couple of months behind, but she would pay very soon. Yes, very soon. Wally sighed softly and smiled, but he didn't say no. Folks have to eat.

When Wally brought my Sunday school class there after Aldrich skating, the "Closed" sign was in the front window. I'd never been in a store after it closed. We entered through the back door, Wally turned on the lights, and then he gave us each a medium paper bag.

"Fill 'er up," he said.

We'd heard that this would happen, but we still couldn't believe it: whatever we wanted, whatever would fit.

"Go ahead," Wally said.

I started slowly, and then I went wild: potato chips, pop, candy bars, gum, baseball cards, Hostess Twinkies, football cards, Hostess cupcakes, hockey cards, beef jerky, a scouring pad for Mom, a lightbulb for Dad, anything I wanted, all that would fit.

Was this, I now wonder, a Sunday school lesson on grace freely bestowed? As I write it, I disbelieve it. Are those brown bags larger in memory?

On that morning, on the screened-in porch of the old house on Lafond, Wally seemed like a ghost rider. I could have broken the reverie and spoken to the image. I may have entered its world. I might have said something to Wally. At the very least, he would have remembered my dad.

But I had the cigarette to finish. And reunions with people I used to go to church with, reunions with people from my evangelical Christian past, tend to take too much energy. What would happen if I made it known to a single Central Baptist member that I was who I was and I lived in the neighborhood? Would I immediately get hundreds of dinner invitations? Would I be asked to explain, with a mouthful of pot roast, why I no longer attend church? What would I say?

Not that Wally would have asked those nagging questions. He was looking too feeble to proselytize. All it would take, though, was one Wally Johnson to say to someone, "I ran into John Anderson's son, Mark, the other day. He's living on Lafond, just off Fry."

"John Anderson's Mark is living on Lafond? Just off Fry? Well, is he ever going to visit us here?" Central Baptist is one block from Fry.

I had no doubt that all around me, in that St. Paul Midway neighborhood, mere blocks from the church of my father's glory years, deep within my mother's thickest nostalgia zone, were people who knew me. Knew me then and would believe that they still knew me. Or had a right to.

And I wanted to remain anonymous on that porch. I didn't want word to get out that Pastor John Anderson's son and daughter-in-law were living in the neighborhood. I know too well my tendency to become the son of my father when the occasion arises. When I feel called to become that son. Would I, out of guilt and obligation, decide to visit Central Baptist on a Sunday or two? I'd already ventured into more of that past than I cared to admit. Where would it begin and where would it all end?

Sometimes it is easier to remain the image that has been created and leave well enough alone. The past doesn't return without a price.

So I said nothing. I let Wally ride on by. I let him pass.

I'd be lying, though, if I said that this was the first time I'd thought of my evangelical Christian past or the first time I'd thought of Wally

Johnson. I'd be lying if I said that Wally Johnson's riding by spun me into this reflection.

One April afternoon in the late eighties, around the time when Julie and I got married, around the time when I started my difficult student teaching assignment at Minneapolis South High School, I stopped into a Minneapolis Goodwill store.

It was one of the first spring days above sixty degrees, and snow was melting everywhere. The snowmelt prompted a "freewriting journal" assignment that I was to give my ninth graders: "Look at what the spring uncovered." I thought this was clever and metaphorical, they thought it was as stupid as everything else. That's pretty much how my student teaching went.

Still, it was spring, I was newly married, and there was a Goodwill store just blocks from our tiny apartment, so how bad could things be?

I was, as always, looking for more records. Some of my favorite records have been found in secondhand stores, like the time I found Prince's first five LPs in perfect shape, a perfect Bob Dylan and The Band *Before the Flood,* and a playable Tony Bennett *Greatest Hits* double set. All on the same morning, all in the same place, each for fifty cents (and double LP sets were priced as singles). I'd mention the location of the store, but then you might go there and find what I should have found. Fair is fair in the world of vinyl shopping: you discover your own little haunt.

Secondhand stores have some of the strangest collections of vinyl. Where else can you find *Hannah, the Ideal Mother,* by the Reverend C. L. Franklin, Tennessee Ernie Ford's *Greatest Hits, I Can Hear It Now: The Sixties* narrated by Walter Cronkite, six copies of the Renville High School Concert Band's *1975 Pops Concert,* and the cover of Elton John's *Friends* with Herb Albert and the Tijuana Brass's *Whipped Cream and Other Delights* inside?

Flipping quickly through the castoffs, I saw one that didn't just catch my eye: it winked (as used records do). That wink. That wink reminded me of my friendly old Sunday school teacher, Wally

Johnson, who sometimes caught me gazing around the sanctuary during my father's invocation. We'd both have our eyes open, but only Wally knew that it was all right to. Wally had worked this out with God, somehow. While most Central Baptist members thought it was most reverent to have their eyes closed during prayer, Wally thought that reverence meant keeping his eyes open.

Sometimes I'd sneak a look around the church during prayer—just to see what people looked like when they were praying—and then I'd meet eyes with Wally. Wink.

I winked back at the wink, then took a closer look.

There it was, in bold letters: *Jesus Sound Explosion: Recorded Live at Explo '72.* A relic from what I remember as the "Jesus Movement." On the cover of *Jesus Sound Explosion,* Johnny Cash (the man in black) and Billy Graham (the man in blue JCPenney slacks) stand arm in arm. Johnny's holding a "One Way" sign (an extended forefinger) and Billy's holding a Bible. For a backdrop they've got a blue pearl-shell drum set, a bass amp, and a mural of sanctified-psychedelic Peter Max–styled doodlings. Giant golden clouds, green stars, red bubbles, free-floating One Way forefingers, a purple and blue arch, and large signs that say "Smile: Jesus Loves You," "You have a lot to live, JESUS has a lot to give," and "Jesus: Like a bridge over troubled water"—all of this, plus Billy Graham and Johnny Cash.

Thousands of cutoff-and-T-shirt-clad young people sit in a large field below a blue sky, Dallas skyscrapers in the distance. Many have long hair, but about every ten feet or so, men and women who are clearly the Bible college graduates and youth pastors stand like guardians keeping the holy hugs and kisses in check. Short groomed hair, buttoned-down shirts, unfrayed shorts (shorts that were always shorts), and black horn-rimmed glasses. They know that the devil-beat of the music could, at any minute, propel this thing into an out-and-out orgiastic lovefest. They read about Woodstock. They shuddered at the pictures. They're trying to be happy that it's a "Jesus Festival," but they still don't feel comfortable associating the two. Jesus, festival.

As I gave the Goodwill clerk a quarter, asked for a bag, and carried the record out, I knew that I wasn't buying it only for the novelty. Without warning, the castoffs from the evangelical Christian past that I'd placed in the Goodwill bins of my memory were right up front again, winking and demanding my attention.

jazzy music
galesburg popscapes

The Parsonage: In the World but Not of the World

We were to be in the world, but not of it. We were of the parsonage, and the parsonage was of Bethel Baptist Church, and Bethel Baptist Church was not of the world, and the world was what came to be known as the sixties. Bethel Baptist Church faced east on Academy Street, and the parsonage faced east on Academy Street. Our side door opened onto the gravel parking lot and into the church, and the church remained with whoever dwelt within the parsonage. We dwelt within the parsonage, and the church was who we were.

There was something of the world called "jazzy music," and whatever jazzy music was, we were not. Jazzy music was any pop music with a backbeat, and any pop music with a backbeat was not us. The world was the jazzy music of the sixties that we did not know, and the place where we dwelt was the parsonage, which was owned by the church that was not of the world that was the sixties.

"Jazzy music" was the name my mom gave to any pop music with a backbeat. Maybe she didn't know the name "rock and roll," or maybe she knew it but didn't say it because she knew that "to rock and roll" meant to fornicate.

Dad didn't even give it a name. He only said, "Those electric guitars sound so twangy."

Mom and Dad didn't want us to know about jazzy music. They didn't ban it from our Galesburg, Illinois, parsonage, our home from 1966 to 1970; they just didn't tell us anything about it. How much did they know to tell? They must have known where jazzy music landed on the radio dial, as they flipped past on the way to the "inspirational" station. Beyond that?

Jazzy music was still too new for Mom and Dad to sanction and too easy for other Baptists to condemn. What might happen if they left the dial on the jazzy music station, if they stayed in that place? They were young and didn't have room in their lives for mystery. They had to be always watchful as they carefully created the "pastor's family" image, the likeness that we aspired to. Dad and Mom couldn't afford the luxury of private lives.

Bethel Baptist was my father's first and most conservative church, and it was always in plain view. We'd look out our north window and there it would be, the limestone church. Hi, church. Hello there. Look out a south window of Bethel Baptist, and there was the parsonage. Hello, Pastor John, Barbara, Marshall, Mark, Marna.

Mom and Dad could well imagine the deacon's meeting or sanctuary choir rehearsal disrupted by a devil backbeat and fuzztone in the distance.

"Where's that awful noise coming from?" someone would ask, looking out the window.

"Why, that's coming from Pastor Anderson's house! Pastor?"

He and Mom would be held accountable.

We'd be watching a variety show on television and the special musical guest would be a rock and roll singer. I'd savor these accidental encounters with creatures from a pop world that I couldn't reach. Mom and Dad, to their credit, wouldn't switch the channel—unless the clothes exposed too much skin or the dancing got, as Mom put it, "lewd." Instead, they sent jazzy music to a purgatory that we Baptists didn't believe in.

Mom: "I just don't like that jazzy music."

Dad: "Those electric guitars sound so twangy."

The Beatles

The Beatles, I'd heard, were the crown princes of jazzy music.

I once got scolded by a kindergarten Sunday school teacher as I ran around the room singing lyrics that I'd overheard another kindergartner singing: "She loves you yeah yeah yeah—she hates you no no no."

"The Beatles," she said, "are very very bad men. Your mommy and daddy would be ashamed if they ever heard you singing a song by them."

My parents never said that The Beatles were very bad men, but they got silent whenever I mentioned them. I wanted to know what bad The Beatles had done.

I asked Mom. It wasn't a question to bother Dad with.

"One of The Beatles said that…," she paused to catch her breath. "One of them said that The Beatles are better than Jesus Christ."

She swallowed and hoped that the Lord didn't only catch the tail end of what she just said.

She might have said "more popular than" instead of "better than," but I wouldn't have known the difference. One of them said they were something more than Jesus Christ. That's all I needed to hear. Case closed, deal done. Still, whenever I heard a song by The Beatles at a school friend's house, I wanted to hear it over and over, so I'd be able to play it in my head later and later.

I had school friends and I had church friends.

School friends knew all about The Beatles. When the movie *Yellow Submarine* premiered, school friends told me that I had to see it.

"It's just a cartoon," they said. "There's nothing bad in it."

Church friends wouldn't even mention it.

School friends didn't know "good" from "bad." They were going to Hell.

In a yellow submarine, maybe.

We were on a family camping trip, and, because it was raining, Dad and Mom decided to take us into a nearby town to see a matinee. Two movies were showing: *Yellow Submarine* and a Disney movie. Which Disney movie doesn't matter.

Hours from Galesburg, far from the eyes of Bethel Baptisters, we thought we might be able to talk Mom and Dad into letting us see *Yellow Submarine.* We begged and begged, they went off to talk alone about it.

They returned, arms folded across their chests. No, they said. We'd go to the Disney movie.

Did they refuse out of fear? The Beatles could, after all, be agents of the Devil, and this movie was a journey with them into the unknown. Or did they refuse out of common sense? We'd tell church friends what we'd seen on vacation, and the church friends would use that as ammunition: "But Pastor Anderson's kids saw it!" Maybe spending hard-earned vacation money—money dropped from the hands of the Bethel Baptist faithful—on *Yellow Submarine* would have been akin to taking the Lord's money, placing it in the Devil's offering plate, and then worshiping in a temple of jazzy music.

What if Jesus Christ returned to find us sitting there? Where would we spend eternity?

Gladys Snow

Bethel Baptist harbored a cargo of hardcore fundamentalists, neo-nineteenth-century revivalists still feeling the sting of public reaction to William Jennings Bryan and the 1925 Scopes "Monkey Trial." Not to mention Lennon's "more popular than Jesus" remark. These champions were determined to restore fundamentalism's good name and popularity.

Gladys Snow, for example.

Gladys Snow was a large, tireless, omnipresent church booster:

banquet organizer, director of the children's Christmas pageant, spokesperson for the Welcoming Committee, Women's Luncheon MC, Vacation Bible School song leader, my first-grade Sunday school teacher.

Every Sunday, Gladys implored her first graders to invite Jesus into their hearts, and she had a seemingly endless supply of flannel board paraphernalia to illustrate what this meant. Her beige cloth board stood on an easel above our heads. As she told Bible stories, she'd pull, from large envelopes, tiny flannel people and places and softly pat them onto the board. Pat pat pat. These were her people, her places, her stories.

"Once, Jesus and his twelve disciples were out on a boat on the sea."

She'd pull out a blue sea, a brown boat, a white-robed Caucasian Jesus, and twelve bearded white men.

Pat pat pat.

"There was a boy among the five thousand who had two fishes and five loaves of bread."

Down came the five thousand, up went a little white boy bearing a basket of fish and bread.

Pat pat pat.

While we were still in flannel storyland, hypnotized, she'd give the invitation.

"Jesus says, 'Behold I stand at the door and knock.' Jesus is standing and knocking on the door of your heart."

Up went a big red heart with a door in the center, and, just outside the door, a forlorn Jesus with a fist raised to knock.

Pat pat pat.

"If you ask Jesus to come inside, the door to your heart will open and Jesus will live there forever."

Another flannel set showed a black, sin-stained heart, a heart in need of cleansing.

"If you ask Jesus into your heart, your heart will become as white as snow."

"Gladys Snow, white as snow, Gladys Snow, white as snow," I

repeated later. "Gladys Snow, white as snow, Glad as snow, white is snow, Gladys snow, white is snow."

Gladys didn't mention to first graders the eternal punishment for leaving Jesus standing and knocking outside the door, but she expected my father to preach hellfire and brimstone every Sunday.

Lay evangelical theologians couldn't agree on "the age of accountability," the age at which a child would, if he or she died, go to Hell for not receiving Jesus into his or her heart; still, Gladys said, no one "of age," no one old enough to understand, should leave a church service without knowing beyond a shadow of a doubt whether they'd go to Heaven or Hell if they died that very day. An altar call, a chance to walk down the aisle to become saved, should be given at the end of every sermon.

Dad didn't agree.

"I want souls to be saved as much as any pastor, and I rejoice each time someone receives Christ into his heart," Dad, a pastor who emphasized God's grace over God's wrath, said to her once. "But I don't happen to think that telling people they're going to Hell every Sunday is the way to go about it. And, frankly, I'm not going to lose sleep over something that's in the Holy Spirit's control."

"Well you should be losing sleep over it!" she shouted at him. "You should be lying awake at night in anguish, praying for every lost soul that's on its way to Hell!"

One morning Mom was at Gladys's house for coffee.

As Marna played in the room with Gladys's son, Gladys railed on about how my father wasn't measuring up to her expectations. Her volume and pitch climbed higher with each new complaint: he wasn't preaching The Gospel; he was letting sinners slide; he wasn't saving enough souls; church membership wasn't increasing enough; people weren't tithing enough; not enough not enough not enough. The telltale sign of Bethel Baptist's moral and spiritual decline? The new youth pastor that Dad hired, a liberally inclined seminary graduate named Dick Johnson, played a Neil Diamond song in a high school

Sunday school class. Few at Bethel Baptist knew who Neil Diamond was, but they knew what he was not: a believer.

"*A Neil Diamond song!*" Gladys screamed, shaking her heavy King James Bible at Mom. "Whatever happened to the gospel message? Why isn't anyone preaching the gospel at the church anymore? Everything we've worked so hard for over the years at Bethel Baptist is being destroyed!"

She stopped and glared at my mother.

"But with you and your husband and that Dick Johnson leading the church, what do you expect?!" As she said the word "expect," she threw her Bible and just missed my mother's head. The Bible hit the wall on the other side of the room and dropped to the floor.

"I think I'd better leave now," Mom said. She got Marna and headed out the door.

As they got into the car they heard Gladys yell, "Wait! Wait!"

Gladys ran up to the driver's side window, peered in, and said: "Barbara, I love you—in the Lord."

The Snows never returned to Bethel Baptist.

The Restless Ones

Billy Graham and his people made a movie, *The Restless Ones,* that came to Galesburg theaters around 1967. The restless ones were living and breathing proof of what jazzy music could do to a life. The restless ones hung out in bars, smoked, drank, played pool, and drove souped-up Ford Mustangs and motorcycles far too fast. Then someone died in a very bad highway wreck, and this sure made everyone think.

Or maybe that was a different Billy Graham movie. Maybe every Billy Graham movie that I saw during childhood has merged in my memory and become *The Restless Ones.* They all had the same ending: everyone accepted Jesus Christ as their personal Lord and Savior and lived happily forever in the hereafter. Except for the foolish guy who died in the car accident. But he was the one who made everyone think. He died for their sins, and all things worked together for the good.

Dad brought home *The Restless Ones* soundtrack one afternoon. The title song had a lite-rock beat and a bunch of men and women singing verses about the wretched lives of the worldly rebels. At the end of each verse, they'd blurt out "the restless ones" in a way that reminded me of another jazzy music song I'd heard, the Batman TV theme. I don't know what happened to the record, but the song in my head goes something like Running and running and drinking and smoking in bars: *The Restless Ones!* Driving and driving their motorcycles and fast cars: *The Restless Ones!*

I played the song over and over, bouncing along with the beat, imagining the terrible places where the restless ones lived their lives and died their deaths.

Hippies

Hippies, I heard, also belonged in the world of jazzy music.

I got my first glimpse of them on a trip my family took to California in the summer of 1967, the Summer of Love. We spent a day in San Francisco and saw guys with hair longer than we'd ever seen (except in some pictures of Jesus), striped bell bottom pants, beards and mustaches, beads, and sandals.

Dad took a picture of a hippie passing out an underground newspaper, and when we showed slides of the California trip to Bethel Baptist Church members, the guy got a good laugh. Hippies were so strange to us that we had to laugh to keep from being scared unto death.

Hippies were the restless ones even Billy Graham couldn't convert.

Hippies got off at the very last exit on the freeway that jazzy music turned into.

Not even a best friend dying in a bad car wreck would make hippies stop and think.

I'm a Believer

Mom and Dad didn't forbid us from watching *The Monkees* TV show. The Monkees kept their thoughts about Jesus to themselves.

Once and only once, I heard them sing a song called "I'm a Believer," and it immediately became my favorite song. The best song I'd ever heard. The words said something about seeing a girl's face and being a believer after that.

A believer. That meant something in my world. Could they get away with that?

Mom might have called the song sacrilegious. Belief in the girl instead of belief in God.

I wanted to hear "I'm a Believer" more than I've ever wanted to hear a song again. I knew it was out there, on this planet for a limited time, but I didn't know how or where to find it. Maybe they played it on the radio, but that did me no good. Maybe they'd rerun the show. I'd probably be at a church potluck that night.

Some potato chip company had a promotional 45 giveaway. The 45s came inside specially marked chip snack packs. I went to the chip section while my mom shopped, and I shook the snack packs until I could see the title of the 45 inside. Most of them contained "Yummy Yummy," a song that I'd heard in passing and hated.

Where could I find "I'm a Believer"? Where in the world was that song?

Less of Messmore

My third-grade teacher, Mrs. Messmore, let us bring in records to play every Friday afternoon.

Mrs. Messmore was my brother Marshall's third-grade teacher the year before. Messmore. Did her name have anything to do with her hatred of anything messy—anything to do with why she demanded perfection from her students?

Mrs. Messmore loved Marshall because he strove for perfection and, of all her students, came closest. This is common among pastors' kids, especially firstborn sons. Marshall was a straight-A student, the most well-behaved at school and church, the star athlete on the playground, the model boy, the one most likely.

Mrs. Messmore hated me because I strove for less-than-perfection and was the messiest of all her students. In comparison to Marshall, I was the unlikely one. I didn't have anything against perfection: I just didn't know how to get there. I got Bs and Cs and now and then As, and I took a ridiculous amount of time to complete my assignments. I didn't understand things, so I daydreamed. I understood things even less, so I daydreamed even more. Especially when we were doing numbers.

Plus, I was a lousy athlete, consistently the last one picked when choosing sides for teams.

Of all my oddities and imperfections, though, my handwriting was the one that sent Mrs. Messmore reeling. The eye-hand coordination problem that made me a wretched athlete also made cursive letters very difficult to loop together. In a parent-teacher conference with my mother, Mrs. Messmore blew up about my sloppiness. She told Mom that she was giving me a D in handwriting, my first ever elementary D.

Mom protested, begged for mercy.

"Mark will be so hurt if he gets a D. He's trying so hard. He just idolizes Marshall, and Marshall only gets As."

Call it concern, call it manipulation, call it negotiation, call it love: Mom tried to talk Mrs. Messmore out of giving me a D.

"It's not my problem that Mark isn't as good as Marshall!" Mrs. Messmore shouted. "Just look at these, just look at this mess! Just look at this awful handwriting!"

She grabbed a stack of my papers, crumpled them up into balls, and threw them at Mom. "How would you like to read these? How would you like to read these?"

Why were Galesburg women always throwing stuff at Mom?

Mrs. Messmore used to say to me, "Why can't you be like your brother Marshall? Marshall was the best student I've ever had. You should try to be more like your brother. Marshall got all As. His handwriting was beautiful!"

Mrs. Messmore once paddled our whole class, every single third grader, for getting too many problems wrong on a math test. One by one, we walked by her desk and she slapped us on the ass with a thick wooden board.

And this Mrs. Messmore was the teacher who let us bring in records to play on Fridays. It seems odd to me now. She had to win our hearts somehow, I suppose. Friday records must have been an essential part of her elaborately messy system of rewards and punishments.

I wanted to bring in the most popular jazzy music song, the song that would change lives and get Mrs. Messmore on my side. I wanted to make everyone in the class feel like I felt when I heard "I'm a Believer," but I owned no 45s.

I asked Mom for assistance. I don't know what I was thinking. That maybe she had a secret stash of jazzy music records?

"I want to bring a record to school on Friday."

"What kind of a record?"

I looked at my feet and mumbled, "Jazzy music."

"Jazzy music? I don't have any jazzy music records. I just don't like that jazzy music."

She said it differently this time. Like it was an issue of personal taste more than morality. Jazzy music itself, that is—not the world to which it belonged. She wouldn't encourage it, she wouldn't play it on the radio, but maybe she'd let us listen to some of it.

Some.

"I've got some records," she said, "that are a little bit jazzy. Well, I don't know if they're jazzy, but they're fun."

Fun records.

She showed me some old records of hers with cartoon drawings of teenagers who looked like the gangly young people on Twister game boxes. The records had titles like "Songs for Young Folks" and "Let's Sing!" Records that she and Dad bought to learn new songs for church youth sing-alongs. I knew right away that they wouldn't do.

I begged her to take me record shopping at a local department store.

"I'm the only one in my class who has never brought in a record to play."

This was a lie, but it worked. Not being of-the-world didn't *have* to mean being all alone. She knew this. She gave me a dollar and we went to the store. She wandered off to the women's clothing section and left me alone to browse. If someone from church saw me and said something to her about it, she could say she lost track of me, thought I was looking at toys.

I looked and looked, but I couldn't find a 45 of "I'm a Believer." Maybe it was only on an album. Might as well be on Mars.

What to buy?

The Beatles were out of the question. The only singer who I recognized the name of was Glen Campbell. I wanted to hear Glen Campbell because his *Good Time Hour* was on TV when I couldn't watch it: during Sunday evening church. That's how I knew Sundays back then: Sunday school, Sunday morning church, Sunday dinner, Sunday evening church. Believers, I knew, went to Sunday morning church and Sunday evening church, which meant that people who had Sunday evening TV shows couldn't be believers. If they were believers they'd be in church instead of tempting Christians to stay home and watch them.

Glen Campbell's *Good Time Hour* was the opposite of Sunday evening church, our Old Time Gospel Hour. He and his guests sang the songs that I longed to hear while we at Bethel Baptist sang for the thousandth time, "Heaven came down and glory filled my soul."

But nothing came down and nothing filled my soul.

The 45 that I bought—my first 45—was Glen Campbell and Bobbie Gentry singing "Less of Me" and "All I Have To Do Is Dream."

When I played the songs, that down feeling came over me. Both were slow ballads, and I wanted what I didn't have a name for yet: rock and roll. "Less of Me" even had lyrics that reminded me of the Golden Rule I'd learned from Gladys Snow: you should think more about other people and not so much about yourself.

I didn't buy a jazzy music 45 to hear another Sunday school lesson.

When I played it in Mrs. Messmore's class, it got a lukewarm response.

The other kids said it was okay and I agreed.

No one believed very much in "Less of Me."

Butch and Mark: Foster Brothers

I had foster brothers for two Galesburg years: Butch and Mark. Foster brothers weren't real brothers, but they knew all the songs on the radio.

Butch and Mark were almost teenagers, a few years older than Marshall and me. Butch had bangs cut straight across his forehead and showed everyone his muscles a lot. Mark was a wiry kid with stringy blond hair. My hair was brown, so Mom and Dad could tell us apart even though we had the same name. Butch liked to fistfight a lot, but Mark was quiet and nice—except when Butch needed help getting Marshall or me to surrender.

Butch and Mark's mother, a sister of a woman at Bethel Baptist, was an unbeliever. She was dying of cancer, and her husband, Butch and Mark's truck-driver dad, died at the wheel a couple of years earlier. Butch and Mark said that he died in his sleep, but Mom and Dad said that he didn't really die in his sleep.

We four boys slept on two bunk beds: Marshall above me, Mark above Butch. We mostly got along after the bedtime lights went out. That's when the songs started.

Butch and Mark sang (softly, so Mom and Dad wouldn't hear) songs that they knew and loved, songs that I longed to hear: "Gitarzan," "One," "And When I Die," "Strawberry Fields Forever," "Yellow Submarine," "Come Together," "Incense and Peppermints," "Hitchin' a Ride," and on and on and on. I'd never heard these songs on the radio, but Butch and Mark knew how to sing them the jazzy way.

I understand now: Butch and Mark were replaying the songs that they'd never hear on our radio, songs that brought back their real family.

Once, after visiting their older sister, who lived alone in their tarpaper shack, they returned to our house with a handful of 45s and one album (Iron Butterfly's *In-A-Gadda-Da-Vida*). Butch and Mark wanted Marshall and me to hear how close they'd come to singing the real songs. Dad and Mom gave them permission to spin them all in the parsonage, as long as they didn't play them too loud.

They wanted us to hear—as their mother died, as we later left them in Galesburg when we moved to St. Paul, as they became two more boys in the Knox County orphanage—that they weren't simply making up the lyrics and melodies of their real home.

Daddy Sang Bass

One evening, Dad came home with a big grin on his face, an "I've got a surprise for you" grin that he normally reserved for side-door entrances after time spent out of town. He pulled out of a brown bag a 45-rpm single in a Columbia Records jacket, the only 45 that Dad ever purchased for himself. As far as I know. He finally found it, he said, the song he'd heard on the Galesburg radio station: "Daddy Sang Bass," sung by Johnny Cash and June Carter Cash.

("What radio? Where?" I wondered.)

We were all happy to see Dad smiling about something different, something that wasn't church. Maybe this would become a hobby. Other dads had hobbies, so maybe Dad would get some too. He'd recently taken up handball with his new friend, Dan Lew, the Jewish oral surgeon across the street, and he could now (thanks also to Dan) name a favorite TV show: *Get Smart.* Dad and Dan would roar like we'd never seen at the madcap antics of detective Maxwell Smart and his evasion of the evil enemy, KAOS. I'd marvel whenever Dan said "Oh God" at something Maxwell Smart did, and then Dad wouldn't correct him for taking the Lord's name in vain.

A new sport, a favorite TV show, a "non-Christian" friend who took the Lord's name in vain, and now, a Johnny Cash and June Carter 45: this was a different Dad than we'd known.

The five of us gathered around the Magnavox console in the living room. Dad started to giggle, got red in the face, as he slipped the 45 onto the turntable and turned the switch to "automatic."

Every time they got to the part where Daddy Cash's bass dipped down into the underworld and Mama Carter's tenor soared to the top of the Bethel Baptist steeple, Dad laughed and laughed.

Because he was laughing so hard, we laughed too. How could

anyone keep from laughing after hearing a voice so low, followed by a voice so high, followed by a preacher dad's uncontrollable laughter?

Johnny and June sang about an unbroken circle in the place called the by and by, and that was Heaven.

And Dad kept laughing and laughing.

Folk Music

A college guy named Gary Hoffman lived around the corner in a gray tarpaper house next to the high school football field. On sunny days I'd see him sitting in the back yard fingerpicking his guitar, singing Top 40 hits, hymns, folk ballads, and camp songs. Marna played house with his little sister and Marshall was good friends with his neighbor Arly, and I used these connections to my advantage. When Marshall and Arly got sick of me tagging along, I'd wander into the Hoffmans' back yard instead of heading home.

Gary wore black plastic rectangular glasses, sideburns, and short brown hair. He didn't smile or say much. As long as I didn't request songs or ask questions, he didn't seem to mind giving concerts. Once, though, when I asked him to play "Sugar Sugar" by the Archies, he gave me an exasperated look and shook his head.

Gary sometimes sang in Sunday evening church. Once he did a version of "Amazing Grace" to the tune of "House of the Rising Sun." I didn't know "House of the Rising Sun" at the time, but years later, when I heard it on the radio, I recognized the melody immediately as Gary's "Amazing Grace."

"There is a house in New Orleans / that saved a wretch like me."

I asked Mom and Dad what they'd call this kind of music with one guy singing and playing an acoustic guitar. They didn't have a name for it. It didn't sound like hymns, but it wasn't electric enough to be jazzy music.

"I think it's folk music," Marshall piped up. "We learned about folk music in my third-grade music class at school, and that's what it sounds like."

My parents nodded in agreement. Now they remembered. Folk music. It was quite popular with the young people a few years back.

The confidence with which Marshall said "folk music" made me think he knew what he was talking about. Folk. My parents were my folks, my grandparents were old folks, we were all folks, and Gary Hoffman played folk music.

That spring, the high school kids from Bethel Baptist had an end-of-the-school-year pizza banquet in the church basement. The special musical guest: a Christian folk singer. Christian folk was the new thing. Mom and Dad said that we three children could attend if we were on our best behavior.

We walked downstairs and smelled the dark, pizza-scented basement glowing in the light of white candles set in Pepsi bottles. Red and white checkerboard tablecloths.

We didn't recognize the room—a room where, beneath fluorescent lights, we'd attended Sunday school, Vacation Bible School, Christmas pageant rehearsals, potlucks, Christian Service Brigade, father-son banquets.

We walked down to the upper room where teens held last suppers. Communion ceremonies with pizza for Christ's body and Pepsi for Christ's blood. I always knew that this room could be found somewhere in the church.

After the breaking of the crust and drinking of the soda, a man with shoulder-length brown hair parted in the middle, a thick mustache, a brown suede leather vest, black ankle boots, and bell bottom denims walked onto a wooden platform and sat down on a bar stool below a mike.

The folk singer.

The folk singer started singing songs about Jesus and the war and Jesus and the youth of today and Jesus and the suffering people of the world and Jesus dying for all of these. As if Jesus had something to do with the world. The folk singer's Jesus was right now. The folk singer's Jesus was here, now, today.

He played this one song about neighbors and friends using Heaven's name to hate and cheat each other, all to find a buried treasure that turned out to be nothing more than the words "peace on earth." After a bloody battle on Judgment Day, this soldier made of tin rode off mysteriously.

The song reminded me of The War that they showed on TV, but it seemed different than The War. The War was normal—there would always be The War—but neighbors and friends should not hate, cheat, and kill each other for buried treasures that no one wants.

It was as I'd been told: things in the world were not right.

But someday there would come a day of judgment. The world would pay for the sins of the world. The world would pay for the hating of neighbors and the cheating of friends. In the name of Heaven: they would pay.

The Longhaired Knox College Guy and the Book Room

My third grade passed most slowly. How could I quicken the pace? I was the slowest in math, always the last one done. By midwinter I was months behind. When I finally finished assignments, I got more right than wrong, but I took forever to get to the end.

Mrs. Messmore decided that I needed special tutoring.

When the cool, young, longhaired Knox College guy arrived with his guitar to teach music for three hours a week, she decided to pull me out of the class. I sat at a desk in a tiny book room with my tutor—Mrs. Messmore. While the rest of my classmates were learning "Leaving on a Jet Plane," "Both Sides Now," and "If I Had a Hammer," I was cooped up with stacks of unfinished assignments and a warped woman who yearned for the good old days of one-room schoolhouses, the years when boys were men, girls were ladies, and punishments were even more severe.

Constantly comparing me to my brother didn't seem to be working as a motivational strategy, so Mrs. Messmore employed a new tactic. Word was out that, come June, we were moving to St. Paul, Minnesota, where Dad would become the pastor of Central Baptist Church.

"When you get to your new school in St. Paul," she said, "you're going to have to do a lot better in everything. It's a big city and the kids there are going to be way ahead of you. The teachers will expect you to be better than you are now, and they aren't going to be as nice as I've been. They won't take this time that I'm taking with you to help you get your work done."

She scared me about the move to the city. The school would be bigger, the kids would be bigger and better, the teachers would be even meaner. Bad kids would beat me up for going too slow with everything, and mean teachers would beat me up for holding everyone else back. Bad kids and mean teachers and me, a real cipher in the snow.

Not Jazzy Music

"I want to bring another record to Mrs. Messmore's class," I said to Marshall on the way to school.

"What kind of a record do you want to bring?" Marshall asked. "None of the other kids in your class will like the music that Mom and Dad listen to."

"I want to bring a jazzy music record. Not Glen Campbell, this time. No one liked Glen Campbell. I want to bring some jazzy music."

"It's not called jazzy music."

"What isn't?"

"What you're calling jazzy music. Mom calls it that, but what you're calling jazzy music isn't jazzy music."

"What is it called?"

"I don't know. Not jazzy music. Jazzy music is jazz. Our music teacher played us a jazz record last year. When we had music class in third grade."

"I don't get to go to music class. I have to do math with Mrs. Messmore."

"That's why you don't know. Jazz is dumb. It's just a bunch of people playing horns really fast, and you can't even tell what song they're playing. If you heard it, you wouldn't like it."

"How do you know?"

"Because it's just dumb. I don't like it, so you wouldn't either."

This was mostly true. With a few minor exceptions, I didn't like what Marshall didn't like. I didn't even have the right name for what I liked, the music I longed for. All this time, I'd been calling it something it was not.

the jesus revolution

The New Parsonage

We arrived in St. Paul on a June day in 1970, and I was surprised to see that our new parsonage was about three or four miles from Central Baptist Church. Could a parsonage truly be a parsonage if it wasn't a stone's throw from the church? That's what Mom and Dad and everyone else was calling it, though: the parsonage.

This new parsonage expanded the definition of what a parsonage could be. The parsonage was only a house that the church owned, a house away from the church that the church bought for us, the pastor and family. It was church *property*, but it wasn't *the church*.

The road from Central Baptist Church was long and winding: down Snelling, past University, over the Midway Bridge, right on Midway Parkway, through Como Park, around Como Lake, down Wheelock Parkway, past Como Park Elementary school, left on Grotto, left on Cottage, and, oops, you passed it. Pull a U-ey at the end of the block, turn around, and it is the second house on the left, the one with the big picture window, the one with the birch and pine trees in the front yard: 748 W. Cottage. Yes, it looks a bit like a cottage. One story with a kitchen, a living room, a dining room, a den, two bedrooms, and a ping-pong table basement with a big bedroom that Marshall and I shared.

The basement bedroom felt so very far away from the church.

The parsonage could only be called "connected to the church" if all of St. Paul was connected to the church. Central Baptist Church people were spread far and wide throughout the Twin Cities, and the church ministry was not, Central people said, only in one building: it was in the whole city. The whole city, they said, was our mission field.

The church ministry was so big.

And Mom and Dad permitted jazzy music (but it's not called jazzy music) radio listening in the new parsonage. Marshall and I bought, with paper route money, an AM/FM clock radio that we could blast in the basement without fear of disrupting sanctuary choir practice.

We could tune into the same station, we discovered, anywhere in the city. Imagine: the same song played in the exact same way on hundreds of thousands of St. Paul radios.

But that song still wasn't of God. That song was of the world. As long as we knew that, we'd be all right. That song was of the world.

The Catholics and the Lutherans

There was a lot of the world between Central Baptist Church and our parsonage, and most of it belonged to the Catholics and the Lutherans.

I didn't consider them Christians, because they didn't call themselves "born-again believers." Most of them drank beer, many of them smoked cigarettes, and they were everywhere you looked. Their leaders gave them permission to do the things that we Baptists couldn't do. Everywhere you looked. Catholics drank and smoked a lot, Lutherans drank and smoked less, and Baptists didn't drink or smoke at all (except in the state of backsliding).

Yes, Catholics and Lutherans were all around us, filling up those miles between Central Baptist Church and the new parsonage, doing the things that world people did. How could they possibly be Christians? There were so many of them. We were the ones set apart, and they were the ones we walked faithfully among.

Yes, the world between Central Baptist Church and our new parsonage was filled, absolutely filled, with Catholic and Lutheran churches. One or the other on every block. There was even a Lutheran church across the street from Central Baptist Church—a Lutheran church whispering to our faithful: "Come and worship with us. If you're ever looking for something much *easier*, come and worship with us." How could so many Lutheran and Catholic churches possibly be preaching anything approaching The Truth?

People at Central Baptist said of the Catholics and Lutherans (the Lutherans, especially, since they seemed less serious about the whole thing), "Church is not really a place of worship to them. It's just a social club."

I remember riding past Lutheran and Catholic churches on Sunday mornings, and I saw men and women standing outside (men and women in their Sunday best) smoking shamelessly, without feeling a need to hide the sinful habit. There they were, the whole lot of them, standing outside the place of worship, smoking and socializing, like it was just any old place to smoke and socialize. Was theirs just a feel-good gospel preached from the pulpit, followed by a hearty, laugh-filled social time?

(Ha ha ha ha ha: Hell will be a very funny place to burn for eternity, won't it?)

Lutherans, Lutherans especially, couldn't fool me. I knew who they really were: Catholics in disguise. No, the Lutherans weren't fooling me with all of their "We're not Catholics, we're Protestants" talk. If they were truly not Catholics, if they were truly Protestants, why didn't they go to a *real* church? Lutherans were people who couldn't commit to Jesus Christ enough to become born-again believers, to become personal with the Son of God, to become Baptists. If they were truly Christians, they'd be us. And they so clearly were not.

At least Catholics gave the appearance of taking church seriously. They took being Catholics seriously. This didn't make them Christians, but it seemed more like faith than whatever it was that the Lutherans called faith.

Catholics built such overwhelmingly huge and present churches, they had schools all over the city and state, and they had a lot of people devoted to the full-time practice of being Catholics: priests, nuns, monks, teachers, missionaries … If you had any question whatsoever about how serious Catholics were, all you had to do was take a drive downtown and see that the St. Paul Cathedral was built on a hill that placed it higher than the Minnesota State Capitol. I toured the cathedral with my parents once, and I thought it was a tragedy that such devoted people, such serious people, people who would build such a monument to their faith, weren't, when it came right down to it, Christians.

They believed that their good works would earn their way into Heaven, so they had tons of people working for them, full-time, all of the time, for all of their lives. They had their best, their absolute best, people on the job. They went to confession regularly, they baptized their babies, they did everything they could to ensure salvation, but they'd never be Christians because they weren't born-again believers. After all of this they still wouldn't enter the kingdom of Heaven.

Those poor poor Catholics. Those poor Catholic kids who had to go to school in those silly matching uniforms. Did they think that uniformity would buy their way into Heaven? Did they think that uniforms would make them more noticed as a group, more presentable to God? Did they think that God would look down from Heaven and say, "Who are those people with the big churches and schools and matching uniforms? Are they ours? Let them all in, I say! Let them all in, every single one of them!"? Afraid not.

Those poor Catholic kids in their plaid dresses and navy blue pants and starched light-blue shirts and black shoes with laces, waiting for the bus to take them across town to their dark dark school. They couldn't go with us to the public schools, where we could wear bell-bottom jeans and tennis shoes and stylish shoes with buckles and sweatshirts and T-shirts and hair over our ears.

Those poor poor Catholic kids. Waiting for the bus in the below-zero February, in their parkas over their uniforms, thinking that all of this waiting for buses and wearing of uniforms was going to earn their way into Heaven.

(How arrogant of them, after all, to believe that they could earn or buy their way into Heaven. Grace was a gift freely bestowed. We Baptists knew that.)

They'd get outside the gates of Heaven and say, "We were the ones building those huge monuments to you, the ones wearing the uniforms, the ones clothing the naked and feeding the hungry."

God, our Jesus Christ, would say to them, "Depart from me! I never knew you."

All for nothing. All for nothing.

And the Lutherans wouldn't even be able to sell the appearance of dedication. What would they say to God, after all? "I was confirmed when I was fourteen years old. I went to church nearly every Sunday of my life."

God, our Jesus Christ, would say to them, "Unless a man be born again, he cannot enter the kingdom of Heaven. Depart from me, you cursed one. This is not a social club up here."

And those were the ones who surrounded us. Those were the ones we lived among.

The Eckerts and The Sure Foundation

Soon after we moved to St. Paul, my parents' best friends from Bethel College, Ron and Carol Eckert, joined us at Central Baptist Church. Ron and Carol were musicians who loved music. It's not a given that musicians love music, but Ron and Carol did. Of all the wonderful music in the world, they loved music the best in the sanctuaries of Baptist churches.

Ever since their Bethel College years, Dad and Ron had discussed this possibility: someday they would be partners in the ministry. Dad would be the head pastor, and Ron would be his minister of music, his closest associate.

If my only option in life was to remain in that evangelical Christian world (when I was much younger, I believed that it was my only option), that is how I would choose to remain there: I would be a minister of music.

Ron's face turned red whenever he directed, and his face turned even redder when his choirs crescendoed or de-crescendoed. He was so passionate, so intense, in his directing that he almost didn't fit into the Baptist setting—yet I can't imagine him fitting anywhere else. Leading the adult sanctuary choir, leading the contemporary youth choir (The Sure Foundation), leading the congregation in the opening and parting hymns, soloing with "His Eye Is on the Sparrow" as the ushers collected the Sunday evening offering: these things Ron was born to do.

He had a soaring tenor voice. I think of Caruso, Mario Lanza, and Pavarotti, but with less of the operatic drama and more down-to-earth Sunday evening gospel. Ron came from Indiana, and he never lost that Indiana in his voice. He might have ascended to even higher octaves, to grander operatic scales, if that had been his goal in life, but his Indiana reminded him that his call was to minister, not to bring more glory to himself.

Carol Eckert was the graceful soul that Central Baptist music moved through. A classically trained pianist, Carol accompanied the choirs and congregational hymn singing. Whenever she played, Carol did a circular rocking dance: she leaned toward the sheet music to glance at what came next, leaned back and half-closed her eyes to play the beautiful notes, smiled gently, leaned forward to read again, leaned back to play and hear and meditate. Wherever Carol was when she played the piano looked like the most joyful place in the world to be.

And this is how I return to Ron and Carol Eckert, the first musicians I knew and loved: they looked like a perfect union, a spiritual partnership, worlds and worlds shared.

In the mid-fifties, Dad and Ron sang together in a traveling Bethel College gospel quartet. I don't know much about the white gospel quartet tradition, but in memory it sounds like a cross between old-fashioned barbershop quartets and the more doo-woppy variety of black gospel: tight harmonies and arrangements that were closer to syncopation than anything else in white evangelical Christian churches. Many of these singing groups were very popular in evangelical spheres, and the gospel quartet tradition might be seen as one of Jesus rock's precursors, what the preboomer generations knew before Jesus rock existed. I'll leave the extensive research to the musicologists, but consider the fact that Elvis Presley (as Peter Guralnick documents in *Last Train to Memphis*) auditioned for and got rejected from a gospel quartet (a junior offshoot of the most popular white group of the day, The Blackwood Brothers, a group that Dad saw and loved) a year or so before his first Sun recordings. And as Elvis was playing barn jamborees and high school auditoriums across America, Dad and Ron's quartet toured Minnesota, did a summer tour in California, and even recorded a couple of ten-inch albums (one of which is on clear red vinyl). Elvis, Dad and Ron's quartet: they may have passed each other on the same stretch of California highway.

Ron and Dad fell in love with and married two women who happened to be best friends as well: Carol Martinson (Eckert) and Barbara Hartman (Anderson). The Eckerts and Andersons got married in the late fifties and spent most of the sixties apart from each other.

While we Andersons were languishing in the fundamentalisms of Galesburg (a small Land-of-Lincoln town that, in memory, seems as far away from the sixties as the late nineteenth century), the Eckerts lived in Fresno, California, just 150 miles south of San Francisco. They were much closer to the pulse of the era, more in touch with all that was relevant and happening. While we watched *The Restless Ones* on the Galesburg big screen, they saw the real migrating restless ones on the freeways, up in the mountains, hitchhiking through Fresno. The four Eckert boys even listened to AM radio and had real memories of the songs that we didn't get to hear in Galesburg.

Out on the West Coast, contemporary youth choirs were the new thing in evangelical Christian churches, and when the Eckerts came to St. Paul, the new thing migrated with them. They formed Central Baptist's youth choir, The Sure Foundation, complete with drums, bass, and electric guitar.

The Sure Foundation performed Christian rock operas with music similar to that of the group Up With People: large choirs singing backbeat-driven songs with uplifting lyrics and rock instrumentation. They sometimes included little dramatic scenes with the restless one

I'll call The Lost Guy. The Lost Guy was a wayward soul who recited short monologues about how confused he was and how it seemed he had nowhere to turn. Everything had been tried, but something was missing. Elvis, Dylan, The Beatles, pot, James Brown, Otis Redding, Miles Davis, San Francisco, Jefferson Airplane, acid, The Grateful Dead, Janis, Jimi, cocaine, the wild side, heroin, and then back to St. Paul: The Lost Guy would try anything once. All of these anythings only added up to this: something very big was missing.

The Lost Guy had his angry side. Sometimes he'd spout wicked diatribes about all the war and suffering in the world that God had turned his back on, all the evidence that God was dead. At first, The Sure Foundation songs only made him more angry, but his hardened heart gradually softened as the choir sang about Jesus Christ being real and relevant and personal and The One Way out of Lost Guy confusion.

At some point he'd have an epiphany and say, "He died for me! Jesus loves me! Jesus is real, man!" Everyone would embrace him, take him in, and The Sure Foundation would go into another upbeat number like "Christ Is Relevant Today": "Christ is relevant today … Christ is relevant today … He can bring you peace of mind—what could be more relevant?"

What could be more relevant than peace of mind? It wasn't a bad question. Not a bad question at all. The song taught me that new and useful word: relevant. What could be more relevant than the very word "relevant," three syllables that you could snap your fingers to?

It's easy for me to laugh at the idea of Jesus rock, but the undeniable truth is that the Eckerts were very courageous, in 1970, to bring drums, electric bass, and electric guitar into the Central Baptist Church sanctuary (only four years after fundamentalists across America burned Beatles albums because of John Lennon's unpopular remark). In the minds of many Christians, the backbeat of rock and roll was of the Devil. Many were careful to point out that this backbeat originated in Africa, not in Europe, and Africa, they assumed, belonged to Satan. That's why we sent so many missionaries there: to convert heathens and build churches and plant seeds and de-Satanize the continent.

Did Central Baptist's staunchest backbeat opponents realize that what they feared would happen was happening? Did the backbeat proponents really know? The backbeat was bringing new rhythms, new possibilities, new liberties, and a whole new groove into the Central Baptist sanctuary. It's true: I heard and saw live rock and roll for the first time at a Central Baptist Sunday evening church service. The Sure Foundation was performing a musical, *Tell It Like It Is,* with their newest member, a drummer named Mike. As Mike grooved his Ludwig (same as Ringo) five-piece set, I made an important discovery: with drums, The Sure Foundation rocked; without drums, they just sang and swayed. Mike's big beat was The Sure Foundation of that choir. It didn't matter to me that this contemporary Christian music was a whitewashed version of black gospel music and a pale imitation of real rock and roll. I can label it cooptation or appropriation, but I can't dismiss this: drums in Sunday evening church was much better than no drums in Sunday evening church.

The place worship first meant anything to me was in that Central Baptist sanctuary, where sacred and secular, African and European, white and black musical forms were all tossed into the mix, all echoing from the choir risers and up to the back pews of the balcony.

One Way

I listen to a distant call-and-response chant as I stand alone outside the big white pillars that hold up Como Lake pavilion. It is 1970 and I am nine years old.

"One Way," voices shout; "Jesus Is The," other voices answer.

The chant floats across the lake, and even the walkers on the other side can hear it on this sunny Sunday afternoon in May. Even the boys fishing for carp to kill can hear it spilling into the dirty water.

"One Way Jesus Is The One Way Jesus Is The One Way Jesus Is The One Way."

As they come around the corner, I recognize The Sure Foundation.

They are holding signs and banners with slogans: "One Way," "Jesus Is The Way," "I Am The Way The Truth and The Life," "Turn On To Jesus," "Jesus Is Right On," and "Jesus Is The Real Thing." As they march, chant, sing, and shout, I wonder: Is this a demonstration?

I'd heard a demonstration on one of the first LPs I ever bought: *Chicago Transit Authority* by the band Chicago. One of the many serious political songs on the album begins with a recording of protesters at the 1968 Democratic National Convention in Chicago.

"The whole world is watching the whole world is watching the whole world is watching the whole world is watching," the demonstrators chanted. I didn't understand what they meant by that, but I liked the rhythmic power of the voices chanting in unison.

The whole world is watching One Way Jesus is The whole world is watching One Way Jesus is The whole world is watching One Way Jesus is the whole world ...

And these demonstrators shout the name of Jesus on a wide-open city street by a lake where both the redeemed and unredeemed walk, bicycle, paddleboat, and fish on a Sunday afternoon.

Jesus, a flannel-board Sunday school secret of mine, is growing, getting bigger.

How big will Jesus become?

The Jesus Movement

All of a sudden Jesus was popular and jazzy music was inside the church, too. That quick, it seemed, and I still didn't have a name for it. Jazzy music was of the world one day, and in the Central Baptist sanctuary the next. People at Central started talking about the Jesus Movement, and I knew what they meant: Jesus was moving in, all around us.

All across the world, born-again believers were calling the Jesus Movement a "spiritual revolution." The young people returning to the faith of their parents, the converts discovering "a personal relationship with Jesus Christ" for the first time, were labeled "The Jesus Generation." Jesus even made it onto the cover of *Time* in 1971.

Rumors spread about the latest rock stars who'd turned their lives over to the Lord: Eric Clapton, Kris Kristofferson, James Taylor, George Harrison (until believers listened closely to "My Sweet Lord" and heard the background voices singing "Hare Krishna" along with "Hallelujah").

America had seen religious revivals before, but none so amen-able and adaptable to what elders had come to know as "popular youth culture."

How big would Jesus become?

The Jesus Movement may have been little more than media hype, but this didn't matter in my early-seventies preadolescence. Why wouldn't I welcome with open arms the St. Paul inner-city Godspell Christ Superstar Jesus, the hip king in big bell blue jeans, rainbow suspenders, a Superman T-shirt, Converse high tops, and curly dark hair combed into an Afro? This half-black-half-white Jesus appreciated The Beatles' hummable melodies, forgave Lennon's remark about who was more popular (because He was, once again), and clapped on the backbeat of rousing gospel numbers.

The church teen guys with long hair, the paisley college kids on the cover of *The Way* (the new *Living Bible* paraphrased for today's young people), the felt PEACE and LOVE banners hanging in front of the Central Baptist sanctuary, the men with sideburns and hair that almost reached their earlobes, the women in pantsuits and Afro perms, the drums the drums the drums: it was all much better than before.

The Wreck

Too many city churches were moving out to the suburbs, and members of Central Baptist felt that their church should intensify its efforts to bring in people from the St. Paul Midway neighborhood. "Inner City Ministry" was the buzz phrase among evangelical Christians in the early seventies, and the secular city was the new mission field. The Wreck, an evangelical flop pad in the church basement, was designed to reach out to city kids: the disaffected, the disillusioned, the troubled, the bothered.

I was about five years too young to hang out at The Wreck, but sometimes Dad let Marshall, Marna, and me just wander through on a Friday night.

The room was painted in fluorescent pastels that glowed under black lights, filled with telephone cable spool tables and black bar stools, and decorated with posters that shouted "Jesus Is Now!" and "Join the Jesus Generation." A white net hung across the ceiling above black velvet posters of the Last Supper and crucifixion of Christ. In a corner, a pink and purple bathtub filled with pillows cradled stoners and spiritually strung-out church kids.

You could come into The Wreck wrecked and come again wrecked, as long as you maintained. You could be broken in The Wreck. If you wanted to just sit in the bathtub and listen to the live Christian folk singers, that would be all right. You could hide in the darkness there. If the room became too sedative—or if you just plain started thinking too much—you could head out into the hall, get a Coke, and play pool, bumper pool, or ping pong in the fireside room next door.

This, according to its planners, was the ideal progression: teenagers would enter The Wreck and discover a new place to hang out, return a second time and become friends with members of The Sure Foundation, join The Sure Foundation, sing with the group at a church service in the sanctuary and decide that it wasn't such a bad place, accept Jesus Christ as personal Lord and Savior, get baptized, and become church members.

The Wreck was not, after all, a place to stay. It was a port of entry, a place to leave.

The Summer of the Jesus Freaks: The Ones That Got Away

These two guys, Steve and Ken, dropped into The Wreck, joined The Sure Foundation, accepted Jesus as their personal Lord and Savior, and in the summer of 1971 found themselves helping out with Vacation Bible School. I assumed that Steve and Ken, two longhairs just out of high school, used to be hippies. I called all longhairs "hippies" until people started calling some of them "Jesus freaks." Then the two became one. That's what I heard and that's what I saw.

"Who are the Jesus freaks?"

"Oh, they're the hippies who accepted Jesus."

So, some of the hippies were going to become Christians? Jesus freaks? Good news. I always kind of liked the hippies. What if Jesus freaks became more popular than hippies? What would John Lennon have to say about that?

Ken and Steve, an instant hit with all the church kids, became the unofficial Vacation Bible School mascots. We sensed that they'd eaten some wild fruit that we longed to taste, as if they'd actually been cartoon characters and knew which faces and goofy walks would make us laugh hardest.

We're on a Vacation Bible School picnic at Newell Park in St. Paul, and about fifty of us are chasing Ken and Steve. They run in giant, loping steps, hide behind trees, lie on the ground for a few seconds, get up and run as we almost catch them, pretend to stumble and fall, always escape. They are The Beatles to us, John and Paul. They hide in phone booths, and when we open the doors, no one's inside. They shrink to squirrel-size and hide in tree holes, then grow taller than the giant oaks and come after us. They're seen in fifty different places at the same time. We'll never catch them, but what if we do? What will we do? What will they do?

Steve and Ken stopped coming to church by December, and I felt this loss. I needed them on my side. Didn't they realize that? Rumors spread that they were "on drugs" again.

I saw Ken and Steve the next summer in the Como Lake parking lot next to the pavilion, where we went after Sunday evening church for the Como Hymn Sing. The hymn sing was a summertime extension of Sunday evening church, a Christian variety show led by Hugo Hagstrom, a round, bald man in his fifties. Hugo Hagstrom was the Twin Cities' evangelical Christian Ed Sullivan. Each week Hugo hosted regional and national guests who traveled the church circuit: the Palermo Brothers (who played Christian polkas on accordions), the Reedy Family Singers (their family name also describes their appearance and singing), the man who wore a kilt and played "Amazing Grace" on bagpipes, countless white gospel quartets and contemporary youth choirs, an occasional black gospel group, and a parade of winsome celebrity evangelists who'd close out the night with yet another sermon and altar call.

Dad and Mom took us to the hymn sings just about every summer Sunday. Because we'd already spent the better part of the day at church, they mercifully let us walk around the lake or sit in the pavilion ice cream parlor while they sang "Give me that old-time religion." The hymn sing was a joke to us kids, and we dubbed it The Hugorama. We'd sit in the parlor and mock the tone of the Reedy Family and sing "Give me that old-time religion" with exaggerated hillbilly accents. Ours was the new-time religion, the now-time religion. We wanted nothing to do with that old-time religion.

Neither did our old church friends, Steve and Ken. They hung out in the parking lot with the burnouts who drank, smoked, and played loud hard rock on Chevy van stereos to drown out the distant hymns.

When I passed and said "Hi, Steve and Ken," they pretended not to recognize me.

The Raptured Electric Guitarist

It's a February Sunday evening at Central Baptist, 1971. The Sure Foundation is performing a Christian rock musical in the sanctuary, and I'm sitting with my front-row church buddies. We're sitting where we always sit when The Sure Foundation performs: across from the drums. The more drums, the less churchy church feels. Drums somehow make church less than church, but larger than life.

On the stage beneath the choir risers stands a tall, thin electric guitarist I've never seen before. He's got long frizzy brown hair and blue-tinted wire-rimmed glasses. He's dancing in place more than anyone else, shaking his long locks to the power chords he strums, swinging back and forth to the backbeat, leaning into his leads.

He's not a church guy. He looks to me like an authentic rock star, and I've never seen one this close up. Maybe he's famous. Maybe he knows The Beatles. How did he wind up in The Sure Foundation? The Wreck. He must have stumbled into The Wreck on a Friday night. That's the explanation for every hippie-looking kid who ambles out of nowhere into the Central Baptist sanctuary.

On most of the songs, he strums rhythm, amp turned low. He looks a lot louder than he's playing.

The choir is in the midst of an up-tempo number, "Christ Is Relevant Today," when I hear a loudly amplified, screeching fuzz-tone from another world—a Sunshine of Your In-A-Gadda-Da-Vida, bottom heavy, ever-loving fuzztone that tickles the high octaves and rings up into the balcony, where it reaches, at last, the bored teens in the back pews who, for that one church moment, sit upright.

The guitarist nods up there, and duckwalks softly back into "Christ Is Relevant Today."

The solo startles me and my front row friends. We turn and look at each other with huge eyes. Even the choir members have big guilty grins. Something's been unleashed. The Sure Foundation has set foot in the most forbidden pop music world: acid rock. Right here in Sunday evening church, the new guitarist just played an acid rock solo. It couldn't have been much longer than four measures.

It came and left so quickly I can almost convince myself that it never happened. I wait the rest of the service for that sound to return to the sanctuary, but it never does.

The guitarist didn't return to church after that night, and I now wonder what happened to him. Was he taken up into the Rapture like a thief in the night? Can this memory preserve him? Was he just a bonus track, an alternate take? Did anyone else record him?

A Testimony in Drums

Mike, a drummer from a family of unbelievers, wandered into The Wreck one Friday night, and this changed my life. Something to remember, something that is too easy to forget: Someone walking into a room can change your life. Someone new walking into The Wreck can save your soul. And you thought for so long that it was the people in the room (or the room itself) offering salvation to the wayward one.

Mike joined The Sure Foundation as an unbeliever. Long before he left St. Paul for a professional drumming career in Nashville, he began calling himself a believer. In the years between, he made a convert of me. I understand now as I didn't understand then: I was one of Mike's disciples. Becoming a drummer wasn't something that I longed to do because of anything that I saw in the secular world. Ringo Starr didn't make me want to play drums. Karen Carpenter didn't make me want to play drums. No, I didn't pay attention to drums until Mike joined The Sure Foundation.

Mike always placed his drums on the floor below the choir risers, beside the communion table. Whenever The Sure Foundation sang, I sat in the front row, directly across from Mike's drums. Mike was the main event as far as I was concerned, and I rarely took my eyes off him. The Sure Foundation was merely a backdrop, a vehicle for Mike's superstardom. I knew which songs Mike played soft and steady and which ones he rocked hard and dazzled.

There in that sanctuary I saw, for the first time in my life, exactly what a drummer did. It amazed me that the drummer used all four limbs simultaneously: the right arm riding the cymbals, the left arm cracking the snare, the right foot kicking the bass drum (with a mallet attached to a pedal, of all crazy things), and the left foot dancing the hi-hats up and down. How was this possible? How did one person coordinate all of these so skillfully, as Mike did?

Curly-headed Mike grooved the choir so smooth, so steady, so cool. We all wanted to be drummers after seeing him: every guy and even some of the girls. Before, the church never had idols like Mike in its midst. Before, the church only had rock stars in the secular world to compete with. Now, real rock stars were sitting in church pews, standing on church risers, rocking at drum sets beside the communion table. It's no wonder that Jesus eventually became a superstar. He had to. We wouldn't have noticed him otherwise.

On a humid Sunday evening in June, The Sure Foundation sang "Greater Is He" in the Central Baptist sanctuary. Worship programs folded into fans waved in the hands of the congregation.

The novelty of drums in the church was waning, and Mike was more and more becoming a part of the choir body, not a mere addition to it. On this night, his drums lifted the choir into the larger-than-life. Soprano, bass, alto, and tenor voices blended and discovered the drummer's deep groove waiting above and below them, accenting their staccatos, filling the wakes their rests left behind. This giant Sunday evening Jesus groove led some in the congregation to later remark, "The Holy Spirit was sure in the room tonight. The Holy Spirit's presence was so thick you could cut it with a knife."

The choir rode the groove, and Mike realized that he was their driver. That's how I've imagined Mike's conversion. How terrifying it must have been to not believe when so many believers were counting on you to drive them safely to the end of each song. Who or what was driving Mike? Not knowing scared him. He saw the joy on their faces, the sweat soaking their clothes, the bobbing heads and swiveling hips bouncing to his steady backbeat, as they sang about God, the greater "He," overcoming the power of Satan, the lesser "he." It occurred to Mike that he couldn't say for sure which force drove his rhythms. God or the Devil? No small question: God or the Devil?

In the heart of this glory, this Sunday evening wall of sound, he found himself wanting the "greater" He to be inside him too. He wanted this "greater" He to drive the rhythms of his heart, mind, soul, and body.

"On the day of Pentecost a rushing mighty wind blew into the upper room and baptized all of them," the choir sang. "With a power greater than any earthly foe, I'm so glad I've got it too, I'm going to let the whole world know!"

After Mike launched into his snare to tom-tom fill, he silently prayed, "Save me Jesus. Forgive me of my sins. I believe in you now. From now on I want you to drive every beat that I play."

Every beat. I realize now that Mike played every fundamental rock and roll drum beat in that Central Baptist sanctuary: straight-up 4/4 time, half-time, double-time, shuffle, shave-and-a-haircut, swing, slow funk ... Mike found a place for all of these beats in the relevant songs that The Sure Foundation performed, and each of these beats changed the sanctuary. They changed that space so much that it was impossible to know anymore where anything or anyone was coming from. The room was free at last to become a sanctuary.

While my church friends and I looked to Mike as a rock star in our midst, adults saw in him all that the Jesus Movement promised. Mike was the Jesus Movement made good. The contemporary evangelical Christian Church could recreate the sound and rhythm and look of popular youth culture without compromising the fundamental message of salvation. Every time Mike publicly shared a Bible verse that he'd read, or asked the congregation to pray for his hellbound family, or shed joy tears for finding salvation (and the best possible place to drum), he reaffirmed that his conversion was genuine and not simply a passing fad.

Who'd have imagined that a young man could be led to the Lord through a choir that needed a drummer?

On a cool late-August evening in the grassy church courtyard, The Sure Foundation performed the final songs of a farewell concert. Mike would be leaving that week for Nashville, where he'd join a traveling gospel quartet named The Keystones. Real professionals. Mike would be doing what he loved, working for the Lord, and earning his living. This was the world he'd created. He'd honed his chops gigging in The Sure Foundation, and it was time to move on to bigger things.

No one wanted to say, but everyone at Central knew: The Sure Foundation would no longer be the real Sure Foundation. They'd never find Mike's replacement (although the impossible job landed in the lap of Mike's thirteen-year-old student, Dan Eckert, the son of Ron and Carol).

Mike walked up to the microphone for one last Sunday evening testimony.

"Pastor Anderson asked me earlier this week if I'd give my testimony tonight, my final night with The Sure Foundation. As I thought about what to say, I realized that words couldn't possibly express how

Jesus Christ turned my life around. I've never been real good with words anyway. So I decided to do something different. I'm going to give my testimony with what brought me to this church in the first place: my drums. This will be my testimony in drums."

I'd waited three years for this moment: a drum solo! Mike was going give a drum solo out in the church courtyard during Sunday evening worship. And he was calling it his testimony. Brilliant.

He sat down at his drums, picked up his sticks, and eyed them strangely, as if he didn't know what they were or how his hands could work them. Where was he? What were the round, brown-striped fiberglass things surrounding him? What was a Ludwig? What could he do with the gold domes that reflected the blue sky? He became the six-year-old boy who'd received a toy drum set for Christmas. He saw the bass drum pedal and slammed his right foot down on it; he saw the hi-hat pedal and slammed his left foot down on it. He banged on the snare and all of the tom-toms and all of the cymbals, randomly. Nothing coordinated.

This, I knew (and was proud to know), was the unredeemed Mike lost in the world of sin, the world where nothing coordinates. The world where there is no rhythm and no belief and everything is random.

He worked his way into a simple 4/4 eighth-note beat. Limbs began to coordinate. Syncopations fell between the beats. When Mike began the thirty-second-note rolls around the drums, the blur of notes from one drum to the next drum to the next drum and then back to the first drum, I knew that this was the redeemed Mike. This was Mike the believer in the Holy of Holies, cutting loose like I'd never seen. He rolled and blurred and never lost his place in his groove.

While Mike was still spinning there in the courtyard, some eye-shadowed, halter-topped neighborhood girls walked past the church, then stopped to watch and cheer. They didn't know that Mike was giving a testimony—they probably didn't know what a testimony was. But they knew a good drum solo when they heard one. They hoooooed and applauded louder than anyone else when Mike stood up and bowed his head at the end of the solo.

The neighborhood girls didn't stay for my dad's sermon, but I imagined them thinking, "That church must be kind of cool if they'll let a guy do a drum solo." Maybe they'd show up at The Wreck and, like Mike, become insiders looking out instead of outsiders looking in.

It's strange to think that I probably wouldn't have chosen to play drums if Mike had never come to Central Baptist Church. Yes, The Sure Foundation might have found a different drummer, but would I have absorbed the beats of that different drummer? When I think about the process that led to my lost faith, the circumstances that led to the end of my evangelical Christian vision of life, I eventually find myself staring at Mike playing those drums in that Central Baptist sanctuary.

The hows and whys I can't fully explain (there is no cause and effect or single-moment theory), but it has something to do with the introduction of different rhythms into my body, mind, and soul. The full-immersion baptism of different rhythms pouring into all that I am and all that I've become. New rhythms become new possibilities become new worlds.

Twenty-five years ago, I might have said, "The Lord sure works in mysterious ways." The ways get more and more mysterious as the decades pass, and I don't know anymore who or what is working the big groove. As my inner punk cringes at the hippie-dippie way this is sounding, I understand what I am writing about: finding my place in a bigger groove. Finding my place in the big groove that makes it all spin. No sacred realm, no secular realm: only a place on the groove that spins me. The groove that spins my flesh and the groove that spins my spirit.

That's the best that I can do.

Explo '72

Explo '72 was advertised in evangelical Christian publications as "the greatest grassroots evangelistic thrust the world has ever known." The greatest grassroots evangelistic thrust: a week of Bible seminars, street evangelizing, Cotton Bowl stadium revivals, and Jesus rock festivals in Dallas, Texas. Much of it was even broadcast on network TV: it was right there for the whole world to watch.

I somehow knew that this was my event, though I couldn't be there. It was so me, so where I wanted to be: music, celebration, thousands upon thousands of believers, superstardom, thousands upon thousands of people walking the salvation aisle, super-oneness in Jesus Christ, Billy Graham with his arm around Johnny Cash, and the overwhelming imminence of a New Jesus Day. It all came together in this tremendous package, this larger-than-my-life spectacle.

As Central Baptist members gave good-bye hugs to the lucky young people who boarded the bus bound for the holy city in Texas, I sat on the curb, wishing I was older. For the first time in my eleven years, I felt proud to be a born-again Christian. We were on the forefront of a new age in America, a reformation, a great awakening. Those teens with their wire-rimmed glasses, striped vests, suede leather hats, and Jesus-hippie slang were exploring uncharted territory, inventing new ways to be a Baptist adolescent.

As I watched the Explo '72 highlights on TV, I kept thinking, "I wish I was there, but I'm not old enough." I'd been left behind, stranded on earth after the Rapture. That's how it felt. Like I'd been stranded in my world on that great day when believers in Jesus Christ were lifted into the clouds, into Heaven; stranded on that great day when unbelievers were left behind on earth to go through the Tribulation.

I longed for Explo '72 more than the Second Coming of Christ. I didn't yearn for the end of my time on earth, Heaven in the sky, eternity with all-and-only the people I'd gone to church with. How boring that would be. This Explo '72, this Jesus Sound Explosion, was what I wanted: a heavenly union on Earth that would grow and grow, become more and more popular, until the whole world would be one big, happy family of God. No sacred realm, no secular realm. Just one realm. I wanted to be in the world and of the world because, way down in my heart, I knew that I was born to love the world. This here-and-now world that I love.

"If a miracle is something so life-changing and so historically significant that men and women can only account for it by saying, 'God did it,' then Explo '72 was a miracle," anonymous liner notes on the back cover of *Jesus Sound Explosion* proclaim. "It was a life-changing, historically significant experience for more than 80,000 college and high school students and laymen from the United States and more than 70 countries ... A Jesus Music Festival attended by 180,000 people climaxed the week. Now we can only account for Explo '72 by saying, 'God did it.'"

The numbers attempt to document Jesus' popularity. In the wake of The Beatles' breakup, Jesus had to reclaim his throne on top of the pop charts; in the years before and after John Lennon's assassination, Jesus had to destroy the secular humanists who would make Lennon's "Imagine" an international anthem. Can the Christian right be seen as mass culture vengeance for Lennon's "The Beatles are more popular than Jesus Christ" remark? The Moral Majority originated in 1979, John Lennon was assassinated in 1980. I'm not trying to invent conspiracy theories, I'm not trying to draw direct connections; I'm only trying to read this strange text. I'll call it "A Pop Life: The Story of Jesus Christ Superstar."

As one young Central Baptist zealot said in a Sunday evening church testimony, "Jesus changed thousands of lives that week. Man, they had to hold Explo '72 outside in the Cotton Bowl stadium, because if you took all the energy the Holy Spirit was generating there and put it in a regular church sanctuary, the place would literally explooode!! America is coming to Jesus! At this rate, America will truly be a Christian nation by 1980, and by the year 2000, Jesus will be worshiped worldwide."

And that was our call: to make our world one Christian world. The Great Commission: "Go ye therefore, and teach all nations, baptizing them in the name of the Father, and of the Son, and of the Holy

Ghost: Teaching them to observe all things whatsoever I have commanded you; and, lo, I am with you always, even unto the end of the world. Amen."

Unto the ends of the earth, until the end of the world: Jesus Sound Explosion.

Backwards, forwards, 33⅓, 45, 78: there's more than one way to spin the record.

With a Billy Graham invocation, a Johnny Cash song, and a distant Richard Nixon blessing, the festival begins.*

The choir (women in flowing white dresses, men in floral print shirts) sings, "One way one way one way one way one wayeeay-eeay."

The brawny lead singer with the frizzy long hair shouts, "Hey! Did I hear someone say that Christians can't rock and roll? Well, here's one for you!"

The solo folk prophet sings about the End Times, Christ's imminent return, the Apocalypse, the last days on earth, the Rapture, the reign of the Beast during the Tribulation.

The lone black gospel group, Andrae Crouch and the Disciples, lays down a big funk groove and shouts, "Let Jesus take you higher!"

The old-time white gospel quintet (three fortyish men in beige suits and black ties, two women in big curly hair) try to sound more soulful than they've ever sounded.

A weathered Kris Kristofferson asks, "Why me, Lord?"

Kris's soulmates, Johnny Cash and June Carter, stop the show with a two-step about the blind man healed by Jesus: "I See Men as Trees Walkin'."

*Historical footnote: H. R. Haldeman's diaries reveal that Billy Graham served as a Nixon operative and sought to organize Christian youth for Nixon; Explo '72 climaxed with a Billy Graham closing sermon on the night of June 17; earlier that day, five operatives from the Committee to Reelect President Nixon were arrested for burglary inside the Watergate office of the Democratic Party.

Are you there yet?

It's time for a Jesus cheer. Give me a "J"! Give me an "E"! Give me an "S"! Give me a "U"! Give me an "S"! What's that spell? Say it again! I can't heearr yooou! For the city of Dallas! For the state of Texas! For America! For the whole world! For all of God's great creation!

Now, brothers and sisters, there are seven acknowledged wonders in the world. You are about to witness the eighth. This man, our leader and servant in the Lord, the hardest-working man in evangelism, needs no introduction. You know him and I know him. Let's give a rousing Explo '72 welcome to *the* Reverend Billy Graham!

Hit it.

The Day Billy Graham Came to St. Paul

Russell's mother dropped us off at the downtown St. Paul Dayton's and went to her appointment. Russ and I rode the escalator and wandered around from floor to floor. We each had a dollar, and we planned on buying 45s in the record department. Somehow we lost each other on the furniture floor.

A teenage guy with long, greasy brown hair, ripped big-bell jeans, and a black muscle shirt walked up to me and asked if he could borrow a quarter. Because Jesus wanted me to, I said, "I only have a dollar, but I can get change for it," and pulled the dollar out of my pocket.

"I'll take the dollar," he said, and grabbed it.

I looked around for an adult, but saw only three guys, friends of the thief, get up from couches and walk over to their buddy, the clever one.

"Heh heh heh. Nice going. Heh heh heh," they laughed as they got on the down escalator.

"Little dumbshit," one of them muttered.

I found Russ looking at 45s and, crying, told him the story.

That night Billy Graham was kicking off his week-long June '73 crusade at the Minnesota state fair grandstands. A Billy Graham Crusade in your town is the evangelical Christian equivalent of a visit from the Pope and, like everyone at Central Baptist, I planned on attending every night. My father and mother got invited, along with other local clergy, to a crusade kickoff dinner with Billy. This made me feel enormously proud. Billy Graham and my dad and other local clergy, all at the same table.

Clergy was a new word. My dad was a clergyman. This sounded more like lawyer, doctor, accountant, policeman, manager, judge, contractor, teacher, and clerk. The things that other dads did. I could say, "My dad is a clergyman. My dad is a member of the local clergy."

As Mom and Dad were getting ready for the dinner, I told them of my terrible encounter with Satan's lost urban tribe. They responded with the correct amount of compassion and gave me a dollar to compensate for the loss.

I imagined them telling the story to Billy and all the pastors and wives gathered at the dinner.

"What a shame!" they'd all say. "What kind of a world are we living in when a young Christian trying to do the right thing has a dollar stolen by heartless juvenile delinquents?"

Billy would ask for my name and say a special prayer for me and my ministry to the troubled teens of the city. The story would stick in his head the rest of the evening, and he'd find a way to work it into his sermon. An illustration of a Christian with a servant's heart wronged by Satan's urban predators.

"Why, just this evening around the dinner table a pastor told the story of his son, Mark Anderson." Yes, he'd mention my name. "Mark, a twelve-year-old Christian, was going to give a quarter to a teenage beggar and the beggar, caught up in a life of crime, a life of sin, stole a dollar from him. The teen beggar grabbed the dollar as Mark pulled it from his pocket. Ladies and gentlemen, young people, boys and girls—this world needs Jesus!"

Afterwards he'd want to meet me. We'd have our picture taken together, his arm around my shoulder. He'd repeat the story at other stops on the crusade. Our picture would appear in his *Decision* magazine with the caption, "Billy Graham and Mark Anderson, the boy who had the dollar stolen."

That night I listened to the sermon, heard not a word of it, waited for Billy to mention my name. He didn't.

When I got home I asked my parents to repeat every word they'd said to Billy, every word he'd said to them.

They were introduced, Dad told me, and they shook hands. They sat at the other end of the dinner table and didn't get to talk. It was a big table, and many of the local clergy were sitting there.

"I was hoping I'd get to say more to him," Dad said.

What I Wanted to Be

While other sixth graders developed addictions to the Hardy Boys and sports biographies, I devoured every David Wilkerson book I could get my hands on. Wilkerson's books had titles worth remembering: *Purple Violet Squish, Hey Preach! You're Comin' Through, Twelve Angels from Hell,* and the best-selling *The Cross and the Switchblade.* These books told "real-life" stories of New York City's pimps, gang members, prostitutes, homosexuals, junkies, pushers, and other sinners too numerous to mention. That's how Wilkerson lumped them, and that's how I knew them all: sinners.

I was allowed to enter this nether world (my first journey through New York City) because David Wilkerson had a special way with sinners. All of his main characters, his new creatures, invited Jesus into their hearts, turned from their wicked New York City ways, found the straight-and-narrow path to salvation, joined Wilkerson's Teen Challenge ministry, and spent the rest of their days trying to lead wayward New York City teens to Wilkerson's Lord.

New York City: that place became, in my imagination, the valley of the shadow of death.

In *The Cross and the Switchblade,* Wilkerson told the story of how he led New York City's most notorious-and-feared gang leaders to Jesus Christ. He later sold the story to Hollywood, and the book debuted as a major motion picture in 1971, at the height of Jesus

Movement hype. Pat Boone played Wilkerson and Erik (*C.H.I.P.S.*) Estrada played Nicky Cruz, former leader of the Puerto Rican gang, the Mau Maus. Nicky Cruz was Wilkerson's most prized convert.

I've lost most of my David Wilkerson books, but images remain.

Wilkerson meets a group of Mau Maus on a New York City street and attempts to share his salvation message with them. Most of all, he wants the soul of Nicky Cruz, the hellbound street tough that he's read about in the newspaper.

Wilkerson tells Nicky that he loves him, and Nicky threatens to kill Wilkerson. Wilkerson smiles and says yeah, sure, he could do that. Nicky could slash him into a thousand little morsels, a thousand tiny bits—and every slice would still love Nicky.

I pictured a thousand bleeding body fragments all saying in voices that no one has heard before, "I love you I love you I love you I love you I love you I love you …" The broken body would have to say "I love you" out loud for Nicky to know that the preacher wasn't lying.

As an eleven-year-old boy, I believed that Wilkerson's zealous machismo was the love of Christ. This was true martyrdom. Mutilate me. I will return your love. How will you return mine?

In his autobiography, *Run Baby Run,* Nicky Cruz attempted to reclaim the story that made Wilkerson and him evangelical Christian celebrities. *Run Baby Run* was a lot more scary and intense and real than *The Cross and the Switchblade.* Yes, of the two books, I strongly preferred Nicky's *Run Baby Run.* Gang initiation rites, drugs, rumbles, sexual innuendos, police chases: Nicky told his story straight from memory, with more attention to detail. Wilkerson told of switchblade threats, but Nicky's story bore the real slashes and scars.

Run Baby Run contained the saddest and most horrifying image that I'd ever read anywhere. Nicky cradles his best friend in an alley after the friend has been stabbed by members of a rival gang, the

Bishops. The friend tries to speak, but his mouth only forms blood bubbles. I read those words over and over to make sure they'd been printed right. Blood bubbles. How? Blood bubbles. The gangster and true friend becomes a gurgling, bubble-breathing infant again, and then he dies.

I never finished *Run Baby Run*.

After Wilkerson converted him to Christianity, Nicky went to a fundamentalist Bible college. In this new school, the God worshiped hated the flesh (the carnal realm, the here-and-now world): women and men were forbidden from talking to each other and professors constantly watched all students to keep them from slipping into sins of the flesh.

That's where I stopped reading.

At the time I thought I was just bored, and I felt guilty for getting bored at the most Christian part of the story. This was more than mere boredom, though. This was tragedy: the Nicky I'd been reading about was a dead man. He'd lost his life to save his life.

Nicky expressed deep gratitude for David Wilkerson, the man who'd saved him from life-in-death and led him to death-in-life. Or was it the other way around?

While I was still obsessed with Wilkersonian lore, I went to hear Nicky Cruz speak at the Minneapolis Convention Center. I imagined a street-smart preacher with greased-back jet-black hair and a black leather jacket. Instead, I saw a more mundane Nicky in Dry Look–sprayed short hair and a blue double-knit suit. I wanted to hear his stories, but he preached—with an unmistakable evangelist accent. As if he did the gigs that David Wilkerson's schedule couldn't fit in.

There he was: a propped-up superstar impersonator condemned to a life of growing up in public.

"I met some so-called Jesus freaks," Nicky said, "who were smoking marijuana and they said to me, 'Hey man—we're all getting high on Jesus.' But that's not what it's about, young people. Your body is the temple of the Holy Spirit, and the Holy Spirit doesn't want those drugs inside of you. Instead, go for the real high, the spiritual high that comes through a personal relationship with Jesus Christ."

Spiritual high. What could that be? I didn't know, but I liked the sound of it. Some secret earthly reward for Nicky, in addition to eternity in Heaven. A sign of life in the here-and-now.

Spiritual high. That's what I wanted.

Soon after I saw Nicky, on a very warm weekday during Easter break, I walked alone to a nearby mall to spend a couple of holiday dollars my grandparents had sent me. I wandered around and eyed every possible purchase: key chains, baseball cards, comic books, 45s, chocolate eggs, sunglasses, goofy hats. Things of the world.

I stopped into a Christian bookstore and admired the Bible verse plaques, the glow-in-the-dark crosses, the Bible verse posters, the Bible verse hand-puzzles, and the glow-in-the-dark praying hands. They could put a Bible verse on just about anything, and they could make just about anything glow in the dark. I only wished I had enough money to buy everything in that store.

Then I saw it: a pocket-sized *Good News for Modern Man* New Testament with a rainbow cover. Only a dollar-fifty. The Lord had led me to it, I was certain. I'd been sensing the Lord's leading lately. Towards what, I didn't know. Towards the spiritual high? The higher ground?

I'd never bought a Bible with my own money before. Never even thought of it. Why would I? Every couple of years, the church gave me a gold-lettered, monogrammed Bible, with a zipper up all sides, for faithful Sunday school attendance. All I had to do was show up every Sunday, and they'd give me another Bible eventually. Dollars from grandparents were harder to come by.

I had to have that rainbow Bible, though. I couldn't explain it. The Lord led to me to it. That was the only explanation. The Lord wanted me to buy it, study it daily, put it in my pocket before school, and read it during lunch. That was God's plan for me. Kids at school would ask me what I was reading, and I'd say loudly and proudly, "The Bible." They'd gather around me, and we'd read it together. I'd answer all of their questions and lead them to Jesus.

As I walked the mile home from the mall, I randomly opened up the rainbow Bible and read verses aloud. I noticed the budding trees and the robins returning from down south. I sang hymns, gazed up at the sun, and saw most clearly what I wanted to be when I grew up: a David Wilkerson. I'd start Teen Challenge Minnesota and spend my life with the lost and unloved souls of the inner city. It was good to have such a clear image of who and what I would become as an adult.

The walk felt like this: Spiritual high! Yes Lord! Amen!

I'd put on the "full armor of God" as I was called to do. Not a gun or a knife, but a Bible. I'd put my life in danger for Christ, confident that I'd be protected. The thousand pieces of my broken body would shout "I love you," but I would remain whole.

And someday I would write and sell my Teen Challenge Minnesota story.

Parable-ized

Dad occasionally used Marna, Marshall, and me in his sermon illustrations. This, we understood, came with the Pastor's Kid (P.K.) territory: our likenesses might on any given Sunday be realized in parable form. Sometimes he'd warn us, sometimes he'd surprise us, sometimes he'd ask permission.

"Mark, is it all right if I use what you said this week about the Good Samaritan in my sermon?" he'd ask on the way to church.

The sermon, I knew, had been written, so my role in the morning service was foreordained, God's Will.

"What did I say about the Good Samaritan? I don't remember."

"You know, when I was driving you kids to school on the day it was twenty below zero."

"Oh yeah. I suppose you can use it. Do you have to say my name, though? Can you just say that one of your sons said it?"

"Say it was Mark," Marshall would say. "I don't want everyone to think I might have said something I would never say."

I'd sit in the balcony awaiting the arrival of my pulpit-life.

"Last Tuesday as I was driving the boys to school, we passed a neighbor who was stuck in snow. You all know how cold and snowy it was last week. Well, I said to the boys, 'I think we should get out of the car and give the Nelsons a push.'

"'But we might be late for school if we stop,' Mark protested."

Smiling congregation eyes shone on me. Through my father's illustrations, I'd been typecast, parable-ized, as the lovable pastor's son who sheds new light on old Bible stories with witty, slightly irreverent remarks. I knew I was loved, I knew I'd been imagined. I knew the parable-boy who walked and spoke in my place, the parable-boy who lived in the house of God, my father and mother's house, the sanctuary, the mind of the congregation.

"'Don't you remember the story of the Good Samaritan?' I asked my son.

"'Sure, Dad,' Mark said to me. 'But it wasn't twenty below in Jericho.'"

Punchline, drum roll, cymbal crash. I'd smile and nod back at the smiles.

Yes, that was me, the boy who said that. I am the boy of the parable.

Maybe a pastor visiting from another church heard the illustration and (since it is fair game for pastors to steal sermon illustrations) I'd become his son in his version of the story. Maybe a boy my age who later became a pastor now uses the illustration whenever he preaches on the parable of the Good Samaritan. Am I his son in the parable? Is his son my brother?

The Missionary Parable

Becoming a missionary was always a possibility. I could see myself doing that. Or, I could see parable boy doing that. The job held a certain appeal that I can now recognize: I wanted to escape at least one of the worlds that I was born into.

I can still remember the title of one of the missionary autobiographies we sold at our church (in the "Reading for Successful Living" book rack): *A Foreign Devil in China.* The foreign devil in China that I heard most about was named Buddha. But the "foreign devil" could live in any place, anywhere missionaries could snap slides of.

I never read any of the missionary autobiographies, but I heard the missionary parable repeated again and again, from many mouths.

The zealous American seminary student and wife accept the call to Africa. In missionary stories, Africa is a country, not a continent. The borders are invisible, the names are irrelevant, the people are savage heathens who dance naked, the governments (broken states, disunited states) are corrupt, the cities are overcrowded, the jungle is wild and dangerous.

The missionaries are scared at first, but confident that the Lord will protect them. A helicopter delivers them to the remote, untamed place not on the map (unreachable by road). There they build a house, a church, a camp, a village, a family, a following. The church grows beyond their wildest dreams. Hundreds are converted. Word spreads from village to village. The building doubles in size. Native disciples don American clothes and build churches throughout the region. Ten little churches in ten little villages. The missionary's church serves as the headquarters, the administrative heart of the ministry.

They have a son and, a year later, a daughter. They are happy, they feel whole. They see the fruits of their labor all around them. They call the fruits "good." All this after only three and a half years in the country. They call it "God's African Miracle" when they write to their friends and supporters. Soon they will return on furlough to their Minnesota home church where they hope to raise three times as much money as they came to Africa with.

But there is always Satan. Satan (the King of the Jungle) gets jealous of their success. His tribal lords, the former rulers of the jungle, have been dethroned and are conspiring to avenge their loss of power, the death of their livelihood. Ten lords from ten villages meet in the shack of their leader, the earthly king appointed by Satan, and they plan the murder of the missionary family. They will try to spare the native converts. They see the natives as dupes, formerly loyal subjects who will return to their true way of life in the absence of the missionaries.

The missionaries and their two children are brutally murdered in the night. The house and church headquarters are burned down. The fire and screams wake up the native converts who, to the surprise of the king and lords, fight for the missionary and family. Three converts and two lords die in the fight.

In the end, the converts prevail and the ministry lives on. And that is the moral of the missionary parable: the converts will prevail and the ministry will live on.

Furlough with Justin, the Missionary Kid

Justin's mom and my mom got together one afternoon and decided that the two of us would become friends. Justin needed someone to show him how to be an American boy his age.

On paper, it was a perfect match: Justin, the eleven-year-old missionary boy, the son of an overseas minister of the gospel, home on furlough ("He doesn't have any friends," Mom said) for a year; and me, the eleven-year-old pastor's kid who was slightly awkward, bad in sports, a bit of a sissy, and should therefore take what friends he could get.

That's how I became friends with Justin Owens, the missionary kid from São Paulo, Brazil.

I always dreaded hanging out with the missionary kids, but Mom urged me to befriend them when they were home on furlough. Furlough: that single year in the United States that followed four in the foreign land. Furlough: that one year in the States followed by four more on the mission field. What can you do, really do, in the span of a furlough?

To most missionary kids, being home on furlough only meant a year in a foreign and horribly alien American school. To missionary parents, furlough meant a year of fundraising, solicitation, peddling, showing slides of triumphs (new converts, new and bigger churches) to congregations across the States. Only to head back out to the mission field for another four years.

A furlough was not a time of rest.

I now know what I didn't understand then. All those Sunday evening missionary slide shows I whispered through had only one goal in mind: to keep the thing afloat by convincing believers that the ministry in the pagan land was worth financially supporting. The missionaries from Brazil might show, for example, pictures of their latest major convert, Antonio. Before joining their São Paulo church, Antonio was a homeless street urchin turned thug turned drug dealer turned pastor of the new church they'd build when they returned to the mission field. If they were able, that is, to raise enough money to build the church.

What would happen to Antonio's church if they didn't raise enough money? What would happen to Antonio if they didn't raise enough money? The more tragic the possibilities, the more the offering plates filled.

And here they are in Minnesota, this Owens family that's been missioning in a foreign devil land for four years. They have three terrified children who have come to accept this as their world: four years at a missionary boarding school with other missionary kids (all the missionary kids that I knew went to boarding schools, miles away from their parents); and then back to St. Paul, to a school no less foreign, to a land (American childhood, American adolescence) no less alien.

The Owens kids don't wear or even know the latest styles, they speak with accents that they can't even hear, and they listen to music that everyone else stopped listening to two or three years earlier. Maybe São Paulo just got the Partridge Family, and the Owens kids proudly own two Partridge Family records. That's their only connection to rock and roll. It's something they know that they didn't know four years ago, back when everyone was still burning Beatles records.

And maybe Justin Owens asks me if I like the Partridge Family. I cringe and hope he never asks me that around any of my school friends. Because I stopped liking the Partridge Family in fourth grade, and I am now in sixth grade, and they've become a joke, a reference point, something that shows how I got from there to where I am now: Chicago, Elton John, Three Dog Night, Bread, The Guess Who, Blood, Sweat & Tears.

"I have two Partridge Family records," Justin says. "If you come to my house, I will play them for you. Do you like the Partridge Family?"

How do I respond to a question like that?

Did I ask for this friend? No! Did I invent his world? No!

Justin wasn't without other typical missionary kid oddities, displacements, and dislocations. He wore far-too-baggy JCPenney blue jeans with the straight legs rolled up at the bottom because they were too long. Even in Galesburg, boys didn't wear baggy jeans with the bottoms rolled up. The only place I'd seen that was in pictures (from the forties and fifties) of my dad on the Houston, Minnesota, farm. The Owenses bought everything much bigger than necessary to make it last. As for them and their household, they would grow into their clothes. They would acquaint their children with the harsh reality: you have to grow into things in this life. In the next life, things will fit.

And no bell bottoms because they didn't want to appear frivolous with money as they solicited funds. They wanted to appear respectable and dignified but slightly out of fashion. How long would bell bottoms be in style compared to the fundamental message of the gospel?

I, on the other hand, was on my second pair of hard-fought-for bell bottoms (the last boy in my fifth-grade class, I might add, to make the switch from straight legs to bell bottoms). And now my mom wanted me to be friends with Justin Owens, the missionary kid who wore big, baggy, overlong, straight-legged JCPenney jeans rolled up above his hard-soled, laced, black Sunday shoes. He hadn't even discovered shoes with buckles!

"He doesn't have any friends, Mark," Mom said.

Well, I wasn't exactly Mr. Popularity either.

And what did Justin want to do when he came over to play? Race my Hot Wheels cars? No. Look at my baseball cards? No. The missionary kid wanted to read my *National Wildlife* magazines. He was far more interested in nature than my car and card collections!

I couldn't understand Justin at all. Nature boy. What was the big deal about nature? What did Justin find so interesting in there?

Family friends kept sending me these yearlong subscriptions to *National Wildlife.* I tried appreciating the magazine. Three Christmases in a row they renewed the subscription. I made an honest effort to read and develop interest in them, but it was all pictures and articles about strange animals and strange bugs and pretty flowers. Nature nature nature. I'd page through, read a little bit here and there, and then, "C'mon c'mon c'mon c'mon c'mon c'mon c'mon!"

I wanted immediate appeal, immediate gratification: Charlie Brown books, Dennis the Menace books, Archies comics (that's where I learned that "C'mon" was actually a word). I wanted punch lines. Or sports magazines, heroics: Hank Aaron or Harmon Killebrew hitting another homer. Baseball cards and sports magazines and sports biographies and comics and Hot Wheels cars and Top 40 radio supplying the soundtrack to it all: that's where I was coming from.

The fact that I was lousy in sports, the last one picked on playground teams, only made me want to enter that boy-my-age world all the more. And it didn't help that Justin was even lousier in sports than I, even sissier than I.

I tried to get him to say something in Portuguese. That was something Justin had. That was different. I'd never heard an American boy my age speak another language. That was the closest I'd ever come to hearing someone speak in tongues.

"Say something in Porchageeze," I'd say to Justin.

"No. I don't want to. Everyone always asks me to say something in Portuguese. That's boring. I'm sick of it."

"C'mon. One sentence. Say, 'I have to go to the bathroom' in Porchageeze.'"

"No!"

"C'mon. Say it. 'I have to go the bathroom.'"

"No. Say something in English. That's what I always say to kids at school when they ask me to say something in Portuguese."

He wouldn't give in. What good is having a missionary kid friend if he won't even speak the other language for you?

Did I ask for this friend?

"São Paulo means St. Paul in Portuguese," the Owenses said in their slide show. "We live in the St. Paul of Brazil. We're sister cities."

This was good for at least a few extra St. Paul offering dollars.

I didn't understand how languages worked back then. Why didn't they just call it St. Paul instead of "São Paulo, the St. Paul of Brazil"? Even if the word "saint" had to be translated into the unlikely "são," why couldn't Paul simply be Paul without the unnecessary "o"? What did Jesus call him up in Heaven? Paul or Paulo?

I was the pastor's kid (P.K.) from St. Paul. Justin was the missionary's kid (M.K.) from São Paulo. I don't know how else to account for the fact that we became loyal friends for that year. He was a missionary's kid and I was a pastor's kid and there was this thing called a furlough. Might as well redeem it by making a new friend.

Still, I can't account for that friendship. I mostly thought of Justin as a geek, a dork, a dweeb, a sissy, an undesirable, a stranger in the land of American boys my age. And I don't have any particularly great or awful memories of the guy.

Maybe it was the sense of suspension in space and time that opened up a new place of communication: the furlough. Justin might choose to call life in São Paulo his real life, or he might choose to call life in St. Paul his real life. Either way, he was far enough removed from his land and mine that we actually managed to talk about something that wasn't sports or cars or animals or bugs or flowers or Top 40 radio: being the sons of ministers. Maybe that's how the friendship began. With him saying, "The thing I hate about being a missionary's kid is that everyone expects you to be better than anyone else. You have to be an example to all of the other kids."

Life as an example. Life in the parable. Something we both knew about. One reason why so many P.K.'s and M.K.'s choose to be negative examples: because they can. They've got the eyes on them. Might as well do something that the eyes will enjoy.

I'd never heard another one like me, another preacher's kid, actually talk about the having to be an example. Was this my first friendship that came from conversation and not play? Is that why I can't think of any Justin Owens stories? I believe so.

Somehow I remember that conversation, even if we never really had it.

I do remember the summer of 1973 moment when the Owenses flew back to Brazil. A whole crew of Central Baptisters came to the airport to see them off. A lot of the adults hugged and cried, but I didn't cry. Friendships came and went frequently at that age, though it seems sadder to me now. I think we would have been good friends to each other in those four years that he was gone: seventh, eighth, ninth, tenth grade. I could have used the son of a missionary to talk to as I moved into that foreign devil land of adolescence.

As the Owenses got ready to board the plane, I said something very odd, something that I'll never forget, something that seemed to come from nowhere. Some deep nowhere inside of me. I must have seen some James Bond movies recently or too many episodes of *Mission Impossible.* For the first time in my life, I saw the airport as a potential site of terror. Anyone walking by, as innocent as they might look, could be hiding a gun amidst clothes or inside a book or inside a violin case or in the heel of a platform shoe. Things weren't necessarily what they appeared to be.

As Justin stood in the last-call-to-board line, I yelled to him, "Justin, don't let them see the machine gun in your suitcase."

He scowled at me, as if to say, "How stupid can you be for saying that?"

Justin knew about airports. Justin knew that the terror wasn't a joke.

My other friends laughed. Even a few adults laughed. This was all the positive reinforcement I needed to say it again: "Hey Justin, be sure to keep the machine gun in your suitcase hidden."

Immediately, an armed guard came bounding over to me and said, "Young man, you'd better not say another word or both you and your friend will be in big trouble. That is not a joking matter. Don't even joke like that. Believe me: if you say another word to your friend about a gun in his suitcase, I will arrest and search both of you."

"It was a joke," I said, near tears.

"I know it was a joke. But that isn't a joking matter."

I wondered why he was making such a big deal of what he knew was only a joke. I know now: He was responding more to the material itself, not so much to the possibility that it was true. He was guarding the border between what was and wasn't a joking matter.

He wasn't treating me as a child, and this terrified me most. He was taking me seriously, as an adult. As a human being capable of killing. As a human being with a friend capable of killing. What I said, though fictional, though a joke, could be taken as real. I could say, "Don't let them see the machine gun in your suitcase," and someone trained to see machine guns in suitcases might see one in that very suitcase.

I had reached the age of accountability, the age at which I could go to Hell if I died.

Shedding

On a May Saturday night during the annual Central Baptist Family Camp weekend, members of The Sure Foundation sit on risers in a large aluminum shed, the Woodlake Baptist Camp chapel. They wait for someone to step up to the mike for a testimony. I sit with my mother, brother, and sister and wait for the testimonies to end, for the singing to begin again, for Mike's backbeat (he can't lose it).

Anyone in the choir or congregation is welcome to walk the cement floor to share a conversion story, Bible verse, prayer request, exhortation of praise, or tale of desperation and deliverance:

The meeting with Jesus after everything was tried but "something was missing" …

The chastisement of John taken to heart: "You are neither hot nor cold, but lukewarm, therefore I will spew you from my mouth" …

The lost former best friend who is searching, groping, "so close to coming to the Lord" …

The miracle of finding a twenty-dollar bill by the Mississippi River just after praying for money to buy a new Living Bible …

The horrible pain of the separation and the divorce, and then the joy of being part of the family of God, one in the Spirit, the family that was always wanted but never had before …

The naked "Praise Jesus" from the person who usually doesn't "say anything at these things because I'm, you know, kind of shy and nervous" …

The mother's prodigal son who keeps running and running from God, taking drugs, smoking cigarettes, stealing money from her purse, hanging out with the wrong crowd, threatening to beat up and kill her—and she was so proud when, in sixth grade, he won the Sunday School Bible verse memorization contest …

The son and the former alcoholic father who used to fight real fist fights, but now, through a miracle of grace, found a personal relationship with Jesus and are beginning again …

Everyone starts crying. First the adults, then the children. Mom starts crying, Dad starts crying when he sees Mom crying, I start crying when I see Mom and Dad crying, Marshall starts crying when he sees me crying, Marna starts crying when she sees all of us crying.

I am terrified. I've never seen so many adults in one room crying, unable and unwilling to stop. They can't stop the tears any sooner than they can stop the next person from standing up to give a tearful testimony. They don't want the service to end because they haven't felt such a bond, such a cleansing, such a oneness before. There's a sweet sweet spirit in this place, they sing. They don't want the night to end until all present have testified.

I want more than anything to hear a closing song and benediction so I can go to bed and put the gravity of the evening behind me. Why is everybody crying? There's some stuff up ahead that I haven't seen, and at this very moment it isn't looking too good.

I hope each testimony is the last. The mothers are crying, the fathers are crying, the tears won't stop, the night won't end, I'll remain in the shed forever, waiting for the choir to sing a closing song, followed by my father's sweet benediction.

those bored looks

Two Roads, One Traveler

On the risers in front of the pulpit, the rejuvenated high schoolers, Jesus Movement activists, sang and bounced to the lite-rock beat of their choir, The Sure Foundation. In the back pew of the balcony slumped the sullen, sunken-eyed late-teen guys whose parents dragged them to church every Sunday. The back pew guys wore their stringy bangs in their eyes; the guys on the risers parted theirs carefully down the middle. The back-pewers' mothers dragged combs through their hair before church, but the sons messed it up on the way to Sunday school and, in case anyone missed the point, untucked their white button-down shirts.

"What's the big deal?" they wondered as they watched The Sure Foundation. "It's still just church. Same song, new beat. A half-assed rock beat. Jesus bubblegum rock. The Association with Christian words."

Mom held up these malcontents as examples of what not to become when, in another year, I entered junior high. She named and described them with one phrase: "Those bored looks."

"They sit back there every Sunday with those bored looks on their faces," she'd say. "They look like they just hate being in church. I hope you kids don't get like that when you're their age."

She saw me moving closer to those bored looks when, on a whim one Sunday, my friends and I decided to sit up in the front row of the balcony instead of our usual spot in the front row of the main floor. In the balcony, I could see the back of her head, but she could only see me if she turned around; Dad could see me from his pulpit, but only if he made a point of looking up. I did my best to use church time wisely: I drew caricatures of church stalwarts on the blank side of the worship program, made up new words for hymns, whispered sarcastic asides to my friends, feeling both in the sanctuary and slightly outside of it.

I could feel the tug-of-war between The Sure Foundation on the risers and those bored looks in the back pew. Two roads diverged and, being one traveler, I imagined a double life.

Four college guys from church, longhaired older brothers and friends of those bored looks, bought a bread truck and drove it to California. I distinctly remember one of the bread truck sojourners. He was very tall, six feet seven. He wore black horn-rimmed glasses and shoulder-length curly brown hair with bangs clipped short and straight across his forehead. His height, his strange bangs, his glasses: if those bored looks had a guru, a Ginsberg, it must have been him.

One summer Sunday after the morning service, I saw the bread truck pull up and park in front of Central Baptist. The bread truckers, elder bored looks who'd been gone for months on a trip out west, stepped out in cutoffs and T-shirts.

Their younger back pew apprentices joined them by the truck. The elders told about their adventures; the apprentices imagined their future, their freedom. In a few years they'd buy a bread truck together and drive away. Maybe they'd return and maybe they wouldn't. If they ever showed up at church again, it would be after the service ended, and they'd wear whatever they wanted to wear.

Or maybe they'd drive to a place where there were no churches and decide to just stay there.

One of the bored looks lived in my neighborhood. Every once in a while, I'd see him walk quietly by with the burnouts as I practiced in the park with the Northwest Como football team. Bushes and trees walled off the field on the north and west sides. South of the spot where, during baseball season, long hits became home runs stood a picnic pavilion built for church potlucks and family reunions. This became the designated after-school meeting spot for the Como Park burnouts. They hung out there to smoke cigarettes and pot, drink beer, and blast rock and roll loud enough for us to sing along.

As we did calisthenics, the burnouts would step out of the woods and slump towards the pavilion. The bored look would see me, the pastor's kid, and give a slight nod of recognition, accompanied by a look in his eyes that pleaded, "Please don't tell your parents that you saw me here, Young Goodboy Mark. I'd cover for you if you were old enough to be here with us. Someday I will cut you some slack."

The bored look grew up and became a Baptist minister. He knows who he is.

I've kept my mouth shut about him for all of these years.

Where's the slack, preacher man?

The Not-Parsonage

My parents wanted a home of their own, and they knew they'd never be able to buy one if they lived in parsonages all their lives. Maybe this was the new Baptist Church trend: no more parsonages. After all, not every pastor and family would need or want the exact same house. If more and more churches were getting rid of their parsonages, Mom and Dad knew that they'd likely have to purchase a house whenever they left Central Baptist. And they'd have no equity built up. Even pastors need a little equity now and then, eventually.

So Central Baptist sold the parsonage and used some of the money to help Mom and Dad put a down payment on a two-story stucco house with brown brick and gold trim. This house, our first not-parsonage, was on Pascal Street, about five blocks east of the Minnesota State Fairgrounds, on the northwest side of Como Park instead of the northeast side.

In those days of neighborhood schools, it meant that we'd go to Murray Junior and Senior High (yes, students in grades seven through twelve went to the same city school) instead of the rougher

Como Junior High. Dad and Mom wanted to save us from Como Junior High, the out-of-control St. Paul school that was making the news as an example of how schools would be ruined by two distinctly seventies practices: experimental sixties-inspired teaching methods and forced busing. The racist implications of the latter were concealed in the usual Minnesota Nice rhetoric.

Como had a bad reputation that seemed to get worse with each new year of the seventies. It was only 1972, I'd begin junior high in 1973, and I'd finish junior high in 1976. There was no telling how bad Como Junior high would get by 1976.

Mom was back at Bethel College in St. Paul, finishing her secondary English teaching license. She'd done some required classroom observation at Como Junior High and was appalled, absolutely appalled, at the lack of discipline there.

"They never picked up a pencil the whole time I was there," she later said of the classroom she was assigned to.

She knew that the risk of her children stumbling and falling away from Jesus Christ would be increased if we became adolescents who never picked up pencils.

No equity, no pencils: we had to get out of that parsonage as soon as possible.

The not-parsonage on Pascal Street had old gray carpeting that I helped Dad remove as we listened to the 1972 presidential election returns. Marshall, Dad, and I pulled and rolled up the ugly gray carpet, pulled and rolled up the foam padding beneath it, and removed the staples from the hardwood floor as George McGovern, the Democrat we were all rooting for, got his liberal ass kicked by Richard Nixon.

And later in the week, the carpet men installed in the living room, dining room, and stairway the thick gold shag carpeting that was perfect for lying down on while listening to records played on Mom and Dad's Magnavox console. It was like lying down on a big gold sheepdog that didn't slobber.

Dad and Mom had their own big second-floor elm-shaded bedroom that overlooked Pascal Street, and Marna had a little bedroom next to theirs. Down the hall was a guest/sewing room with a foldout couch, a second bathroom, and a porch overlooking the back yard. Outside of the living room we had a porch with a swing, and in the den we had a little red Sears fireplace.

Marshall and I lived, once again, in the basement on bunk beds. Whoever lived there before us remodeled the basement to accommodate a Bethel College student or two, so we had our own shower, our own bathroom, a refrigerator, a little stove, a ping pong table, and a workroom-closet where we hung our clothes on plumbing pipes. We never used the refrigerator or stove, but just knowing they were there made us feel older. We didn't have to live on our own yet, but it seemed feasible.

I began to feel unmoored, untethered, in that big house, that not-parsonage, that place freestanding, apart from the church, on its own, alone in the world.

And we were, it seemed, richer than we'd ever been, in the big old house, the not-parsonage with the floors paved in heavenly gold shag.

When I Was Lukewarm

I had my school friends and I had my church friends. Two sets of friends, two worlds, one sacred, the other secular. The lines weren't drawn so straight and clear, but I tried to imagine them that way: church, school, sacred, secular.

My two best church friends were Russell Reynolds and David Koenan. I confessed my sins to Russ and Dave, and they did the same. That was the definition of a close church friend: someone to whom you could confess your more serious forays and stumblings in the world of your school friends. We didn't chastise one another—because we knew how much we Baptists struggled and strove in this hostile and dangerous territory, this land of Catholics and Lutherans.

The confessions provided some absolution, but we were equally (if not more) interested in simply hearing about the sins. If I told Russ and Dave that I got drunk the Friday night before, they'd want to know what that was like. What goofy thing did I do this time?

Well, it so happened that I rode my ten-speed, no-handed, across ten front lawns in St. Anthony Park. Then I fell and got back on the bike and rode some more. Then I made out with some girl's second cousin from Brainerd. How far did I get? Somewhere between second and third base. The memory is blurry.

"But I felt really guilty about it the next day," I'd say. "I don't want to do that anymore. I'm going to rededicate my life to Jesus Christ again at camp this year."

"Me too," Russ would say.

"So am I," Dave would say.

"Let's all do it at the same time. We can all go forward on the same night."

Rededicating your life to Jesus Christ was what the Baptist kids did. Camp was the time and the place for decision, and we needed something to decide. We'd all accepted Jesus into our hearts in our childhood years, but a falling away from the faith, an adolescent phase of backsliding into the hands of Satan, was expected. And when the camp pastors asked, at the end of each sermon, if there was anyone out there in the audience who needed for the very first time to accept Jesus Christ as personal Lord and Savior, they also pleaded with those of us who'd done that very thing years before: "Maybe you've fallen away from the faith, into sin, and you need to come forward and kneel at the altar tonight to ask for forgiveness, to rededicate your life to Jesus Christ, to renew your covenant with the Lord."

Opportunities for covenant renewal were infinite. You could renew, rededicate, repent whenever you needed to—although, if you did so publicly more than once a year, people would begin to doubt the sincerity of the rededication and say among themselves that you only went forward so that everyone would look at you, or you only went forward to win the heart of that devoutly Christian girl you had the crush on.

I tended to renew my covenant annually at camp. In between, in private, I'd renew it maybe twenty or thirty more times.

School friends didn't know about any of this.

A lot of guys at St. Paul Murray Junior and Senior High School went to church, but this didn't make them act any differently. That's what I would have expected, since they were mostly Catholics and Lutherans.

Murray drew from two main neighborhoods: Northwest Como (on the east side of the Minnesota State Fairgrounds) and St. Anthony Park (on the west side of the fairgrounds). The St. Anthony Park families were more white-collar and Lutheran, while the Northwest Como families were more blue-collar and Catholic. I was a Northwest Como Baptist who hung out mostly with the St. Anthony Park Lutherans. My best friend at Murray, Jerry Bergman, the son of a St. Anthony Park carpenter, didn't go to church at all.

The Bergmans' church was their cabin on a lake in Wisconsin. They went to their cabin every weekend, without fail, whether or not Jerry chose to go along with them. And Jerry usually didn't go. He was left alone in the house, unsupervised, nearly every weekend. Jerry didn't neglect the responsibility that this presented: he became the king of the St. Anthony Park partiers, and the Bergman house on Raymond Avenue became the St. Anthony Park party castle.

I heard rumors and saw traces of Jerry's older brother, the adult of the house when Mr. and Mrs. Bergman were gone. He'd graduated from high school and still lived in the basement. I spent many afternoons and evenings listening to records and playing pool down there, but I can't remember what Jerry's older brother looked like. Still, I believe that the mystery older brother was a formative influence in my life. He'd perfectly designed and furnished the Bergman basement for what I now know as the seventies: huge stereo speakers, turntable, tape deck, records and tapes galore, brown simulated-leather couch, a La-Z-Boy recliner, an enormous color TV, state-of-the-art plywood paneling, shag carpeting, a bumper pool table, a regulation-sized billiard table, a foosball table, a well-stocked bar with a black linoleum counter surrounded by long black stools, and a bathroom with piles upon piles of *Playboy* and *Penthouse* magazines.

The Bergman basement had everything you'd want in a youth drop-in center. And no adults. Jerry's basement was the secular equivalent of The Wreck.

School friends, church friends, Jerry's basement, The Wreck. All of this shuttling back and forth between worlds made me fear becoming one of the lukewarm spewed ones that my school friend, Pete, warned me about.

Pete was the only friend of mine who blurred the clear-cut school friend/church friend distinction. Like me, he lived a few blocks from the state fairgrounds, had parents who'd graduated from Bethel College (as he and I did years later), attended a Baptist church (not my father's Central Baptist, though), and struggled fiercely with the wondrous temptations that the world had to offer. Like me, he spent much energy feeling guilty and planning the next rededication-to-Jesus opportunity.

Pete and I got drunk together, listened to the same music (Bad Company, Led Zeppelin, Aerosmith, Uriah Heep, Yes ...), went to the same concerts, played on the same basketball teams, made out with the same girls, and shared the same evangelical Christian anxiety: a persistent sense of never being where or who we should be.

Pete discovered the Bible verse that shook our worlds, Revelation 3:16: "So then because thou art lukewarm and neither cold or hot, I will spew thee out of my mouth."

"I'm feeling," Pete said after reading the verse to me, "pretty lukewarm spiritually these days."

"So am I," I said. "I'm feeling a little bit colder than lukewarm."

Lukewarm, a little bit colder than lukewarm, either way the message was the same: we weren't just right. This was precisely what we'd always feared, that God might spew us out of His mouth if we weren't on fire, if we were in that icky lukewarm middle state.

This little verse challenged the once-saved-always-saved assumptions that we'd grown to believe. That's what we were told as children: once you accept Jesus into your heart, He never leaves you. Once you've been granted the gift of salvation, it can never be taken away. Once you've been promised eternity in Heaven, you won't go to Hell.

Hardcore backsliders took full advantage of these guarantees.

"If it's a certainty that I'm going to Heaven," they said, "I might as well sin on Earth."

This was, Sunday school teachers told us, missing the spirit of the gift. If you've been given salvation, if you're a true believer, they said, you should strive, positively burn, to live the kind of Christian life that is pleasing to the bestower of the gift (who is God in Jesus Christ, Our Lord).

This is where things got confusing.

If you emphasized living a Christian life as evidence of salvation, you could fall into the salvation by good works camp: Catholics and their ilk. These so-called Christians claimed, our teachers said, that they could earn their way into Heaven. This was, at best, fallacy, and at worst, heresy. Because of our innately sinful nature, we could never live right enough to earn our way into Heaven. Never ever ever. The very thought was an insult to God; it implied that we could eventually be perfected. It led to a notion that we could become gods.

We were saved by grace through faith alone, "not by works," the Apostle Paul said, "lest any man should boast." No, we didn't want to be pious boasters, braggarts, who had the audacity to claim that we'd actually earned our way into Heaven.

Still, that begged the question: could someone receive the gift of salvation as a child but live like a non-Christian (cuss, drink, smoke, screw, etc.) later in life (as a wayward teen, as a lost adult) and still wind up in Heaven? Sunday school teachers tiptoed around this question with another question: "Was that person ever saved in the first place?" But if they asked that question, the once-assured child might say, "Well, you said that he was."

And then it became an issue of false advertising. Bait and switch. Sure, the teachers and preachers and troubadour evangelists would guarantee the certainty of a hereafter in Heaven, eternity with Jesus, if it would get us to receive Him. They were selling a product, and what good was a sale without a guarantee of satisfaction? What incentive would there be to receive Jesus into our hearts if they admitted that our decision could be revoked? Would this admission bear results?

Results: the evangelical enterprise.

Maybe other Sunday school teachers had, in ages past, unsuccessfully tried the truer explanation: that no one could know for sure who God would let into Heaven. That God could decide that the childhood decision meant nothing if the saved-one turned out to be a murderer or a rapist or a drunk or a promiscuous fornicator or all of these.

Why didn't anyone know how bad you could be before God said, "Enough is enough. I take your salvation back"? Was or wasn't God's love truly unconditional? Apparently, it was more fickle than Pete or I would have guessed.

Yes, lukewarm we were. We hadn't out-and-out rebelled. Neither of us was an out-in-the-freezing-cold sinner. We rebelled covertly. We still obeyed our parents, mostly; we went to church every Sunday morning, Sunday evening, and Wednesday night; we went to Thursday night Bible studies and all youth group outings; and we tried to forget all of the above when we were least afraid of getting caught.

Lukewarm, yes, but were we spewed? How could we know beyond the shadow of a doubt whether or not we'd been spewed?

"I'm not going to risk being lukewarm. I'm going to get hot for the Lord again," Pete said. "When I get to camp this summer I am going to rededicate my life to Jesus Christ."

That was the only sane thing to do, we agreed: get on fire for Jesus again. And it was a given that we would wait until camp. We wanted to enjoy that lukewarm state while we still could. We needed to get out of the world and into camp in order to get the world out of our systems.

The Almost-Burnouts

Mom now remembers my fourteenth year as the year of our not getting along at all, the year everything she did and said sounded wrong to me. I suppose it was normal adolescent turf-marking, accompanied by all-too-common experimentation with drinking and drugs, things that had to be kept hidden—and hidden all the more so from the Baptist minister's wife who happens to be your mother.

Other church moms told stories of their formerly sweet and docile children turning overnight into demons who smoked, got drunk, swore at them, stole money from their purses, and blasphemed the name of Jesus. The hazards of my adolescence were, Mom knew, compounded by my inescapable role as a pastor's kid. We were easily typecast as saints or reprobates. I was trying to be both in different places. She sensed that, but she didn't have any hard evidence. Yet.

Sirens went off in her head when, during my lonely and confusing seventh-grade year, I started hanging out with Jerry and his band of roving drinkers and pot-smokers, the St. Anthony Park almost-burnouts. What could she do, though? I needed friends, and none of my church friends went to my school.

Jerry was a nice enough kid, a kid who would smile and say, "Hi Mrs. Anderson," when he came over to our house. He wasn't a smartass, not one of those sullen and despondent mutterers-under-breath. I'd had trouble making friends, and he wanted to be my friend. Friends are friends, and as a teen you take what you get or die trying to ascend to the next level of popularity.

Marna and the Concert Kit

The four of us told our parents that we'd be gone all day on a bike trip to Stillwater, a Minnesota town across the river from Wisconsin. We all had ten speeds, and teenage boys frequently went on Saturday bike trips from St. Paul to Stillwater, so they had no reason to doubt. On Friday night I packed a bag lunch—a peanut butter sandwich and a big bread bag filled with the leftover popcorn that my sister Marna and her overnight guest, Becky, had made earlier in the evening.

"Why are you packing a bag lunch?" Marna asked as she and Becky sat in the kitchen.

"I'm going on a bike trip to Stillwater tomorrow with Jerry, Brad, and Paul. We're leaving at about ten in the morning, and we'll be gone all day."

"You're going on a trip to Stillwater? I'll bet you're going on a trip to Stillwater. I wonder if they'll even make it there," she said, turning to Becky.

"Shut up. What do you mean by that?"

"Oh, nothing."

"We're riding our bikes to Stillwater, that's all. And you better not say anything to Mom about us doing anything else. Because we're not."

"Yeah, Mark. Like I'm really going to say something to Mom."

Marna hung out with younger siblings of my party friends, and she had plenty of information to blackmail me with. I never knew how much she knew—just that she knew more than I could write off.

"You're so stupid, you probably would tell Mom," I said.

"You're so paranoid, Mark. Just go to bed and quit bugging us."

Typical teen conversation between Marna and me. Early in childhood, we'd given up on getting along. I now wish that we'd been allies instead of rivals, but she lived on the second floor, in her own room, next to Mom and Dad's, and I lived in the basement with my brother. The distance between our lives was great, and we hadn't yet learned how to talk to each other.

The next morning, the guys stopped by my house and we headed to our real destination: a park a few miles away in Roseville, an inner-tier suburb of St. Paul. "Trip to Stillwater" was, as Marna knew, code for "trip to a wooded area to get stoned."

A mile out of St. Paul, Jerry, the guy who was supposed to supply the pipe and screens, discovered that he'd forgotten both. We stopped into a novelty shop in Rosedale Shopping Center, a store that sold strobe lights, black lights and posters, battery-operated laugh boxes, nasty cards, sex games, and smoking paraphernalia.

For three dollars we found "The Concert Kit," a clear blue plastic rectangle containing a small wooden pipe, screens, rolling papers, and a roach clip. The Concert Kit: a good indication of what the sixties drug culture had become by 1976. Drug paraphernalia was mass-produced and packaged, along with corporate Album-Oriented-Radio, for The Burnout, a ready-to-smoke self that could be donned like a favorite concert T-shirt. Even suburban shopping malls had head shops. That's one reason why so many people who went through adolescence in the seventies claim to have been burnouts at one time or another, and it's also why so many of the real seventies burnouts—the tragic burnouts—are still stuck in that decade. So much depended upon one's ability to get into and out of the clear blue plastic rectangle.

We rode to a secluded wooded area where we felt confident that we'd be able to smoke in peace without getting busted. Jerry loaded the pipe bowl with very dry, brown-green weed as a transistor radio played "The Boys Are Back in Town."

"This is some strong shit! Did you hear it crackle? It's not going to take much for us to get gone," he said as he passed the pipe to Brad.

The pipe went around and everyone said "Strong shit" as they drew from it. It scorched my esophagus, and I coughed.

"Mark coughed," Jerry said. "He's gone."

Time slowed. We finished the bowl, then lit another and another. Smiling, eyelids drooping, we left the woods and sat down on a hill. Swift walkers, joggers in sweat suits, kids on stingrays, and teens on ten speeds circled the lake. We looked around and started laughing uncontrollably.

I moved my head from side to side: slow circling frames froze and shifted, froze and shifted … I'd been high before, but never *stoned.* Terrified and laughing, I remembered the junior high health class drug movie starring the guy who freaked out on bad acid at an after-school party and never returned to normal.

"III FEEEEEL REALLLLY WEEEIRRRD. IIII'VVE NEVERRR FELLLT LLLIKE THISSS BEFOOORRRRRE."

I pulled my peanut butter sandwich out of the ziploc baggie, and as I took a big bite, I felt something very hot and wet, something that didn't have the texture of peanut butter or bread. I looked at my sandwich and saw a shiny yellow-green tongue hanging out—a tongue, I guessed, of a demon that had crept up from the underworld to find a home in the peanut butter.

"AAAUUGGGHH!" I yelled as I spit out the bite. "There's a green demon in my sandwich!"

I'd been learning a lot about demons that year.

I threw the sandwich as far as I could. My friends rolled hysterical in the grass.

"It's not funny!!" I said.

They seemed to be in on Satan's cruel joke. I cooled off my tongue with a sip of lukewarm Shasta root beer. Shaken and hungry, I got out my bag of popcorn, grabbed a handful, looked at it, and saw tiny black beetles crawling in the crevices.

"Black bugs! There's black bugs in my popcorn!" I shouted, tossing the bag.

My friends were hyperventilating somersaults in the grass.

Demons! Demons everywhere! Where could I seek refuge? I couldn't hop on my bike and head home: if I even made it that far, I'd be caught by Mom. I fell back onto the soft grass, closed my eyes, saw the shiny green tongue, the black beetles, and the wide mouths of my laughing friends.

I woke up late in the afternoon. I almost felt normal. My friends were asleep.

I found the sandwich and popcorn. The demon and beetles? Pickled green jalapeno peppers and black pepper kernels.

"Did you enjoy your lunch on your trip today?" Marna asked when I got home.

My Spiritual Walk

It was a brief conversation that Marshall remembers, a brief conversation that I'd forgotten until he reminded me.

Marshall had taken on the role of saint, and I was trying hard to keep him from hearing about my sin. Between the running-and-hiding and the paranoia about him finding me out, things got tense between us. What he remembers: things got particularly tense after the brief conversation we had about my walk with the Lord.

"Mark, I've been thinking about your spiritual walk lately," he said one afternoon. "Do you ever read your Bible anymore?"

I was lying on the top bunk, listening to Led Zeppelin's *Houses of the Holy*. The question roused me from my full metal stupor.

"If you ever ask me that again," I said, "I will kill you."

I didn't see the look on his face.

I heard him walk upstairs to the kitchen, I heard him walk through the living room, I heard him walk upstairs to Mom and Dad's room. He had something new to report about me.

I guess I told him. He didn't ever ask me that again.

A Way of Escape

To celebrate the end of ninth grade, Jerry and company were going to be drinking at one of the two main spots: in Jerry's basement or under the Highway 280 bridge by the railroad tracks. I assured them that I would join them this time, no matter what. And I wasn't going to let anyone stop me. They'd been bugging me about not getting drunk with them more often.

I needed Mom's permission to go to the gathering, and I knew that she wouldn't be thrilled about it. She had reason to worry, but I needed to convince her otherwise. This much I didn't lie about: there would be drinking. The lie: I promised her that I wouldn't drink.

"Isn't it hard for you to not drink when everyone else is?" she asked. "I get worried about you."

I'd learned to ease Mom's worries by quoting scripture. A well-timed Bible verse could work wonders.

"Yes, Mom. It gets hard, at times. But isn't this what we as Christians will face all our lives in a world of unbelievers? I learned a Bible verse in Sunday school this week that I've been thinking a lot about. 1st Corinthians 10:13. 'There hath no temptation taken you but such as is common to man: but God is faithful, who will not suffer you to be tempted above that ye are able; but will with the temptation also make a way to escape, that ye may be able to bear it.' This means that whenever I'm tempted, God will provide a way to escape."

"Oh Mark," she said as she hugged me, "I'm so proud of you. You can go—but be home by eleven o'clock. You're probably a good influence on your friends."

Did she think I'd be the party evangelist?

As I recall this lie, I'm struck by a couple of things. First of all, I can't believe how deceptive, how plain old bad I was to use a Bible verse as a means of lying more effectively to my very own mother. Second of all, the word "escape" is deceptive in the verse. The most difficult temptations that I've been confronted with in life have involved sex, alcohol, and drugs, and "escape" has usually meant simply walking away or saying "No thank you." These are, of course, the most difficult things to do in the first place—so what's the escape? The verse leads the reader to believe that a secret door will open, that the tempted one will slide down a hatch and find himself or herself back in the realm of safety.

About five of us made our way to the railroad tracks below the 280 bridge and commenced with the drinking to celebrate the end of school, the beginning of summer. I downed five beers in less than fifteen minutes. Guzzled, took a breath, then cracked open the next one. The first two were a challenge, but by the third, my brain and body were ready for anything.

We made noise, blasted the transistor radio, sang along with whatever the airwaves offered us, welcomed the handful of girls who decided to join us, hoped to make out, and when that didn't happen, we took to the streets. St. Anthony Park, with its hills and big houses and green alcoves, was great for roaming, and you could remain easily hidden. The roads there tarried and offered ample opportunities to get lost. Teens ran wild in St. Anthony Park.

We eventually made our way to Dan Griffin's big white house, the place that came to be known as The Tramp: a big backyard with a trampoline, a shack in the distance, and a wooded area beyond it. Packs of teens came from nowhere, got drunker in the shack, then headed onto the trampoline. I don't remember parents ever being around—and, amazingly, I don't remember anyone dying or breaking bones or winding up paralyzed from the neck down. Drunk kids would flip, backwards and forwards, and there were no spotters to toss the fallen back onto the bounce.

Things at The Tramp got more and more out of control, and it was all a lot of fun until the clock struck ten and I remembered, "I have to be home in an hour, and Mom will be waiting up for me." Mom always waited up for me.

"Better walk it off," Jerry said.

I spent the next forty-five minutes walking alone, up and down the hills, sweating off what I could. By ten forty-five I felt relatively sober, but my breath still reeked, so I bought a pack of Wrigley's Spearmint gum to chew. I put three sticks in my mouth, chewed and chewed.

"What does my breath smell like?" I asked Jerry when I got back to The Tramp.

"Wrigley's Spearmint—and beer," he said, and gave a smirk that said, "You're dead."

I'd have to sneak in and hope that my parents were asleep. Unlikely. They'd be waiting up, I knew, and Mom would want to talk. She'd ask me about the party and if everyone was drinking and was it hard to be the only one not drinking.

I rode my bike home through the dark of the Minnesota State Fairgrounds. I had, by then, six pieces of gum in my mouth.

All of the upstairs lights were on in the house. I spit out the gum and walked in the side door.

I'd sneak quickly down to the basement. I'd spend a long time in the bathroom, get undressed, run to my bed, get under the covers, turn my face to the wall, and pretend that I was asleep. If Mom or Dad came down and tried talking to me, I'd say, "Whaaaah? I was asleep."

Before I got down the top step, Mom opened the door to the basement.

"Hi Mark. How was the party?"

"It was okay. I felt really tired though. I'm really tired. I think I'll just go to bed."

"You're really tired?" she asked, and looked hard into my red eyes.

"Yeah, really tired."

Her eyes filled with tears. She knew.

"You've been drinking," she cried. "I could smell it as soon as you walked in the door. You've been drinking. I know that smell."

She knew that smell because her Uncle Howard was, for years, a pathetic and vicious alcoholic. I'd heard the stories: Howard ruining family functions and holidays with his drunken pathos and rage, Howard wetting his pants in front of Mom and her friends as they jumped rope in front of her parents' Denver apartment, Howard even showing up drunk on Sunday morning and evening at Calvary Baptist Church.

"My greatest fear on my wedding day," she once told me, "was that Howard would show up drunk and make a scene and ruin my wedding."

Well, he didn't, and he later sobered up. By the time I came around, Howard was a friendly teetotaling bigot who worked at the bank and gave us children fifty-cent rolls of pennies whenever we visited him.

"John! John!" Mom yelled. "Come down right away."

She sobbed and sobbed, and Dad came downstairs to assist with the crisis.

"What's wrong?" Dad asked.

"Mark's been drinking."

"I only had one beer," I said.

I was sober enough to lie about how much I'd had without fear that they'd observe otherwise. I started crying. The booze spinning in my head, Mom crying, the shame of getting caught, Dad's saddened eyes: it was impossible not to cry this time, so I did.

"I only had one," I kept repeating. This made no difference to Mom. It didn't matter how much I had: I'd given in to the temptation of the world. I hadn't escaped.

"I was so proud of you," she said, "when you left and read that verse from 1st Corinthians about God providing an escape from temptation. I thought you meant it."

I told her that I did mean it, every word of it, that this time the temptation became too much to bear and I couldn't see the way to my escape. Except leaving altogether and heading home—which I didn't want to do.

"I only had one," I repeated.

Dad didn't say much through all of this. The parental discipline pattern was that Mom would overreact (and apologize later) and Dad would underreact (and not mention it later).

"Why don't we go downstairs and talk," he said to me. "Or maybe you should take a shower first."

My red eyes, my powerful breath, and my insistence that I'd only had one led him to believe that I probably had more. He never said so, but I suspect. Dad somehow knew that a good hot shower would be the best mode of detoxification. It might have been something that he learned in seminary—part of the "Urban Ministry" lesson about how to deal with the church drunk. Or maybe he had to assist once or twice with the detoxification of Uncle Howard.

We went downstairs. Sobbing hysterically, I disrobed and climbed into the shower.

When Mom saw me in the morning, she apologized. Maybe, she said, she'd overreacted a little bit. It was just that smell, that horrible smell, and those awful memories of Howard.

"I know that smell anywhere," she said.

Smell memories last a long time. That was one reason why I could smoke pot without getting caught: the smell conjured no memories for her, and it was easily erased by a pack of Wrigley's.

"How much did you drink last night?"

"I had one beer. And I started another, but I poured it out when I remembered that verse in 1st Corinthians."

What a lying little wretch I was. It worked though. The pouring-out of the second beer indicated a guilty conscience, a conscience that I'd listened to long before I got caught. I felt guilty on my own, long before I saw her tears. What was this pouring-out of the second beer if not an escape in operation?

"It must have taken a lot of strength to pour out that second beer," she said.

Timber

A few days after I got caught, I headed up to Trout Lake Baptist Camp for the month of June to volunteer on their work crew, a position that my parents and youth pastor had recommended to me months before.

I vaguely remember filling out an application that included a personal statement of faith and being thrilled when I got the letter back saying that they would be pleased to welcome me onto the Trout Lake Camp Summer Youth Volunteer Staff for the month. I thought little of this at the time, but it now strikes me as strange: I gladly went up to a Baptist camp for a whole summer month to do grueling physical labor, and I earned nothing more than my room and board, things that I never had to work for before. I must have really needed to get away from home.

Except for my week at camp, the summer before was mostly tedious and boring. I was at that place in life where it seemed like there was never anything to do. What did a guy do for a whole summer? Too much of nothing. Might as well volunteer to go away for nothing.

I now wonder: was there an element of at-risk-youth prevention going on here? "At-risk" hadn't yet entered the concerned-adult lexicon, but I think my parents were worried about the risks, the stumbling blocks, the stones in my passway. Mom and Dad feared that all the deadened summer time, combined with my lack of interest in much of anything except listening to records (I didn't read much, I didn't write at all, I only played drums now and then), multiplied by the time I'd surely spend with my drinking friends, would lead to many more nights of not escaping temptation.

I remember riding up to Trout Lake Camp with Mom and Dad, just the three of us, and stopping at some diner in Brainerd where they had, at each table, a little jukebox that played whole albums in addition to singles. You could pay a dollar to play the album, or pay a quarter and play three songs from it, or pay a dime for one song. People were thinking less and less about singles, more and more about long plays. Because there was so much time to fill.

I chose a few selections from the Rolling Stones' *Goat's Head Soup:* "Dancing with Mr. D," "100 Years Ago," and "Coming Down Again."

The three of us didn't have much to say to each other. We didn't want to think that anything much would be different about our lives. Just because I'd be away for a whole month (as a work crew guy) and a week (as a camper), the longest I'd ever been away from my family. Nothing much could change in a month and a week.

Eventually we arrived at Trout Lake Camp on that dry and sunny June Saturday. My memories of the camp have the dry heat texture of a cult compound, but it's been twenty-six years since I last visited the place. As I've moved further and further past my evangelical Christian years, the summer camps have acquired that cultish aura. Still, every conscious Minnesotan knows that Minnesota summers are humid, not dry.

Dad and Mom helped me unpack and move into my cabin, a cabin in the deep woods where the work crew guys stayed. Our cabin was much deeper in the woods than the camper cabins, and we had to wind down a wooded path to get to it. Twelve guys stayed there: ten guys my age and two college guys who served as counselors by night, crew supervisors by day. They were our wise elders, the ones who presented devotions, led prayer times, and gave us new Bible verses to memorize. We could ask them questions about girls and Jesus that we weren't comfortable asking our parents or Sunday school teachers.

This cabin held four separate bunk rooms (one in each corner, with a shared living room in the middle) and it was usually an awful smelly mess. Except for the counselors, everyone was away from home for the first time. My memory of that place: dirty clothes scattered all over the floor, a bench press and weights in the living room, and the commingling stink of jock sweat, four or five flavors of mosquito repellent, and campfire smoke from the night before.

From the cabin we walked to the dining hall and had a sloppy joe and potato salad lunch.

Then good-bye to Mom and Dad. They remember me looking sad and forlorn as we hugged good-bye and exchanged "I love you."

I'd see them again in a month and a week.

How did we work crew guys spend our days? We did a lot of logging.

The dozen or so of us loaded onto the flatbed work crew truck and headed into the forests surrounding Trout Lake Camp. We swung axes, pushed and pulled two-man saws, chopped and cut down nameless tree after nameless tree, yelled "Tiimmmberrrrr," and realized that loggers really did, after all, yell "Tiimmmberrrr," because that's what was falling. The supervisors taught us how to cut the trees so that they'd fall in the direction we wanted them to fall, but I never got the hang of it. The trees I axed always seemed to fall backwards. That's what happened if you swung too high and hard.

"Tiimmmberrrrr! Hey! You guys! Timber! Timber!"

The work was exhausting. It wasn't the exhaustion that follows an adrenaline rush, but lethargic exhaustion. I could say that all of the falling and dying trees sapped my own energy, but I certainly wouldn't have said that back then. I didn't care about the trees. I cared not a whit for nature. Nature nature nature, blah blah blah. The fact that trees were there, the fact that there were trees, was reason enough to chop them down. Chopping down trees was as interesting as the next thing.

The next thing was stripping the logs. A dump truck would drop a bunch of them into Trout Lake to soak; we'd pull them out, set them on the workhorses, and strip off the bark with hammers and chisels. We'd then pull the bark off in strips until we had a plain old bare log in front of us. After the log-stripping, we chiseled away all of the knots, all of the nubs, all of the outgrowths. One of the guys invented a name for the task: "nipping noobies." We'd shave those logs clean and smooth, sand them, and pile them high.

I don't remember what they were going to be used for. What happened to all of that timber? It wasn't going to be firewood. Where was it sent? We saw the whole process, except for the creation and construction of the next thing. What was the next thing?

There were girls there too. They did girls' work (cooking, laundry, place-setting) and they were called Marthas. I made out once with the Martha named Alexia. She said to call her Lexy.

For a half hour in the morning, each and every camper and staff member headed for an empty spot by the lake to have quiet time with the Lord. Quiet time meant reading the Bible and praying. I found a nook beneath a tree, the same nook every day, where I tried my hardest to read, pray, concentrate, meditate, and wait upon the Holy Spirit. I was easily distracted.

The Holy Spirit never came upon me like I thought it would, but I never minded the quiet. I tried to ignore all that was there for me to ignore.

Staff members were expected to be the leaders of this new world that the campers were entering. We were to be examples of Christ-centered living. Every morning before the campers got up, we (fifty-plus believers, wage-earning adults and volunteer teens) met for Bible devotions and prayer for all of the lost souls. All staff members were expected, at least once during the summer, to lead the rest of the staff in morning devotions. The devotions were seen as the fruit of our morning quiet time, the indication that we had something that could be called a "spiritual walk."

What had I learned in that time of meditation? The contents of my spiritual walk: Was I hot, was I cold, or was I lukewarm? Was I spewed, or was I not-spewed? And that's what I shared when it was my turn, the verse that still weighed heavy on my heart, months after Pete first read it to me: Revelation 3:16.

I stood before the staff members and gave a testimony about something that happened to me earlier that year. My Central Baptist youth pastor, Lloyd, came up to me one Sunday evening and told me how pleased he was at the spiritual growth that he'd seen in me that year. I must have been having some real fruitful quiet times with the Lord, he said, because I seemed so much more mature than before. I was starting to show some real leadership qualities.

"Keep up the good work," Lloyd said.

And I told the staff about that. I told them about how it made me feel like such a hypocrite, because the truth was that I hadn't been having quiet times at all. I'd only started the quiet times at camp that month, and I'd learned so much, so much, in those special quiet times.

I didn't mention all of the times I'd been drunk or stoned that year, but I hinted. I hinted: "There are some things I did last year that I feel really bad about."

That's when I brought out the verse, my verse. My verse. I read a modern translation of it so that everyone would understand, and I added the verse before and the verse after for more context. No one would miss the point and risk the consequences of remaining in a lukewarm state.

"I know your deeds, that you are neither cold nor hot. I wish you were one or the other! So, because you are lukewarm—neither hot nor cold—I am about to spew you from my mouth."

When my friend Pete read that verse to me, I told them, "it really hit me. Struck me right between the eyes." Almost every staff devotion had a "really hit me" in it. That was the moment of clarity. The blinding light on the road to Damascus. It really hit me. When I say it now, I imagine a hand reaching out from the Bible to club me on the head.

"And I realized," I said, "that, hey, I was taking advantage of the situation. I was taking God for granted because I didn't think salvation could be taken away. And it really really hit me: God could spew me right from His mouth … So, this morning I'd like to challenge all of you to check your own spiritual growth and see if you are hot, cold, or lukewarm."

Any good devotion had to end with a challenge, something that its hearers could do in response. My challenge: you'd better check yourself. Hot, cold, or lukewarm? You'd better check yourself.

As nervous as I felt up there, my words seemed to have an impact. I didn't think I was saying much of anything, but I could see plenty of adult nods of recognition. I didn't know if my words would bear results, but it sure looked like I was having an impact, convicting with my convictions.

Later in the day, the supervisor of the Marthas, a pretty Bible college woman with long brown hair, came up to me and said, "I didn't get to hear you speak this morning, but I heard from others that your devotions were right on! Everyone I talked to said they were very very powerful."

My words, like all words spoken in public with conviction, had a way of holding me accountable to my hearers, my audience. My testimony was out there, in other heads. I'd better check myself.

Yes, I'd better check myself.

The Bicentennial After-School Special

Stephanie and I met at Trout Lake Baptist Camp in the summer of '75, the summer "blooping" became the camp practical joke. A girl would walk up to a guy and say, "Hey, do you want to go blooping?" The guy, thinking that "blooping" was a new slang word for making out, would, without hesitation, say, "Sure." The girl then led him to a remote spot on the lakeshore, sat down next to him, picked up a small stone, tossed it in the lake, and said "bloop" as it hit the water.

"Did you hear it go bloop? That's blooping," the girl said, then walked away.

The guy sat there all alone, knowing he'd been had.

Before long, though, blooping came to mean making out or, at least, the possibility of it. Some guy would come back to the cabin and tell about a girl who took him blooping and, after throwing the stone in the water, started kissing him on the lips. So, we gathered, the girl might mean what you hoped she meant, or she might just be playing a joke. You wouldn't know until you got alone with her, but the potential payoff was worth the risk of humiliation.

Some guys took matters into their own hands and started asking girls to go blooping. Its origin as a practical joke made it seem less risky. Guys bragged about how many different girls they'd blooped with during the week. Then, one pious guy claimed that when he said "blooping," he meant "quiet time in prayer." Other guys picked up on this.

"You read me wrong. See, I'm just looking for a sister in Christ to pray with."

One guy, according to rumor, invited a girl to bloop after lights out. The two sneaked out of their cabins and skinny-dipped under the stars.

Practical jokes, making out, praying, skinny-dipping: by the end of the week everyone wanted to bloop, but nobody knew for sure what blooping meant.

My romance with Stephanie began at the peak of this blooping confusion. One thing led to another.

A small group of guys and girls from Central Baptist in St. Paul and Olivet Baptist in Robbinsdale were hanging out after a hot dog and baked bean picnic supper. These youth group alliances happened when the guys from one church were placed in a cabin with the guys from another—and the girls from one church would be placed with the girls from yet another. Soon enough, you'd have three or four youth groups intermingling, communing, then dispersing to couple.

The Olivet and Central teens started talking about who had and who hadn't been blooping, and Stephanie was the only one who hadn't. Stephanie, a school friend of a girl from Olivet, came from a non-churchgoing family. Because she wasn't a born-again believer, she stood among us, but not of us. The group unanimously agreed that it was up to me to show blooping to Stephanie. Stephanie didn't even know what blooping was.

Stephanie, just over five feet tall, wore a braided black leather choker beneath her long blond hair. She had blue eyes and saddle shoes.

The two of us walked down the hilly path that led to the lakeshore and sat down beneath a birch tree. I picked up a small stone.

"Okay watch, this is blooping," I said as I tossed the stone in the lake. "Did you hear it go 'bloop' as it hit the water? That's all blooping is. It's just a stupid joke."

"It is stupid," Stephanie said. "You brought me all the way down here to show me that?"

To redeem myself and the situation, I suggested talking for a few minutes. She said she was getting bored with the stupid picnic anyway.

We began at the beginning: how young was she, how old was I? She was going to be in eighth grade, and this seemed very young to me. I was going to be in ninth. We moved from our distance in time to our distance in space: I was from St. Paul, blocks from the Minnesota State Fairgrounds; she was from Golden Valley, a suburb near Theodore Wirth Park.

"That's about six miles from where I live," I said.

A small sailboat tipped over in the middle of Trout Lake.

"Six miles," she said, and laughed.

I thought we'd nearly exhausted possible conversation topics, when Stephanie asked the question that opened all doors.

"Do you like listening to music?"

"That's one of my favorite things to do!" I said.

The sailor stood on the keel and the boat plopped upright again. He hopped back in, and off it went.

Stephanie said her favorite singer was Elton John, and she had two of his records. My favorite, coincidentally, was also Elton John, and I had three of his records. She liked him more than anyone else, even though some people said he was a fairy. Especially guys, which was why she was surprised that I liked him. I didn't know about that. I didn't know what a fairy was, so I pretended that I knew and I didn't care.

And it didn't matter that Elton John was, in 1975, the most popular singer in the world: Stephanie didn't know any other guys who called him their favorite singer, and I couldn't, at that very moment, think of any girls who called him theirs. We liked something the same, and it was a way into a world. Liking the same singer was as good a reason as any to start a romance when I was fourteen.

"What's your favorite Elton John song?" she asked.

I thought hard. She seemed to be testing me. Anyone could name the most popular singer on earth, but narrowing his output down to one favorite song would separate the wheat from the chaff, the true follower from the commoner.

"'Funeral for a Friend/Love Lies Bleeding,'" I said.

"All right! That's my favorite too! It's actually two songs in one. You're a real fan, and not just someone who only likes songs if they're on the radio. Most people say 'Bennie and the Jets' or 'Crocodile Rock.' Those are his two worst songs."

This was an important mutual discovery: we were album listeners, not 45 listeners. For some reason, most girls I knew bought 45s, while guys bought albums. I accepted this, but I couldn't explain it. The intense and short-lived community of one three-minute song that everyone knows the lyrics to, versus the big-lonely-forty-minute-basement-bedroom-album. Marna and her friends would sing along with radio hits at top volume, while I'd be lying silently on my top bunk, hoping that the fifteenth minute of side one would lift me out of my world and into a heaven of its making.

But Stephanie liked albums. The possibilities for this relationship were boundless.

"You're not at all like I thought you were," she said as the chapel bell rang.

"Want to sit together?" I asked, as I took her hand.

"Sure," she said.

Evangelical Christian summer camp is designed to be, as my father told me a few years ago, a "high impact" week. This was a term routinely used by ministers and Christian educators. Wasn't "high impact" also a military metaphor, like so much of the religious language that I grew up with? Night after night, the camp evangelist, the primary human impactor, the bomb, would exhort, humor, charm, and scare the living sin out of a captive audience of teens. High impact. Toss in some rousing, big-voiced, contemporary chapel songs backed by guitar and drums, and the desired effect would surely be produced: an explosion of faith, a Jesus Sound Explosion.

By the end of the week, the guest evangelist would, if he was any good at all, be the most popular person at camp. The camp spirit would radiate from him (and the evangelist was, back then, always a he), and earnest young cabin counselors would, when the day was done, reiterate more intimately his message of salvation. Lamplit bedside devotions prompted discussion of teen and God things and more conversion. There were always, always, more souls to win—and the Holy Spirit never went to bed. The Holy Spirit might visit in the morning, in the noontime, in the twilight, in the night, or late in the midnight hour. We could never know when that very Holy Spirit might dispatch high impact.

Camp planners knew that sermons, sing-alongs, and devotions wouldn't, alone, draw hormone-charged teens to the point of highest impact. Trout Lake Camp attracted campers with a mix of recreation, frivolity, romance, and guilt. In the afternoon, we'd play miniature golf, ride horses, sail, water ski, canoe, swim, high-dive into the lake, play softball and basketball, attend Bible seminars, or take nature hikes with new girlfriends or boyfriends. After evening chapel, we'd participate in group bonding activities: skit nights, talent shows, indoor relay races.

The most popular relay race was the one where a row of campers passed an apple or orange, held between the chin and neck, from one camper to the next. We'd line up, as in, "All right now, get in four lines and stand boy-girl-boy-girl." (Every once in a while, a counselor would slip and say "girl-boy-girl-boy," and it sounded weird, wrong.) This race was designed, I'm convinced, to encourage romantic heterosexual intimacy and, at the same time, tease us with sex that would be sinful to consummate. Counselors laughed and said, "It's easier if you hold on to each other's waists," as they watched the relay that visually resembled the necking they'd go great lengths to prevent at the end of the night.

It's true: staff members would wander through the woods with flashlights and disentangle kissing couples. "Bushwhacking," they called it. The next night we'd entertain them with the relay where the boy-girl-boy-girl lines passed lifesavers with toothpicks held in our mouths.

I have to wonder what these adults were vicariously experiencing through us. America's Puritan heritage lives on in the strangest of ways. We already know this, though, don't we?

On Friday, our last full day at camp, Stephanie and I went canoeing during afternoon free time. We paddled on a small bay through water lilies as dragonflies flew around our heads. Horseflies bit our arms and legs. The bay led to a stream canopied by trees. I asked if she wanted to see what was up the stream. She said she'd like that—the way the sun was shining through leaves onto the water. It looked pretty. I liked that too, I said.

As we headed upstream, we discovered that we were, for the first time, completely alone. Conversation got slower with each paddle. She was from Golden Valley, I was from St. Paul. Golden Valley was about six miles from St. Paul. Probably closer to seven, she said. We both had bikes. Ten speeds. My second-favorite Elton John song was "Tiny Dancer." She didn't have a second-favorite Elton John song. Or maybe she did, but she'd have to think about it.

I saw a big snapping turtle—nearly as big as a 33-rpm album—walking from the sandy shore into the water. I thought it was huge until Stephanie said that she'd seen pictures of bigger ones in *National Geographic*—huge turtles that lived on islands off the coast of South America.

"They're about eight times as big as that one."

Eight times as big. Most people would have said ten. Stephanie was different. She made me want to read *National Geographic.* And *National Wildlife.* What was happening to me?

Soon the stream narrowed and the water was too shallow to paddle. To our left, a portage path led to an empty sand beach on another lake. I'd been a Trout Lake camper for four summers in a row, but I'd never been upstream far enough to see the other lake. We didn't know if we'd get in trouble if someone from camp saw us, but neither of us could remember anyone saying where we could or couldn't canoe.

We beached the canoe, picked it up, carried it through a winding path, set it down on the beach of the other lake, and sat down in the sand. There were no people or cabins nearby—only sailboats in the distance.

"I like you, Mark."

She said my name.

"I like you too," I said.

We put our arms around each other and kissed once on the lips. Then we kissed again. Each kiss broke the previous record for the longest kiss of my fourteen years. She put her tongue in my mouth, and we fell back into the sand. Our hands snuck beneath clothes and found places both unpermitted and unforbidden. Anything that stopped short of all the way was all right, as far as I knew, and Stephanie hadn't grown up hearing about sin, so the rules meant nothing to her.

When we faintly heard the camp dinner bell floating across the water, we realized that we'd lost track of time.

"Oh no. I've got sand in my pants," Stephanie said, and laughed.

"Me too," I said.

The camp week always ended with the Friday night campfire, the culminating event where some zealous, bearded counselor led songs with a guitar. Campers stood up, one by one, and gave testimonies about how sinful they were before camp, how they'd accepted Jesus or rededicated their life to Him during the week, and how they were really really (really this time) going to change their lives after camp and lead everyone in the world to Jesus Christ.

Without fail, somebody would start crying, and within seconds just about everyone there (all but the degenerate cynics) would be wiping away tears of Jesus joy and tears of sadness. The campfire would end and they'd return to the same smelly old unredeemed world, that awful place to be in but not of. They'd board buses back to nowhere, they'd lose contact with all the friends they'd made from other churches, they'd lose the new boyfriends and girlfriends to old school flames, they'd lose that feeling of oneness in Christ. And in the heat of the campfire, they'd promise not to get drunk, stoned, naked, and stupid ever again. Where would they find relief, a resting place? In the Lord? That was the right answer, but it wasn't much comfort.

Or maybe they'd just backslide faster and further than before, and all of these promises would be broken.

That was my constant dilemma: how could I possibly sustain the intensity of that camp spiritual renewal? I always came home from camp charged up, ready to lead a new life: I'd stay away from pot and booze and heavy petting, I'd witness to all of my school friends, I'd keep up with daily Bible study and prayer, I'd stay out of fights with my brother, I'd be kind to my sister and mother, I'd feel proud of my father, and I wouldn't be a lukewarm Christian. I wanted a constant camp high, a Friday night campfire that wouldn't go out.

My stumbling and backsliding didn't prevent me from being dogmatic about my faith. My beliefs remained, even as my behavior changed. More than anything else, I believed that I needed (as absolutely everyone did, no matter who they were or where they came from) to become born again in order to enter the Kingdom of Heaven. Rebirth requires a place from which to be born, and that place, I knew, was the state of sin. Guilt about backsliding and accompanying dogmatism: the cycle made more sense than I realized at the time. The dogmatism was another way of saying, "Don't make the mistakes that I made. Don't tread where I trod." Yet the person receiving the message had to first tread in that place in order to hear the message.

That's where Stephanie didn't follow me. She, quite simply, didn't believe that the place existed, and she couldn't understand my evangelical Christian angst. She thought (God bless her soul) that the campfire scene was very weird. She said, as we sat by Trout Lake afterwards, that she only went to Olivet Baptist because one of her best friends from school went there.

"Some of the youth group activities are fun," she said. "They get me out of the house. It's something to do."

She was the sanest person I'd ever known, though I didn't realize this at the time.

I told her that I wished I could be a better Christian around my school friends, and she wanted to know why I didn't consider them Christians since, after all, America is called a Christian nation. They were, I said, Lutherans and Catholics, but not born-again Christians. And if they weren't born again, they weren't really Christians.

"I'm not born again, but I think I might be a Christian," she said.

"If you're not born again, you can't be a Christian. If you don't know for sure, then you're not one. It says so in the Bible."

She wondered if my definition of a Christian meant that she was going to Hell. I ignored the question and put my arm around her. I couldn't bring myself to tell my new girlfriend that, yes, according to what I'd been taught and what I believed, she'd go to Hell when she died if she wasn't born again. It's just not very romantic to say, "You're going to Hell—now kiss me, you fool."

I tried to kiss her. She backed away.

"You didn't answer my question. You just want to make out. Do you think I'm going to Hell?"

"Well, I don't know who will be in Hell. Only God knows. My mom told me that some people think the Jews will get a second chance to ask Jesus into their hearts, so maybe everyone will get a second chance. Maybe you'll get a second chance."

"Lucky me. This Baptist stuff is all so weird. I never really went to church before going to Olivet—just a couple of times with my mom and dad, and I don't remember what brand it was. But you're all so serious about it, and I don't feel that way. I mean, I've never kissed a guy who thought I was going to Hell."

"I didn't say for sure you were going to Hell. I said you might get a second chance."

"Okay. A second chance. It doesn't matter. This is getting too serious. I still like you a lot. Let's kiss."

We kissed and kissed until the get-back-to-your-cabins bell rang.

The next morning we exchanged phone numbers.

We calculated miles and figured out that downtown Minneapolis was about halfway between her part of Golden Valley and my part of

St. Paul. We'd meet there on our bikes sometime next week. Maybe at the IDS Building, Minneapolis' only skyscraper.

We kissed good-bye and boarded church buses bound for the world.

The rest of that summer flew by. We met weekly at the IDS, then rode our bikes around the chain of Minneapolis great lakes: Lake of the Isles, Lake Calhoun, Lake Harriet, and back around. We made out in the woods. She came to a few Central Baptist youth group functions, and I came to a few Olivet outings. We talked nightly on the phone. In late August, we met at the Minnesota state fair and, afterwards, walked the three blocks to my house, where we sat on the couch and listened religiously to all four sides of Elton John's *Goodbye Yellow Brick Road.* Mom brought us lemonade, Dad drove us back to her home in Golden Valley. I escorted her to the door and gave her a last summer kiss.

When the November cold and snow hit, when it became too cold to ride bikes, I broke up with Stephanie to go out with a Central Baptist girl. Jody broke up with me a month later, and of course that served me right.

Stephanie and I met again at camp in July of '76, the week of the Bicentennial Celebration, the week of my fifteenth birthday.

When she got off the Olivet Baptist bus, we said "Hi" but didn't hug. I nobly offered to carry her bags up to the cabin, and she graciously let me. I felt my forehead, arms, hands, and chest dampen with sweat. I said something about the humidity—not so much the heat. I asked her how the bus ride was.

"It was a bus ride," she said.

After setting her bags in the cabin, she said what we both meant: "Wanna go blooping?" It had its original meaning again, and we didn't know what would happen.

"I was going to say that," I said.

"Yeah, but you wouldn't of. I could tell you wanted to say it, but you wanted me to say it first."

She was right, as usual, and I didn't deny it.

We walked down a pine-needled path, stopped at the lakeshore, checked for poison ivy, and sat down.

"Which one of us is going to throw the rock in the water?" she asked.

"He who is without sin cast the first stone," I said.

"What?"

"Haven't you ever heard that story in the Bible?"

"I don't read the Bible. Do we have to talk about the Bible?"

I didn't want to talk about the Bible. Stephanie thought I was trying to make up for her lost time away from church. She hadn't forgotten that I'd broken up with her to go with a Baptist girl. I'd betrayed her—this I knew.

She shook her head and said, "I don't know about you people. How did I end up at this camp?"

I didn't know that we were a people until she said so. And this camp—this camp, a world that had ended her up. I couldn't think of what to say, other than, "God sent you here," which would have been precisely the wrong thing to say.

I stood up and grabbed a cattail. Cattails reminded me of a weird counselor at Camp Shaubena, a camp near Galesburg, Illinois. I sensed that I was one funny story away from winning Stephanie back over to my side.

"I'm thinking," I said, "of this goofy counselor at Camp Shaubena in Illinois. Did I ever tell you that I lived in Illinois for four years?"

"Yes Mark, you've told me your whole life story at least a couple of times now. Tell me about the goofy counselor."

I don't remember how, exactly, I told the story to Stephanie. It's about a missionary from Ethiopia who, while he was home on furlough, served as a camp counselor. I remember him pulling cattails from the sand, taking big bites out of them, chewing them up, and saying, "Mmmm! I just love pronto pups. You kids ought to try them!"

We'd laugh and laugh and ask him to eat another. He'd pretend to, but he wouldn't really. I saw him skip into the woods and spit them out while we weren't looking.

Missionaries: some of the strangest people I've ever met.

"That's always the worst thing to hear my mom say on a Sunday morning," I said. "'By the way, kids, we're eating at missionary so-and-so's house this afternoon.' Sunday dinner at a missionary's always takes the whole afternoon—because they don't know or even care how long anything takes. And then my parents get mad if we don't at least try a little of everything they serve. Some of that missionary food—ooh, I don't even want to think about it. If we eat a little of everything and don't complain, my parents will take us to Bridgeman's for ice cream and french fries after Sunday evening church."

I'd gotten used to a strange world.

"That missionary counselor," I said, "probably got so used to eating anything people served just to be polite that eating a cattail didn't seem like such a big deal. And there was one curious camper who wanted to eat one too. The missionary tried to stop him, but who could blame the kid?"

"I'll bet," Stephanie said, "the kid was you. I can just see you thinking you could eat a cattail."

She was right, but I had to deny it. My story was supposed to be about the goofy missionary, not about me. What would she think if I told her that I'd actually considered becoming a missionary when I grew up?

"It wasn't me," I said.

"Yeah it was you. It was you. You wanted to eat a cattail. Ha ha—Mark wanted to eat a cattail."

"It wasn't me. I'm not a cattail eater."

"Yeah you are. I want to see you eat one. I'll forgive you for breaking up with me last fall if you do. By the way, are you still going with what's-her-name from your church?"

"No, she broke up with me about a month after I broke up with you."

"Ha! Serves you right! Serves you right! The church girl broke your heart!"

"Yeah, I was pretty hurt at the time."

Stephanie held up her thumb and forefinger, rubbed them together, and said, "You know what this is?"

I didn't know.

"This is the world's smallest violin playing 'My Heart Bleeds for You.'"

I pretended to laugh. Ha ha ha.

She had some things to get off her chest, she went on to say. After I broke up with her, she stuck pins in my school picture and found other creative ways to hate me for a few months. My picture as the dartboard bull's-eye. Drawings of me in art class that she later poked holes into with a sharp pencil. She even made some sort of voodoo doll Mark with stuffed socks and rubber bands.

No one had ever hated me that much before. She must have truly loved me.

"I started going out with this jerk named Ed," she said, "who only wanted to get drunk and make out. We never had anything to talk about. He didn't even like music. Except Kiss. He thought they were really cool. He went to their concert and had their posters all over his bedroom. Do you like Kiss?"

"No. I've always thought they were stupid."

"Good. I got so sick of them. He'd get mad if I put anything else on. I don't know why I went with him. I suppose just for something to do. It got me out of the house. We didn't have anything in common, though."

I wondered how much we still had in common. For one thing, she was growing into more mellow music: America, Hall and Oates, James Taylor, the Eagles, Linda Ronstadt, Joni Mitchell, Jefferson Starship. She now had forty-two albums, and only three of them were by Elton John. Mellow music calmed her down after fights with her mom, she said. And she had a lot of fights with her mom.

I meant to ask what she fought with her mom about, but I wanted to talk more about music. I had one James Taylor album, but I hadn't fully explored the mellower spectrum of things. I was getting heavily into hard rock. I wondered if she liked hard rock or if it bugged her. That's where I was: Led Zeppelin, Lynyrd Skynyrd, Aerosmith, Bad

Company, The Who, Bruce Springsteen, The Rolling Stones, Yes, Uriah Heep, Thin Lizzy.

"I have almost one hundred albums now."

"Well, you're a year older than me," she said. "I'll have that many by next year. I like hard rock too, every once in a while. I like it when I'm feeling good. I just haven't bought much of it. It's more risky. When I'm feeling rotten, I have to be more careful about what I buy. Especially when I only have a few dollars to spend."

It wasn't that she didn't like hard rock. It was more a matter of how she felt at the time relative to how much money she had. That made sense to me. When I didn't have much of my paper route money left to spend, I bought music that felt, more or less, like I did. When I had a little extra, I bought how I wanted to feel.

I couldn't believe how well things were going between us. It was as if we could talk about anything. A year had passed and things were less junior high, more high school. We could talk about our feelings. If we wanted to.

I tossed the cattail over my shoulder and sat down next to her.

"Wait a minute! You still haven't eaten the cattail. You have to eat the cattail before you sit down next to me."

"I'm not eating it."

"Well, I suppose I'll let you sit here if you say, 'I'm sorry, Stephanie, for breaking up with you to go with a church girl.'"

"I'm sorry, Stephanie, for breaking up with you to go with a church girl."

"I forgive you."

We held hands and kissed.

"We should probably find out what time it is. We might miss something," Stephanie said. "Hey, we still haven't officially blooped. Get a stone and I'll get one and we'll toss them together at the count of three."

We found stones.

"Okay," she said. "One, two, three."

After breakfast on the morning of July Fourth, the camp director announced that we'd be having an extended sing-along hour, a "singspiration," in the recreation room after chapel that evening. Stephanie and I looked at each other, and I knew right away that we'd be skipping.

"I can't believe that," Stephanie said, as we walked to our morning Bible class. "It's July Fourth—the Bicentennial—and they planned something at the same time that the fireworks will be going off across the lake. I'm sure they did it on purpose too. There shall be no fireworks at camp! It's not like I'm into all the Bicentennial stuff, but I always like watching fireworks on July Fourth. And it's your birthday, forgodsake. If anyone should be able to watch the fireworks, you should."

"Let's just not go. Let's skip. What could they do to us if they caught us, anyway? I suppose they could call our parents and tell them we skipped the singspiration to watch the fireworks. My parents might be a little mad—but I could win them over to my side by telling them it wasn't fair that I had to miss the Bicentennial fireworks on my birthday. How could they argue with that kind of patriotism?"

"My parents wouldn't care. They're just glad to have me gone for a week. My mom would probably think it was funny. But how can we get away without getting caught?"

I pointed to the woods down beyond the boys' restroom. If you kept walking in that direction, north, you'd eventually be off the campgrounds. We needed to get completely off the campgrounds or the bushwhackers would catch us. We knew that an army of staff members would be out in the woods on the night of July Fourth, searching for too-frisky couples.

"I don't know if I like the idea of leaving the campgrounds," Stephanie said. "Then we'll be on private property."

"It's either that, or singing every camp song we've ever learned in the recreation room."

Stephanie didn't argue.

The sky was beginning to darken when chapel ended that night.

"So how are we going to do this, Mr. America?" Stephanie asked.

"Just walk by my side. There's a tree I've been meaning to show you over there on the other side of the restroom."

"Wasn't that the tree you were telling me about earlier in the day?"

"Yep, the tree I was telling you about earlier in the day."

"The one with the leaves and the branches and the bark and the roots?"

"That's the one. But I'm having trouble seeing it in the dark here. Maybe it's up in those woods there."

"Let's look."

"I don't see anyone around, do you?"

"No."

"Run!" I whispered as we stepped onto a winding path.

Holding hands, we sprinted beneath the pines and birches, past overgrown bushes that scratched our arms and faces. Did I know where we were going? I thought I did.

We couldn't see Trout Lake Camp anymore, so we slowed down to a jog.

Up ahead, a "No Trespassing" sign on a barbed-wire fence blocked the path. We stopped. That wasn't supposed to be there. We wondered if we should turn around, but we knew we couldn't go back. It was too late for that. If we walked into the singspiration hot and heavy and scratched, they'd assume the absolute worst.

I folded my hands and held them down for her.

"Step into my hands," I said.

She stepped into my hands, and I boosted her over the barbed wire.

I stood stranded on the other side. How would I get over?

"Here," she said, as she pushed one slackened wire down to the ground with her foot, and pulled another up with her hand. "You can crawl through."

I bent down and crawled through.

We stood together, for the first time that summer, on ground that wasn't camp ground. This was the world.

We walked on until we saw a dry, empty beach, sheltered by long green reeds and cattails. A dark, vacant-looking cabin stood far enough away to forget it was there, but close enough to be reminded. When we sat down, we couldn't see it anymore. We put our arms around each other.

"Happy birthday to you happy birthday to you," Stephanie sang in a whisper, "happy birthday dear Marky happy birthday to you."

"And," she said, as she goosed me, "a pinch to grow an inch."

We kissed. The fear of getting caught made the kiss feel stolen, so we kissed again.

"I really care for you," I said. That's the closest I could come to saying, "I love you." Earlier in the week, the camp pastor told a group of us guys that the words "I love you" should be saved, along with our virginity, for our future wives. We could, however, say, "I love you—in Christ." Stephanie wouldn't go for the "in Christ" part.

"I really care for you, too," Stephanie said.

We heard a loud explosion in the distance and looked up to see a spray of red.

"Fireworks!"

"I'm going to give you a really big birthday kiss," Stephanie said.

We embraced, kissed, and, as the fireworks went off over our heads, we fell back into the sand. We kissed and rolled. The kisses led to buttons popping, shirts off, zippers down, belts unbuckled, pants at the knees.

"You can," Stephanie whispered, "if you want."

I wanted. I'd go to Hell. I wanted, so I did.

How possible was this? Stephanie closed her eyes, I kept mine wide open, neither of us said a word. There we were: Stephanie and I, on the Fourth of July, on the two-hundredth American Independence Day, on my birthday, naked in the sand, skipping a singspiration, letting freedom ring on someone else's private property, as fireworks, fireworks that we sincerely meant to watch, exploded all around us.

And that was it. That's what it was like.

Was that me? I couldn't say for sure. I felt outside of time.

We got dressed. The sky was quiet, and we didn't know what to say to each other.

"Oops," Stephanie began. "That was sort of stupid of me. This is a bad time of month for me to be doing that. This time of the month I could get pregnant really easily."

I shivered. Pregnant easily. This time of the month. What did that mean?

Well, according to Stephanie, there were certain times of the month when it was almost impossible for girls to get pregnant, and other times when it was easy for girls to get pregnant.

This was news to me. I didn't know why it was so, and I certainly wasn't going to ask her to explain. Why didn't she stop me? That was supposed to be the girl's job. That's what the camp counselors and pastors said—and I wouldn't dare ask them to explain about the easy and impossible times of the month. They'd wonder why I wanted to know. These weren't matters for a teenage Baptist boy to consider.

"Yeah, that was sure stupid of me," she said. "Right now it would be very easy for me to get pregnant."

Pregnant. Pregnant. Why did she have to keep saying that word?

"Pregnant?" I asked.

"Yeah—you know, when women get fat and have babies."

I knew about that. How, roughly, it happened—if not necessarily how and when, exactly, or why. I'd studied some of the finer details in a Christian book that my parents gave me on my eleventh birthday: *Almost Twelve.* The book had pictures of naked stages of body development that I stole peeks at when the mood hit. Sure, I knew a little—and I guessed the rest. Boys had penises, girls had vaginas, both got pubic hair, girls developed breasts and curves and became women, men put their penises in women's vaginas, women got pregnant and had babies.

Not always, though. Guys at school bragged about doing it to girls, but I never saw any of those girls get pregnant. Except one. So, I gathered, pregnancy happened mostly to adult women and the occasional, one-in-a-number, unlucky teenage girl—the unlucky girls I saw smoking, down the street from our house, outside a St. Paul boarding school for unwed teen mothers.

I pictured Stephanie in a baby blue maternity pantsuit, smoking with the teen moms at the boarding school. I wouldn't be with her, though. I'd be miles away at the juvenile reform school to which my parents would banish me, the troubled middle son. Then, next July, when the baby turned three months old, I'd pass my driver's test, get my license, and the three of us would drive away together. My old lady, my kid, and me. Tramps like us. Born to run.

"I'm sorry," I said.

"Don't apologize. We both did it. And it's not like I haven't done it before," she went on to say. "It's just that I wasn't thinking ahead this time."

This time? And she wondered why I broke up with her to go with a church girl! I was just another "time" to her. At least church girls laid down the law. They upheld standards. They knew when to say no. I only had one thing to say to her, one thing that would—despite whatever she thought about the dirty act—communicate my own disgust: "I feel really guilty about what we just did."

"I don't," she said. "I'm a little worried about being pregnant, but I don't feel guilty. It's just what two people do when they care for each other, isn't it?"

When they care for each other? Care for each other? It didn't matter, I knew, it didn't matter, I'd been taught again and again, if they liked each other, cared for each other, or even loved each other, if they weren't married. Where was this girl's moral compass?

"But it's a sin!" I said. "It's adultery! The Bible is very clear about sex before marriage being wrong."

"The Bible," she said, exasperated.

"It's not just the Bible—it's what my parents think. If you got pregnant and they found out, they'd be so hurt and angry with me. I don't think I could ever face them again. I'd probably kill myself."

"You're being a little dramatic about this, Mark. We don't know if I'm pregnant yet. Just try not to think about it, because there's nothing we can do except wait."

We heard the get-back-to-your-cabins bell ringing in the distance, so we ended the discussion and headed back to Trout Lake Camp.

We got there as other couples were heading into the woods for one last kiss. Or whatever else they did.

"Try not to worry about it, if you can," she said. "I'll try not to worry too. No matter what, we still have each other."

We kissed good night.

The next morning when I saw Stephanie, she had a big smile on her face, and good news to accompany it—news that I rejoiced to hear. After Stephanie got back from our outing, her counselor Mary asked, during cabin devotions, how many of the girls in the cabin had accepted Jesus into their hearts already and how many of them still needed to. All of them, Mary reminded, did need to. It wasn't a matter of "if"—it was a matter of "when." Because it was a matter of time that involved the longest time span of all: eternity.

Stephanie was the only girl in the cabin who hadn't accepted Jesus into her heart, and she didn't want to be the only one in the cabin anymore than she wanted to spend eternity in Hell. She was sick of being the only one of things: the only girl in her family, the only youth group girl whose parents didn't go to Olivet Baptist, the only blonde in a family of brunettes, the only one who absolutely adored Hall and Oates's albums and not just their singles.

"I'm sick," she said, "of being the only one of everything. So, I decided to accept Jesus into my heart. I figured, 'Why not—it's worth a try.' Now I'm a Christian, like you and all of the other people here."

"That's great!" I said. "You know, if you die now, you'll go to Heaven. And if we both die, we'll both be in Heaven together."

I wanted to make sure that Stephanie understood all of the nuances of the deal she'd bought into.

"Yeah, I know. Like I said, it's worth a try. There's nothing to lose."

"And there's everything to gain. Did your decision," I had to ask her, "have anything to do with what we did last night?"

"Not really. No. It just seemed like the right thing to do. Maybe I'll be able to relate to you better now."

Well, we could always relate to each other better. There was always more relating to do. No doubt about it.

My heart was glad. I almost felt redeemed. At the very least, I felt vindicated. Guilt to grace to guilt to grace to guilt to grace: the ageless conundrum works, as they say, in mysterious ways.

The next day we bused back to the world. We promised not to break up again when we got there.

Riding my bike to the Wax Museum record store, flipping through used records from A to Z in search of gems, lying on the living room gold shag as Led Zeppelin and Aerosmith destroyed the speakers of my parents' console, going to arena rock concerts with Stephanie: that's how I remember the final weeks of the summer of '76.

Despite Stephanie's new born-again status, nothing much changed in our relationship, except our confidence that, yes, we'd be in Heaven together when we died. She discovered a few weeks after camp that she wasn't pregnant—but then we did it again, and my awful guilt renewed its covenant with me. This time, though, Stephanie said she was ninety-nine percent sure that she wouldn't get pregnant.

"How can you be so sure?" I asked.

"Just trust me."

What did she mean? How could she know? I looked for answers in *Almost Twelve,* but none of this stuff was mentioned. That one percent possibility. What about it? In the middle of the night, I woke up screaming from nightmares of me holding the sobbing baby before my hysterical parents: "This is our child, your grandchild."

To keep from stumbling further and deeper into sin—with Stephanie, with my almost-burnout school friends—I needed less risky modes of transcendence. No drugs, no booze, no sex—only rock and roll. I needed it bigger and louder and more in my face and body than ever before.

I had a big problem, though. I didn't have enough money to buy the object that stood highest on my list of desires: a stereo for the basement bedroom that I shared with Marshall. I could save money from my morning paper route, but that would take months or maybe years. I wanted immediate gratification, and Mom and Dad's Magnavox wasn't getting the job done. For one thing, the thoroughfare of the living room too often disrupted my sanctuary. Worse, Marna caught me dancing in the full-length mirror, pretending to be Robert Plant, Roger Daltrey, Mick Jagger. Of the three, getting caught playing Mick in the mirror was the most humiliating: the pouty lips, the hand-on-the-shoulder hip-wags, the trampy prancing about, the limp-wristed waves. No, I didn't like it when my little sister caught me being Mick. What would she do with that eyewitnessed brother spectacle?

I needed to listen to the noise alone in order to the find the peace that I longed for, the secret silence in the center. No, that's not it. I needed my own place to be pummeled. A basement listening space. How could I save the hundreds I'd need to buy a turntable, receiver, and knee-high speakers?

I saw a billboard advertising the Great Minnesota Getogether, the state fair. I'd get a job, any job, at the state fair. The Minnesota State Fairgrounds was, after all, the center of my universe, the no-man's-land between my home and my school that stood empty for most of the year.

I asked Dad and Mom, and they granted permission.

A school acquaintance who'd taken tickets at the haunted mansion the summer before told me how he'd landed the job. It was, I thought, a pretty good job, and its place in the midway limelight made him a St. Paul Murray celebrity for the duration of the fair, and a month or so into fall semester.

I could, he said, apply through the fair employment office, but they usually only took people sixteen or older. Since I wasn't sixteen, he thought it best to skip the employment office and go straight to the midway a day or two before the fair opened.

"As the men are setting up the booths and rides," he advised, "find out who's in charge and ask if they need any help. That's what I did. Oh yeah—if they ask, tell them that you're sixteen. They won't bother checking."

The next morning, I headed to the under-construction midway. I wandered from the squirt gun car race to the penny-on-a-plate-toss to the double Ferris wheel to the haunted mansion to the short man booth to the fat man booth to the tilt-a-whirl to the Amazon woman to the pronto pup stand to the Matterhorn and got the same response: no help needed.

Across from the Matterhorn, I saw a skinny man with greased black hair and mirror shades setting up an iron-on T-shirt booth. One by one, he stapled up multicolored transfers of my heroes. The guy had everyone: Yes, Zeppelin, Skynyrd, Springsteen, Elton, Steely Dan, the Eagles, King Crimson, ELP, Chuck Berry, the Stones, Little Richard, Bowie, James Brown, Dylan, Parliament, ABBA, Jefferson Starship, Hendrix, Jefferson Airplane, Janis, the Doors, Black Oak Arkansas, Neil Young, Black Sabbath, Clapton, Earth Wind and Fire, even Thin Lizzy. And that's just a partial list.

He was the man I wanted to work for. Who wouldn't want a job selling rock and roll T-shirts across from the Matterhorn, the most popular ride at the fair, the ride that played, nonstop, the best hard rock? I was certain he'd have no openings.

"Do you need any help? Are you hiring?" I asked.

He eyed me from head to toe.

"How old are you?" he asked.

"Sixteen."

"Sixteen, huh? Ever operated one of these machines before?" He pointed to the open-mouthed transfer iron.

I said I hadn't.

"Well, I need a quick learner. Cuz, see, if you mess up on one of these transfers when you're putting it on, I lose money on the T-shirt and the transfer. There's not a damn thing I can do with them either. See this box full of T-shirts?"

I nodded.

"These are fucked up T-shirts I can't use. Rejects. Money down the drain. So I've got no time for dinks who can't get it right after a couple of tries."

"I learn quickly," I said. "I've seen people working those irons before and it looks easy."

"Easy? Easy? I suppose it would look easy to a kid standing there thinking 'Oh, that looks fun. That looks cool. That looks easy.' But keeping this thing at the right temperature, putting the transfers on straight, keeping the handle down long enough that the transfer sticks but not so long that the T-shirt burns, pulling the paper off so there ain't no bubbles, and doing all this while you've got twenty people lined up—and they all want a different T-shirt—does that sound easy to you?"

I said it didn't sound easy anymore.

"Well it isn't. It isn't just fun and good times and rock and roll—it's a lot of work. If you want easy go get a job taking tickets at the Fun House. See, I get these boneheads who come here thinking 'Oh—T-shirts. Cool. I can hang out with all the cool T-shirts and pick up foxy chicks.' Cool guys. Then they maybe start talking to a chick who just wants the Shaun Cassidy T-shirt, and they turn around and then 'Oh shit—I burned the T-shirt.' Then they try another one and talk to the girl some more—and she's just a thirteen-year-old anyway and they're like sixteen or seventeen trying to impress this thirteen-year-old who just wants to get her Shaun Cassidy T-shirt and go. And then 'Oh shit, I burned another one.' Goofy fuckers. I get these goofy fuckers who just want to be cool guys. You aren't one of these goofy fuckers are you?"

I could be a goofy fucker, now and then, but I generally wasn't one, so I said, "No."

"Well, let me tell you then. I've got a job for you, if you're willing to work fifteen hours a day at two-fifty an hour. That's eight A.M. until midnight for seventeen days. Seventeen days straight. Think you can handle it?"

I couldn't believe it. I'd be working seven more hours a day and making twenty-five cents more an hour than I expected. I'd have a stereo in no time.

"I want to, but I need to check with my mom to make sure the fifteen hours is all right." I was thinking, in particular, of the Sundays away from church.

"He needs to check with his mommy. He needs to check with his mommy. Listen, maybe you're not ready to start working for me.

There are plenty of guys who'll be able to start right away who won't need mommy's permission. I need a yes or a no right now, because I've got work to do. Opening day is tomorrow."

"Okay, then. I'll start now."

"That's what I like to hear. You're hired. Come on aboard!"

He smiled for the first time and reached out his hand to shake mine. I'd made it through my first job interview.

"I'm Lenny. What's your name?"

"I'm Mark."

"Come back here, Mark, and help me fold T-shirts and put them on the shelves. Then I'll show you how to operate the transfer iron. Let's see—it's eight-thirty now. Listen, if you need to call your mom, go ahead. I'm not really such an asshole. I can be, but mostly I'm not. I actually like you mama's boys. You're usually better workers. Call mom and be back here by eight-forty-five."

Although she was concerned about the fifteen-hour days and my having to miss church two weeks in a row, Mom agreed to let me work.

I still had a few minutes, so I woke up Stephanie to tell her.

"Fifteen hours?" Stephanie said. "You're going to work fifteen hours a day? Seventeen days in a row? By the time I get to see you again, school will be starting." She paused. "I'm happy for you, though. You'll get a nice stereo. Can I visit and have lunch with you?"

"Sure. I'll get an hour lunch break."

"Summer's pretty much over for us, huh?"

Yes, summer was pretty much over for us.

I'd get up at five to do my paper route, finish by six, go back to bed for an hour, shower, dress, eat, get to work by eight, take an hour for lunch, finish work at midnight. I had no time for guilt. I couldn't even go to church.

Lenny also hired a chubby, red-haired, Marlboro-smoking Ramsey High junior named Mike. Each morning, the two of us set up the goods with the front hatch shut, and we'd finish with fifteen minutes to spare before our eight-thirty opening time. Mike would lean against the back counter, light up a cigarette, offer me one, and, since no one could see, I'd accept. A cigarette in the morning before a long day of work. It wasn't bad. I kind of liked it.

While the two of us worked hard, Lenny only unlocked the booth in the morning, locked up at midnight, and came by a few times daily to collect his piles of cash and see if any more shirts had been added to the reject box. Mike and I came up with a foolproof way to keep Lenny from finding our accidents: we'd hide them and tell friends to stop by for free T-shirts. Lenny didn't keep careful inventory, and friends wouldn't care about the glitch on the lower lip of the Rolling Stones logo or the bubbles by Jimmy Page's left leg. They loved us, and Lenny said, "You guys are the best workers I've ever had." Then he'd go to his trailer to drink whiskey and watch TV.

As far as Mike and I were concerned, Lenny had something good figured out. He was set.

"He's got the life," Mike said.

"Yeah," I said, "I wonder how much he brings home."

We'd open the hatch and see The World's Fattest Man and The World's Shortest Man get out of a Cadillac and head for their long days behind plexiglas.

The Matterhorn operator warmed up the engines and cranked "Can't Get Enough of Your Love" for the empty sleds spinning through the Swiss Alps. I played air guitar and let the spinning take me back and forth through time until the first customer arrived.

In no time we'd have a crowd, and I'd lose myself in real time: the spinning, the mini-donuts and french fries, the chugging motors, the Matterhorn DJ shouting, "Do you want to go faster? I can't hear you!" and the third rotation of "Fool for the City," the mothers pushing baby carriages, the girls in cutoffs and halters, the steam rising from the iron, the T-shirt folded, the money taken.

Before long, I wasn't selling T-shirts—I was hawking them.

"Step right up folks, git yer T-shirts. Yessirree, we've got T-shirts for sale here folks. Hey you over there! Yeah you! You look like you could use a beautiful blue Aerosmith T-shirt. No? You're making a big mistake. Step right up! You name it, we got it."

I became The T-Shirt Guy.

"Who are you trying to be?" Stephanie asked, as she walked up to the booth on opening day.

I suddenly became myself again.

"I was being," I said, "a guy who hawks T-shirts at the fair."

When the crowd died down, I left with Stephanie. A lunch break with my girlfriend: it felt like an adult thing to be doing. We ate pronto pups and corn on the cob by the grandstand bridge, headed over to see the prize pig lying with its piglets, rode twice on the double Ferris wheel, found an empty and quiet place to sit arm in arm and make out. We got as much as possible accomplished in one state fair hour, and then I headed back to the T-shirts.

When night fell, the lines for T-shirt buyers and Matterhorn riders got longer and longer. I'd close the iron on another Rolling Stones transfer to the tune of "Tumbling Dice" as the Matterhorn DJ shouted, "Are you going fast enough yet? I can't heeaaar you! Let's go *backwards* this time."

At midnight, Lenny returned to bag up bundles of money and lock up shop.

The Fat Man and The Short Man climbed into the waiting Cadillac, rolled off, and headed to a nearby motel bar for last call.

The fair ended and school began again.

I bought the stereo, and Stephanie rode her bike from Golden Valley to my basement to see, hear, and touch it. Turntable, fifteen-watt receiver, AM/FM tuner, giant speakers: it was gorgeous. I blasted Yes "Relayer," and Stephanie said it sounded loud, but clear, and whispered that she for sure wasn't pregnant.

Our rendezvous became less frequent as the October chill set in.

I bought two tickets to the Lynyrd Skynyrd concert at the St. Paul Civic Center, and a school friend with a driver's license agreed to taxi from St. Paul to Golden Valley and back—if I bought him two large beers at the show. I looked old enough to drink (eighteen) with my new mustache and sideburns.

Stephanie and I shook our asses and puffed joints as Skynyrd played their songs in the exact same order as on the live album that I bought the week before. Even the rapport-building stage banter was the same, but that didn't bother us. In fact, we would have felt cheated otherwise.

"Free Bird" was, of course, awesome. And nearly twenty minutes long.

Stephanie was irritable on the way back to Golden Valley, so I asked why.

"I've been looking forward to this for weeks, and now it's over and I have to go back home to my bitchy mother and I probably won't see you again for a long time."

"Concerts are always too short," I said, "no matter how long they are."

A couple of days later, I called and Stephanie wasn't home. I left a message. She usually returned my calls promptly, but this time I waited a few days before calling again.

Another week passed.

I turned on the TV and saw the opening credits for "Hard Rain," a Bob Dylan concert special. Dylan live on network TV. I hadn't heard much of his music besides "Like a Rolling Stone" and "Knockin' on Heaven's Door," but I'd been meaning to give him a listen. I called up Stephanie to see if she was watching too. We could talk and watch and, together, decide: what about Dylan? Worth all the bother?

Her mom answered.

"Is Stephanie there?"

"Mark," she said. She'd never said my name before. "Stephanie's not here. And I might as well tell you: we haven't seen Stephanie for over a week and a half. She ran away and didn't leave a note. We were actually going to call you to see if you knew where she was. We thought she might turn up at your place. We don't have a clue about where she might have gone. Have you spoken with her?"

I said I hadn't. I didn't know anything. Said I was shocked, sorry.

Told her to call if she found out anything—anything at all. Told her to please ask Stephanie to call me if she came home or phoned.

Who was Stephanie to me, really?

I barely noticed my own trouble, so how would I notice hers?

I remember feeling loss when her mother said she'd run away. Maybe even shock.

Attachments are less strong with fifteen-year-old couples. Aren't they?

I told everyone all about Stephanie running away when I got to school the next day: "My girlfriend ran away."

I wanted to say it. It was something to say: "My girlfriend ran away." It reminded me of an away-she-went song by Lynyrd Skynyrd, "Tuesday's Gone."

This was of that: my girl ran away. Ran away and left me. Left me here all alone. And here I am to tell you about it. I could almost say it like I'd say, "I rededicated my life to Jesus Christ." My girlfriend ran away. Where'd she go? I don't know. Away. Away is all.

The boys said, "That sucks."

The girls put their hands on my shoulder and said, "I'm sorry. I'm really sorry about that."

So I kept saying it all day: "My girlfriend ran away. She ran away! I don't know where in the world she went."

I'm sorry, the girls said. They imagined her alone. They imagined me alone. They imagined themselves away away away. They put a hand on my shoulder.

One girl asked, "Did that surprise you? Did she ever talk about running away? Did you notice anything different about her?"

Different? Like what? She said she wasn't pregnant. What else could be different about her?

"Not really," I said. I wasn't going to be a dad.

No, I didn't notice. I didn't notice a lot. Not much different. It didn't even seem that much different, by the end of the day, having her so far away. Knowing she was away didn't seem much different than anything else.

The next day was even more different: my life almost felt normal again.

Satan Worship

Nolan McCormack rode into camp on a Harley that August in 1977. He wore mirror shades, a denim jacket with a big patch that read "My God isn't dead—Sorry about yours," faded Levi big-bell blue jeans, black leather cowboy boots, long sandy hair, and a mustache. Girls said he looked like Kris Kristofferson, and boys thought he sounded like Clint Eastwood. We knew right away that this man wasn't like any other camp evangelist we'd ever known.

A career youth evangelist, Nolan was almost one of us. Most of our dorky youth pastors were committed to adolescents only until they finished seminary and became head pastors of their very own small-town churches. They had to become older and more stuffy, more mature, or else they'd get railroaded out of town for being too young. Not Nolan. Nolan wouldn't sell out to adult staidness and stability. Camp to camp, youth retreat to youth retreat, spaghetti banquet to spaghetti banquet, revival to revival: Nolan, a renegade for Jesus, motorcycled across our big nation doing the Lord's work in Satan's greatest recruitment camp.

Because Nolan spent most of his time with teenagers, he expected more from us than our only-in-it-for-the-experience church youth pastors. They had to win the hearts of our parents, so they were more willing to excuse our stumblings and indiscretions. They needed for us to like them. Nolan, on the other hand, wouldn't kowtow. Who were we to him? Church punks, that's all. Besides, he was charismatic enough to know that we'd end up loving him after the first night, no matter what he said, so why pander?

Not one to buy into the "Once-saved, always-saved" Sunday school maxim, he made it clear that if we didn't turn our lives around we'd go to Hell, and all of our party friends we didn't witness to on Earth would be there with us. And it wouldn't, as heavy metal lyrics promised, be one big party down there. Nolan preached Christian carpe diem: seize your youth, your chance to tell your unbelieving friends about Jesus, or tomorrow you will all die and go to Hell.

No, Nolan didn't beg for our approval—only our souls.

"When you are trying to lead someone to the Lord, be very careful and attentive when you get to Christ's resurrection," Nolan said. "Satan will be working extra hard to distract the situation so that the story ends with the crucifixion."

A faithful group of high schoolers gathered in the A-frame chapel for a seminar on "Witnessing to Your Friends and Strangers." Attendance at the seminar, held during afternoon "free recreation time," was not mandatory. Those of us who'd chosen to attend knew that we were the cream of the zealous young Christian crop. We could be swimming, sailing, canoeing, horseback riding, playing softball or miniature golf, taking back-to-nature walks with camp sweethearts. Instead, we were being coached in how to lead the world to Jesus.

"No," Nolan went on, "Satan doesn't want unbelievers to hear about the risen Christ—he'd like the story to end with the death of Christ, so that he appears victorious. Let me tell you a story to illustrate."

Nolan had a way with sermon illustrations. The best sermon illustrations took stories from real life, distilled them, highlighted their moral nuggets, and, whenever possible, included a good laugh or two.

"One Fourth of July," Nolan said, "I was witnessing to a young man, and things were going smoothly. He was very open to the gospel message, very interested. I told him about Jesus Christ dying on the cross for his sins, and I was just about to tell him about the stone rolled away from the tomb when, out of nowhere, a bottle rocket came whizzing between our faces. Man, that rocket came so close to hitting both of us. Knocked us right on our butts."

He knew we'd all laugh when he said "butts." Nolan could get away with that. Our youth pastors had to say "rears" or "rear ends." The more earthy ones might say "buns" or "rumps." But not even Nolan could say "asses."

"But then—oh the Devil is so clever sometimes," Nolan went on, "then we got sidetracked and spent the rest of our time together talking about the rocket. We were so startled. Then, the man said he had to take off, and just after he crossed the busy street, I thought, 'Satan, you wise fool. You didn't want that man to hear about the risen Christ and you used that bottle rocket to steer us off course.' So, that's my advice to you when you're witnessing. Be very aware and attentive—keep a watch out for Satan as you approach the resurrection."

Those words echoed in my mind for years: "Be very aware and attentive—keep a watch out for Satan as you approach the resurrection."

Keep a watch out for Satan. No one needed to remind me to do that. Ever since my shameful Bicentennial night the summer before, I'd been obsessing about Satan, demons, and demon possession. Stephanie had disappeared, I felt responsible for everything, and I had no one to turn to. I feared the Devil more than I knew the Lord.

The Satan obsession really gathered momentum after I had another conversation with my faithful Baptist school friend, Pete.

It was almost too cold to be on foot in the November twilight, and because there was no snow on the ground, we called the season "fall." As usual, we walked home from basketball practice along the "pig path," a path between the fields, silos, fences, and barns of the University of Minnesota's agricultural campus and the Minnesota State Fairgrounds. Two countries hidden within the city: on one side, fields of corn, cattle sleeping in the thick grass, pigs in troughs; on the other, empty streets and vacant buildings that would, come August, be filled with people from all over Minnesota.

Earlier in the week, Pete went to his church, Bethany Baptist, to hear a former Satan worshiper speak about "Satanism in Rock and Roll." For months it was all he could talk about.

"This Mike guy used to be some sort of bigwig in the Church of Satan—a high priest or something," Pete said. "And then he became a Christian. He said that when he was worshiping the Devil, Satan got him millions of dollars, women, drugs, pretty much anything he wanted. In return for Mike's faithful service. That was the bargain. He said that he was more powerful than the president, and if Satan said he wanted the president dead, Mike could have gotten him killed, no problem."

"Why did he become a Christian?" I asked. Although I was supposed to rejoice when someone converted to Christianity, it baffled me that someone would give up that much money and power for Jesus.

"He said he had so much power that it actually scared him. What if Satan really did ask him to kill President Ford? He was getting so much for nearly nothing, and he knew Satan would ask for a big payback someday. He didn't want to find out what that was. Plus, he was unhappy because he wasn't living the life that he wanted to be living. Something was missing inside."

Something missing inside. I should have known. That's what rich and famous guest speakers (usually retired professional athletes) always said in their Sunday evening conversion testimonies. They had everything they ever wanted, but something was missing inside. They'd tried drugs, alcohol, sex orgies, sports cars, and all that the world had to offer, but they were driven nearly to suicide in their quest for something more. Everyone thought that they were happy and successful, but they were really the most miserable people on the planet. Then Jesus came into their hearts and filled that "empty space." And whenever the rich and famous guest speakers came to our church, the empty pews and offering plates were filled too.

I took some comfort in hearing that a Satan-centered life would lead to that same empty space.

"I'll bet," I said, "that Satan wasn't happy when Mike made the switch to Jesus."

I opened the gate that led off the pig path and into the empty state fair midway.

"Satan was so furious," Pete said, "that he got his other faithful followers to come after Mike. Satan wanted him dead. He was a marked man: number one on Satan's hit list."

Pete went into a long story about the Satan worshipers coming after the one who got away, the traitor. Mike got followed and chased everywhere he went. He couldn't find a hiding place, and he thought his days were numbered. After a bunch of chases and narrow escapes, he sought out the Baptist pastor who led him to Jesus, and the pastor let him hide out in the church for a few nights.

We walked past the grandstand and boarded-up mini-donut and pronto-pup booths of the ghost town fair.

"The first night there, Mike locked all the doors and windows in the church," Pete said, "so there was no possible way for anyone to get in. He just knelt down by the communion table and prayed. He couldn't sleep. Then, at about one in the morning, he heard the front door open. This guy came into the sanctuary with a huge butcher knife. The guy didn't even break the lock on the front door or anything. He just opened it, even though it had been locked!"

"No way! He just opened it?"

"Opened it, no problem. With the help of Satan. So the guy came after Mike with the butcher knife, and he was about ten feet away. Mike shouted, 'Satan, in the Holy Name of Jesus Christ I command you to leave this room.' The guy stopped dead in his tracks, dropped the knife, and ran as fast as he could out of that church. Because he wasn't acting on his own—he was only obeying Satan, and Satan couldn't stand up to the power of Jesus. He knew he'd be crushed. So Satan ordered the guy to leave Mike alone. And that was the end of that. They've left Mike alone ever since."

I saw no good reason to question the truth of the story. I wanted to believe in the presence and power of Satan as much as I wanted to believe in the greater power of Jesus. "Satan, in the Holy Name of Jesus Christ, I command ... " I could think of a lot of situations in which those words would come in handy. Especially if the Devil was truly lurking in every nook and cranny of human experience.

Still, one good story wasn't enough to justify a ministry. Every effective evangelist needed a desired outcome, a call to greater commitment. According to Pete, Mike's goal was to get teens to see and understand the reality of Satan in rock and roll music. We'd heard the rumors and warnings, but Mike had spent time on Satan's inside track, so his word was worth more. While he didn't completely condemn rock and roll, he read a list of Satan-worshiping rock and roll bands that all good Christians should stay away from.

"At the end of the meeting," Pete said, "Mike had everyone stand up and commit to being more careful about what we choose to listen to. I stood up and made the commitment."

This commitment put Pete in a serious moral dilemma. High on Mike's list of Satan's bands was one of Pete's favorites: the Eagles. The news of who the Eagles really were came as a shock to everyone at the meeting. They expected Black Sabbath, another band on the list, but the Eagles? That band epitomized the laidback, lite-folk-country-rock sound of 1970s California. Their name alone evoked American patriotism. Yet, Mike said, in that very large state of California, the Eagles got involved with some dangerous Satan worshipers. Satan worshipers, as it turned out, were all over California. They looked normal, dressed and spoke like everyone else, but they secretly worshiped the King of Darkness.

"You know the song 'One of These Nights'?" Pete asked as we passed the penny arcade.

"What do you think? It was only played on the radio about every five minutes last year."

"Well, it's really about searching for the perfect girl to sacrifice to the Devil." He started singing some of the lyrics softly, and I began to hear the song differently. The Devil, demons, Hell, everything I feared most: it was all in there.

"Geez," I said. "I never even thought of that before, but now that I do, it makes perfect sense. It's weird how you can hear a song so many times and not even try to figure out what it means. It reminds me of that verse in the Bible about Satan coming disguised as an angel of light. I mean, the Eagles of all bands! They have those sweet harmonies and catchy melodies and everyone just about likes them. Little sisters, burnouts, just about everyone."

"Well, I made the commitment and I'm going to follow through this time. I'm going over to Derek's tonight, and we're going to burn all of my Eagles albums in his backyard. You can come over too if you want."

Derek, a church friend of Pete's, lived in a Roseville house with a huge backyard.

"I don't know," I said. "I mean, I think it's the right thing to do, but I don't want to be there when you do it."

"Yeah, I can understand that. I was thinking we'll probably see and hear some shrieking demons when we throw the records in the fire. They might even try to come inside us, since we're destroying their old home."

The possibility of seeing and hearing real demons was more than enticing—maybe even a once-in-a-lifetime opportunity. I'd almost given up on ever seeing an angel. Father God, Jesus Christ, the Holy Spirit, angels: all of the supernatural forces on my side seemed content to remain invisible. When I asked Sunday school teachers why that was, they said that there would be no need for faith if we could see and prove everything. Okay. Faith. But why were Satan and his demons so much less discriminating in their cameo appearances? Were they only seeking negative attention? Sunday night missionary speakers, for example, spoke to and cast out demons more often than my parents made long-distance calls to their siblings. I never doubted the existence of "evil spirits" in missionary stories—although the foreign settings made them seem slightly less real, like pictures of naked people in *National Geographic.*

Shrieking demon faces flying from a friend of a friend's backyard bonfire would be something altogether different, something that would surely turn my backslidden life back onto the straight and narrow path. There were two problems, though: I wasn't quite ready for the straight and narrow path, and the thought of seeing live, unleashed demons scared the shit out of me.

"I think I'll pass on going to Derek's. I'm just not ready."

"Well, I'll be ready for them," Pete muttered.

We walked quickly and watchfully through the vacant lots of Machinery Hill, the place where, during fair time, farmers eyed the latest-model tractors, pickups, and plows. The headlights of a car approaching from behind sent us sprinting all the way back to the world as we once knew it.

That night, Pete got all of his Eagles albums and went over to Derek's. They built a big bonfire in the backyard and, one by one, tossed the albums and covers into the rising flames. As cardboard curled and vinyl dripped, they took a step back, looked carefully for shriveled little faces, and listened for shrieks.

The Eagles, their first album. Nothing.

Desperado. Nothing.

On the Border. Nothing.

Ceremonial pause.

One of These Nights cover. Nothing.

Ceremonial pause.

One of These Nights vinyl. Nothing.

Hotel California might have been the magic one, but Pete hadn't bought it yet.

"I burned them last night," Pete said when I saw him in the hall the next day at school.

"Did anything happen?"

"We didn't hear any shrieks or see any flying faces or anything," Pete said, trying not to sound disappointed. "But I'm just glad they're gone. I couldn't sleep with them in my bedroom."

"You did the right thing," I said, calculating the total cost of the records in my head.

I retold the story of the former Satan worshiper to my Central Baptist youth group, and soon everyone was asking our high school minister, Lloyd, about demons, Satan, the occult. This was freaky stuff, and we didn't know what to do with it. One misstep was, apparently, all it took to go from safety to demon possession to a life of Satan worship. None of us wanted to someday find ourselves alone in the Central Baptist sanctuary after midnight, hiding from a man with a butcher knife.

What, we wondered, might open wide the door for a bored demon to enter? Getting drunk or stoned? Masturbating? Heavy petting? Sexual intercourse? Simple light petting? Singing the lyrics to the wrong rock and roll song? Lloyd quickly ran out of answers, so "Satan and the Occult" became one of the topics he scheduled into the high school Bible studies that he hosted in his living room every Thursday night. He enlisted the expertise of Dr. Graham Lewis, a Bethel Seminary professor who'd spent many years on foreign mission fields and had cast out many demons.

By lamplight, we sat in a circle on the hardwood floor and listened, three Thursdays in a row, to Dr. Lewis's stories of demons encountered in countries that I knew about only from Sunday evening missionary slide shows: Ethiopia, Argentina, Nigeria, Thailand, Sudan, Madagascar, Nicaragua ... these places were so nowhere in my mind that they could have been anywhere.

Dr. Lewis, a man in his fifties, spoke with a trace of a British accent, an accent that made his stories sound more believable. I couldn't imagine such a dignified-sounding man telling me anything less than the whole truth.

"In order to cast out a demon," he said, "one must first find out its name. Demons will, most often, take the name of their task. For example, if the demon's task is to encourage lust for women, it will take the name 'Lust.' If the demon's task is to urge a person to kill, it will take the name 'Murder.' So I will ask, first of all, 'Who is your master?' It will say, 'Satan is my master.' Then I will ask, 'What is your name?' and it will say, 'My name is Lust,' or 'My name is Fornication,' or 'My name is Murder.' But one must first find out the demon's name, as a doctor must first discover the sickness before providing a cure."

The demons in his stories always spoke in English and had English names, and Dr. Lewis's repeated moral was that demons possess people worshiping gods other than Jesus Christ.

"If you are living according to Christ, following His divine will," he said, "you needn't worry about a demon entering you."

Living according to Christ. Following His divine will. But what if I stumbled?

"Should you ever discover the presence of a demon in yourself or someone else, or sense the presence of Satan nearby, remember these words: 'Satan, in the Holy Name of Jesus Christ, I command you to leave this room.'"

Well, I already knew about those words—words that would, if the situation might arise, serve as a demon disinfectant. But if the demon was inside of me, would it even allow me to speak them? And if I was in a place where a demon felt so inclined to enter, would anyone nearby know the words to say? Would anyone nearby know the words that would free me?

I came from Dr. Lewis's series with a lot of questions, more wild stories, but no certainties—nothing new to keep me from harm. The straight and narrow path to salvation was looking more and more like the only safe option: no more weed, no more booze, no more cussing, no more heavy or light petting, no more masturbation, no more french kissing, no more Led Zeppelin or Aerosmith, no more of anything that I couldn't imagine Jesus doing. No more of anyplace where I couldn't imagine Jesus entering.

Instead, more Bible reading, more prayer, more witnessing, more thoughts of Jesus dying on the cross for my sins.

I walked the straight-and-narrow path for much of the winter, but the way seemed to widen with the arrival of spring, around the time I saw Led Zeppelin at the St. Paul Civic Center. In the spring of 1977, the months before we were to move to California, I was living on the outskirts of burnoutdom, backsliding while I could.

I had a late-summer camp "rededication to Christ" planned. Then I'd completely reinvent myself in California, become the worthy pastor's son that I always knew I could be. In the meantime, I had to seize the day and party heartily in Minnesota. I decided to ride out my backslide until I got to camp at the end of July, in the summer of '77.

I wound up at camp sooner than I expected. A Trout Lake Camp counselor got sick and I, barely sixteen, got talked into replacing him.

My age didn't dissuade the camp directors from placing into my care the souls of twelve fifth- and sixth-grade boys. That's what worried me most: their souls. The fun and frivolity would take care of itself. Canoeing, sailboating, horseback riding, high and low diving boards, softball, skit nights, miniature golf, a canteen well-stocked with candy and pop: Trout Lake Camp had just about everything that appealed to fifth- and sixth-grade boys. Even the boys who'd already discovered girls still relished a week without them. My main job, then—and it was a tough one—was to get these fellows to go for God before they went crazy for girls. My success or failure as a counselor would be judged by how many campers of mine made "decisions" for Christ during bedside devotion time.

"At some point during the week," the lead counselor said to us at a new counselor orientation, "you need to talk to each boy in your cabin alone and find out if he's accepted Jesus into his heart—and, if he hasn't, if he'd like to. Here are the forms you need to fill out for each kid."

The forms included the boy's name, address, phone number, church sponsor, and boxes indicating whether the camper had accepted Jesus Christ before camp, had accepted Jesus during camp, or, simply and stubbornly, refused to accept Jesus. At the end of the summer, the statistics were tallied and published for all Minnesota Baptist Conference members.

This fell heavy on my heart. I didn't know how to save a soul.

I only knew that I hadn't been the zealous young Christian I'd annually promised to become. I'd never, not even once, accomplished the king supreme of evangelical Christian goals: getting an unsaved person to kneel and say the prayer of salvation, the sinner's prayer. My sixteenth year would mark the beginning of my lifelong crusade. Someday I'd give a testimony with my counseling week as its turning point: "And it was that very week as a counselor at Trout Lake Camp that I began my ministry."

As a counselor, I'd make up for my lost years of complacency and reimburse God tenfold for my shameful Bicentennial night.

I got out my monogrammed Bible and searched for the perfect passage to share with my twelve on the first night of devotions. It needed to be something with the reminder of death, the offer of salvation, and the promise of eternal life in Heaven. The obvious choice was John 3:16, the verse that every evangelical child learns before the Pledge of Allegiance: "For God so loved the world that He gave His only begotten Son that whosoever believeth in Him should not perish but have everlasting life." The verse was a quick and easy commercial for the importance of accepting Jesus and an efficient barometer for measuring who was and who was not saved.

After all of the boys returned from the final bathroom stop, got on their pajamas, and slipped into their sleeping bags, I turned off the overhead light and turned on a reading lamp next to my bed. I wanted the verse to ease us into an intimate counselor-campers "Who is God and where will I go when I die?" discussion.

I remembered late-night cabin devotion sessions of summers past. Our counselor would read the chosen verse, comment on it, ask if we had any questions, and the discussion would go on for hours. We'd pick his wise college brain with questions that we didn't feel comfortable asking anyone else: "Will we have hair in Heaven?" "Are angels men or women and do they wear anything?" "Is it a sin to pee outside?" "One of my friends asked Jesus into his heart, but he takes girls to his dad's tool shed and gives them candy to show him their things. Can he do that?"

I read the verse and asked, "How much does God love the world, according to John 3:16?"

Silence.

"Well, let me put it this way. What did God give us? What was His gift to us?"

No answer.

"How about this: What does it mean to have everlasting life?"

One of the boys sat up and said, rubbing his eyes, "Will you turn off your light?"

I looked around the cabin and noticed that just about everyone was asleep or pretending to be, so I turned off the lamp.

The next morning before the ceremonial flag-raising, before the youngsters lined up at attention, we counselors gathered beneath the pole to discuss our first nights. Most of the others were four or five years older than me, and they boasted about how many campers asked Jesus into their hearts during devotions. These vets knew what they were doing and how to do it right. They'd learned about high impact, and they got results.

Two of one guy's boys accepted Jesus, and the rest of the counselors responded with enthusiastic praise the Lords, amens, and hallelujahs. I missed the cue that time, so when the next guy said that four of his fellows asked Jesus into their hearts, I added a hearty "Amen." Three of another's accepted Jesus, and the guy assured us that his remaining unbelievers seemed "real close."

"How did it go for you, Mark?" someone asked me.

"My guys were really tired and fell asleep before I was even done," I said.

I felt like Charlie Brown in the *Peanuts Halloween Special.* After all the other kids tell about the luscious treats dropped in their bags, Charlie says, "All I got was a rock."

Sunday night's devotions went worse.

One boy farted, and everyone started laughing. Then came the arm farts.

"Let the Holy Spirit take over—let the Holy Spirit speak for you," advised my elders as we gathered before flag-raising the next morning. Small scale revivals, great awakenings, were taking place in all of the other cabins. All agreed: something exciting was going on with this group of boys.

I couldn't explain, then, why the Holy Spirit was avoiding my cabin. Maybe the Holy Spirit had two lists of counselors: naughty and nice.

Monday night's devotions bombed, and on Tuesday night the kids whined, "Do we have to have devotions again tonight? Can't we just skip them for once?"

So, I loosened up and told a couple of fart jokes instead. A good laugh was better than nothing, but the guilt kept me awake all night. Who'd be laughing in Hell?

It was Wednesday morning and I still hadn't led a single camper to Jesus. My elders expressed concern about the doomed souls of the boys in my cabin. They all tossed in bits of advice to The Kid, The Rookie.

"Here's what I do," said one pragmatic counselor. "When it's time for devotions, I turn the lights off and light a vanilla-scented candle. Then I tell the kids to gather on the bunks by my bed for devotions. It creates a real intimate atmosphere, and then the Holy Spirit takes over from there. You ought to try it. I even brought some extra candles, so I can give you one."

The right atmosphere, apparently, was an invitation to the overworked Holy Spirit. Why hadn't atmosphere occurred to me before? I just needed a good passage of scripture, a sure-fire soul-saver, and Wednesday night would be my night.

After the campers got into their pajamas, I invited them to gather by my bed for devotions.

"Why?" they asked.

"Because," I said, "tonight I really want us all to share our thoughts and feelings about the scripture that I'm going to read, and I think sitting closer together will make it easier."

I turned off the lights and lit the vanilla candle as they moved closer. The boys were silent.

"Tonight I am going to read a verse from James—James 2:19. Listen closely. James says, 'You believe that there is one God. Good! Even the demons believe that—and shudder.'"

The boys were awake and attentive. I knew that would hook them. I read the verse again: "You believe … the demons believe … shudder." Candlelight glowed on the white faces that surrounded me.

"How many of you know what a demon is?" I asked.

One boy raised his hand and answered, "A demon is one of the Devil's helpers."

"That's a good way of putting it," I said. "Demons are the Devil's helpers. Another way of putting it is that demons are the soldiers in Satan's army. They do the fighting for him. They do his dirty work. This verse says that even Satan's helpers, demons, believe in God—and shudder. Does anyone know what the word 'shudder' means?" No one raised a hand.

"'Shudder' means," I said, "to tremble or shake in horror. If you were going to use the bathroom late at night and a bear jumped out at you, you'd shudder. If I told a really scary ghost story, you'd probably shudder at the end. Well, according to this verse, demons believe in God and shudder at the name of Jesus. If demons believe in Jesus and you don't, I'd say you've got some serious thinking to do. Let me tell you some stories."

As the candlelight flickered, I went on to tell Pete's story of Mike, the former Satan worshiper. I included everything: Mike's decision to worship Satan, the money, the girls, the drugs, the power to kill the president, the power to blow up the whole universe, the fear of that power, Mike's conversion to Jesus, his running and hiding, the locked door miraculously opened, the man with the butcher knife, the knife at Mike's throat, the words shouted as the knife grazed his Adam's apple: "Satan, in the Holy Name of Jesus Christ I command you to leave this room."

"… And at the name of Jesus," I said, "the demon inside the man shrieked and he dropped the knife and ran straight out of the church. No one has come after Mike since. Not once."

"Wow!" one boy said. "Do you have any more stories?"

"I've got lots more. But keep in mind, these aren't just scary ghost stories that I'm making up. These are real. Every word that I'm saying is true."

I told every story that I could remember from the Graham Lewis

Bible study series: the one about the demon in Africa that jumped out of the man and entered a nearby horse that went crazy and ran straight into a huge bonfire; the one about the Buddhist demon in Thailand who smashed all of the precious china in the room; the one about the urban demon in Brazil who cursed the missionary up and down, back and forth, and named himself "Addiction"—because he entered the São Paulo woman to keep her addicted to heroin.

"You see, demons take the name of their task. They take the name of whatever Satan has assigned for them to do. If you usually have trouble staying awake during devotions, it might be because of a demon named 'Sleepy' whose task is to make you sleep when you aren't supposed to. If you talk back to adults, it might be because of a demon named 'Sassy.' If your mother asks you to take out the garbage and you don't do it, it might be because of a demon named 'Disobedience.'"

One boy, frantic, near tears, said, "Well, how can we get rid of the demons? How can we make sure that we don't get demons in us?"

The very question I was waiting for.

"There's only one way," I said. "You must accept Jesus into your heart to be your personal Lord and Savior, and the demons will stay away. And if you someday fall back into your sinful ways and feel the presence of a demon, say this prayer: 'Satan, in the Holy Name of Jesus Christ, I command you to leave this room.'"

All of the boys were wide awake in the vanilla as I gave the invitation.

"How many of you would like to ask Jesus into your heart tonight?"

Five boys raised their hands.

"Repeat this prayer after me ... " I said. "Jesus, come into my life ... "

I joyfully listened as the five repeated, in unison, my prayer: "Jesus, come into my life ... I want to receive you as my personal Lord and Savior ... I believe that you died on the cross for my sins ... Forgive my sins so that I can live forever ... Help me live my life for you so that the demons stay away."

"Five of my boys accepted Jesus into their hearts last night!" I said to the counselors gathered beneath the flagpole.

Congratulations and hugs came from all sides.

"I knew you'd get the job done last night," said the counselor who provided the vanilla candle.

I stood unashamed among my elders. At last, my fear bore results. It's amazing what you can accomplish when you believe—and shudder.

The very next week I was a camper again. The Junior Boys left, the High Teens arrived, I stepped away from my evangelizer position, and I became one of the evangelized. I could sit back, take notes, watch it all happen, marvel at Nolan's charisma and soul-saving prowess, join the throng of teens who believed every word that he said. My week as a counselor gave me a new appreciation for the evangelist's art.

And Nolan got results: twenty souls saved on Sunday, thirty-some on Monday, forty or so on Tuesday, fifty-plus on Wednesday. I'd never before seen a camp evangelist break a hundred, but if anyone could, it would be Nolan. His Thursday night sermon had an additional factor in its favor: it was, he told us the night before, going to be a very detailed account of the crucifixion and resurrection of Jesus Christ.

"I'll warn you," he said as he began on that humid August night, "this sermon will be very graphic. I'm sparing nothing. So if you don't think you can handle it, you ought to go straight back to your cabin right now. Jesus Christ's death wasn't pretty."

Three hundred-plus high schoolers packed the A-frame chapel. I sat with my church buddies Russ and Dave, but the three of us were so enthralled with Nolan that it didn't matter who we were sitting with. He commanded that kind of attention. You didn't want to be looking elsewhere when his eyes sought contact with yours.

The lake beyond the birches faded as Nolan opened in prayer.

"Oh Lord, tonight let your sweet Holy Spirit fill the room as we meditate upon your death on the cross and glorious resurrection. Let us concentrate on the meaning of your death; let us comprehend the depth of your great great love for us Redeemer, Holy Creator, Everlasting Father ... "

Nolan opened his eyes and asked us to turn in our Bibles to Matthew 27:11–26. He might have begun the story anywhere, but he chose to commence with the entrance of the New Testament's arch villain-wimp, Pontius Pilate.

"Pontius Pilate. Pontius Pilate," he said as we found the passage in our Bibles. "What, young people, are we to make of this Pontius Pilate?"

What are we to make of this Pontius Pilate? It remains a compelling question. Among other things, Pilate has come to represent every spineless politician who ignores conscience and kowtows to the masses.

Nolan gave a brief synopsis of the scene: Before a bloodthirsty crowd of spectators, Pilate asks Jesus if he is the king of the Jews, and Jesus answers, "Yes, it is as you say." Pilate repeats other accusations, and Jesus chooses to remain silent. Following the Passover feast tradition of releasing one prisoner to the public, Pilate gives the crowd the choice of Jesus or the well-known criminal, Barabbas. The crowd chooses Barabbas and demands the crucifixion of Jesus. Pilate says that he doesn't know what crime Jesus has committed, the crowd insists on Jesus' crucifixion, and Matthew writes, "When Pilate saw that he was getting nowhere, but that instead an uproar was starting, he took water and washed his hands before the crowd. 'I am innocent of this man's blood,' he said. 'It is your responsibility.'"

Nolan was well aware of the symbolic impact of this story, and years of evangelism had shown him that the present-day Pontius Pilate was none other than us: the youth of today.

"Guys and gals," he said, "why did Pilate decide to crucify Christ and free Barabbas, a known criminal? Why? Because, young people, he was giving in to peer pressure. Yes, peer pressure. What else can we call it? And, my friends, doesn't it remind you of yourselves and all of the ways that you hand Christ over to the crowd to be nailed upon the cross, again and again and again. Remember that time when your buddy said, 'Hey, just one toke, just take one toke of this joint, man.' You refused at first, but then you gave in—and before you knew it, you were one toke over the line ..."

Yes, I remembered that time and time again when I forsook conscience and took the toke that put me one over the line. Nolan knew me well, he told me about me: nothing got over. To drive the point home even more, he sang refrains of rock songs that I knew—songs that I'd hum as he woke me up to the realization that I was the real killer of Christ. I claimed innocence, I refused to take responsibility, as I handed Christ over to my reprobate friends, and they nailed Him back up to the cross. I forsook Christ to follow the crowd that took the dead body down from the cross and sealed it forever behind the unmovable tombstone. Call me Pilate.

Nolan didn't end with Pilate, though. Pilate was only the beginning.

Slowly and methodically, Nolan highlighted every pain, every torture that Jesus endured before, during, and after his crucifixion. He elaborated on the scant details that Matthew's account gave, all but saying, "This Matthew guy just didn't do this story justice."

"Matthew writes in chapter 27 verse 26 that Pilate had Jesus flogged. Oh yes, young people, they flogged him all right. What Matthew doesn't say is that the whip used on Jesus, according to historical accounts, was made of leather and had bones and hooks on it that bruised His body and tore literally chunks of His skin out ... Matthew says in verse 29, 'After weaving a crown of thorns, they put it on his head.' But, man, they didn't just 'put' the crown of thorns on His head; they shoved it, they slammed it on His head so that the thorns—thorns that were four to six inches long—dug deep into His skull ... Historians estimate that the cross weighed well over one hundred pounds and Jesus carried it after He'd been weakened, nearly passed out, from the severe whipping ... The nails used in His hands and feet weren't little nails like the ones you'd use to build a table or chair. Oh no, young people, they were closer in length and width to railroad spikes ... Those punished by crucifixion didn't usually bleed to death, though. They suffocated. They suffocated."

Nolan wanted this catalog of details to engage, sicken, and overwhelm us. Then, at the height of the description, just before we numbed ourselves, he said, "And He did it all for you! How dare you, how can you even think about, how can you look at your face in the mirror in the morning knowing that He went through all of this pain and suffering to save you from your sins so that you can live eternally with Him in Heaven—and you still won't let him into your heart! How dare you! And, worse yet, those of you who claim to have Him in your hearts are afraid to tell your friends about all Christ went through for them, because you might not get invited to so and so's party on Friday night! Well, I've got news for you, young people—this ain't no party down here, this ain't no picnic, and if you think it is, you've got another thing coming: eternity in Hell with Satan and his army of demons."

I was with Nolan all the way. This sermon was, without question, the greatest sermon on the crucifixion I'd ever heard. The man was turning up and letting loose—as if he had inside information that the Rapture was going to happen that very night. How many would go forward? One hundred, two hundred, two-fifty? Nolan had only Christ's descent into Hell and resurrection to go, and then he'd bring it on home.

"And behold the veil of the temple …" Nolan read from his Bible, but he stopped without finishing the verse, as campers turned away from him and looked to the ceiling. From the balcony to the front row, loud whispers filled the chapel.

"Satan's up to something," I thought as I kept my eyes glued on Nolan. "Don't these people realize what's happening?" I quickly glanced up to where fingers were pointing and saw a large black bat flying back and forth in the peak of the A-frame. Hoping that Nolan didn't notice my momentary lapse in judgment, I turned and faced him once again.

"Guys and gals, guys and gals," Nolan said, trying to regain the control he'd lost.

Half of the campers were still gazing at the bat—they thought it was just an ordinary bat. I knew better. The bat was the Devil,

Satan, Lucifer, Beelzebub, in the most concrete form I'd ever encountered.

"I want you all to take your eyes off the bat, young people," Nolan said, "and bow your heads silently in prayer. Just take your eyes off the bat and bow your heads."

Most of the campers obeyed. The chapel got quiet again.

"We have a minor disturbance in here right now and there's no doubt in my mind about who the source of it is. Let's pray. Jesus, let your Holy Spirit fill this room. Oh yes, let your sweet sweet spirit fill this place, dear Lord. Satan, that conniver, that wrecker of souls, that fallen trickster thought he could come in here tonight and steer us away from the truth of the resurrection. But Jesus, we need your power to get rid of him."

I sat with my eyes tightly closed and my sweaty hands folded reverently, ready to hear the holy order.

"Satan," Nolan shouted, "in the name of the risen Lord and Savior Jesus Christ, I *command* you to leave this room right now!"

We couldn't keep our heads bowed any longer, and Nolan didn't urge us to, as we looked up to the ceiling and saw the bat take a quick swoop toward the pulpit, turn around, fly toward the rear of the chapel, and leave through a hole that we couldn't see. It didn't return.

"Let's bow our heads and pray again," Nolan said. "Lord, we thank you, we praise your Holy Name for conquering death, for conquering Satan and rising again, for rolling the stone away from the tomb. We're reminded, once again, that Satan cannot stand up to your power; you'll always be the victor.

"Lord, Satan feels defeated and depressed right now, and I know you'd like nothing more than to make him feel even more defeated and depressed by having everyone who has not yet received you as personal Lord and Savior come forward to your altar and invite you into their precious young lives. And those believers who have fallen away from you, those believers who have fallen back into sin through peer pressure and now find that they've been dazed and confused for so long, let them also come forward tonight. Let them find their way back onto your One Way to Heaven.

"If there's anyone here tonight who needs to accept Jesus Christ as personal Lord and Savior, or needs to rededicate him or herself to the Lord, I invite you to come forward down the aisle now to kneel and pray."

The pews emptied as nearly half the campers walked proudly down the aisle to be saved. I really wanted to go down there too, but I'd knelt at the altar earlier that week, and I didn't want to look like just another wannabee. The front of the chapel, below Nolan's pulpit, was, without a doubt, the place to be that night. Timing is everything.

I didn't feel right sitting, though. I wanted to shout, "I knew the bat was Satan before any of you. If the bat was still flying up there, you'd all be looking at it, but I'd have eyes right on Nolan."

The Return of Justin, the Missionary Kid

Justin returned for furlough in August of 1977, when he and I were sixteen. He returned as I was cleaning up my act again, trying my best to walk the straight and narrow path. My family was preparing to leave St. Paul for southern California, where my dad had been called to La Crescenta First Baptist Church. The move to California only intensified my desire to become, as I used to say, a new man in Christ. I was ready for a major personality and lifestyle overhaul, in the Holy Name of Jesus.

Justin and I had written to each other a few times while we were both seventh graders, but we abandoned the ritual around the time of Nixon's resignation, the summer before eighth grade. I started hearing about Justin's rebellion a year or so before the Owenses returned for their second St. Paul furlough.

"It sounds like Justin is having a hard time in Brazil," Mom would say after reading another letter from Jane Owens. "He's going through a real rebellious stage. You should write to him sometime. You could be a good influence."

She didn't realize that I was, at that time, going through my own covert rebellion. What did I have to say to Justin about that—other than "I know"? At least he had, apparently, made friends.

I imagined him with other missionary kids, stashing high-grade weed in the boarding school lockers. And why not? That's what I would have done if I was miles and miles from my parents, in South America, the land of drug kingpins and cartels. Might as well take advantage of the nearness to Colombia. If the kids couldn't be saints, if they couldn't be the children their parents wanted, if they couldn't even be near their parents, they might as well be sinners. Might as well use the freedom of being in a foreign land to really fuck themselves up good.

In addition to Justin's fall from grace, the headline news from the Owenses in São Paulo, the news that Central Baptist members were repeating joyfully, was that Jane Owens had healed miraculously from a disease that had, for months, kept her from using her right arm. A mysterious disease had paralyzed the arm, and doctors told her that she'd never be able to use it again. It was dead, useless, and they even discussed amputating it. Then, a bunch of members of their São Paulo church got together and laid hands on it, prayed for it, and it healed. Within the month, she regained full use of it.

People at Central Baptist who'd been praying regularly were absolutely gleeful about Mrs. Owens's arm. A modern-day miracle was proclaimed. And who didn't want to believe in a miracle? I sure wanted to believe. I wanted (despite my stumblings and backslidings and shadows of doubt) to believe in miracles, to believe that the age of miracles had not (as so many curmudgeons insisted) passed. Who wouldn't want to believe in the miracle of Mrs. Owens's arm?

When he returned at the age of sixteen, Justin was one pissed-off missionary kid. I got together with him a few times between his return and my departure, and I felt scared both of and for him. He wasn't the stereotypical happy go lucky burnout without a clue. He was a variety of burnout that I hadn't seen: a particularly disturbing missionary kid interpretation of burnoutdom. He hadn't learned how to be a burnout in an acceptable midwestern way—a good-natured St. Paul burnoutdom that involved a party-hearty outlook, feigned stupidity, an air of spaciness, and a relatively groomed appearance. Long hair, sure, but feathered symmetrically and shampooed daily.

Justin's hair was past his shoulders and greasy, knotted, uncombed, and washed only when it had to be, in the early stages of dreadlocks. His face had long strands of peach fuzz, as if no one had ever bothered to tell him that the peach fuzz must be shaved off before the hard stuff, the real whiskers, can grow. In place of the goody-goody sixth grade geek, last furlough's unfashionable nerd I didn't want my school friends to meet, walked a social misfit—once more an outcast I didn't want my school friends to meet.

My St. Paul Murray High School friends were drinkers and pot smokers who still tried to get Bs in school, still tried to be kinder than not to their parents, and still planned on going to college. When I told them, after camp, about my most recent rededication to Christian ways, they said, "Well that's cool, I guess. If it works for you." And they kept on being my friends.

And Mom was urging me to spend quality time with my old friend.

"He doesn't have any friends, and I guess he's going through a difficult, rebellious time."

All of this only made me glad that my family was moving to California. I wouldn't be around to witness Justin's greater descent—or worse, be pulled down with him.

I'm pretty sure that Justin was the only person—the only person who had anything to do with Central Baptist Church, anyway—who didn't believe in his very own mother's miracle arm. I found this out the first time I got together with him. We were walking down to Lake Johanna in New Brighton, the suburb where they'd found a home to rent for the year, Justin's junior year of high school. I didn't know what to say to this angry son who'd returned, so I figured I'd mention the most obvious conversation piece: the miracle arm. Congratulate him for being the son of the miracle mom.

"Hey, that's great about your mother's arm healing," I said. "People at Central have been talking all about the miracle."

"You believe that?" he asked. "You actually believe that bullshit about my mother's arm being a miracle? It ain't no fuckin' miracle. It's all a bunch of superstition. Just a bunch of coincidence and superstition. I'll tell you what the miracle is. The miracle is that I haven't killed the bitch yet."

I didn't know how to respond. Justin's rage was so intense that I wanted to run straight home and hug my own mom, the mom who'd pleaded with me to spend time with this M.K. mutant. This M.K. monster.

Justin, at that moment, seemed scary and mean and cruel and evil beyond all comprehension. What kind of a person, I wondered, wouldn't want to believe in the miracle of his mother's arm? What kind of person would call that mom a bitch and feel like killing her? His very own mom who brought him into this very world!

This latest incarnation of Justin sounded and looked like an anti-miracle. That's what he'd become in the four years he'd been away: an anti-miracle, a boy-man who was letting nature run its course. This Justin was letting wild and cruel nature lead him into a complete state of degeneration.

After I sat my mom down and explained to her just how angry and bad Justin had become, she eased up on the suggestions to spend time with him. Not completely, but a little.

"I wonder," she'd ask, "how Justin is doing? Have you talked to him lately?"

If I said no, she left it alone. Because she didn't know if I would become his Christian witness, or if he would become my stumbling block. She wanted to believe the former, but she'd blame only herself if the latter happened. And she stopped saying, "He doesn't have any friends," because she knew what I'd say, what I once said: "Well maybe he doesn't deserve any friends right now."

I really believed this, too. How could a guy who denied the miracle of his mother's arm, who called her a bitch and said he wanted to kill her, deserve any friends besides the lowest of the low, the bottom feeders, the toasted ones Justin eventually found his place among?

But I couldn't shrug Justin off. I couldn't erase him from my mind, couldn't count him as one of the lost and leave it at that. I'd given him my phone number and he kept calling and asking me to get together. Because he didn't yet have any friends. And how sad it must have been to be, again, a stranger in a strange land without a single friend.

So I got together with him a couple more times. Once at his house, and once at mine. He mostly talked, I mostly listened. When we ran out of things to say, we got out the Pink Floyd and Led Zeppelin records. He got some anger off his chest, and I assuaged some of my own guilt about not being Christlike enough.

Justin told me about how much he hated his parents, how much they were hypocrites and phonies who made him sick, how much he hated being an M.K., how much he hated returning to Brazil four years ago, and how much he hated leaving Brazil for this latest worthless furlough.

"And they're going to expect me to go back to Brazil for my senior year of high school, just when I get adjusted here," he said. "I hate this life."

He built a case that I couldn't entirely dismiss. A year in the States, four years on the mission field, a year in the States, four more in the field, a year in the States, four more in the field, and here he was in the States again. Uprooting after uprooting after uprooting. The child would have to become convinced that his parents were truly following God's will and come to see himself as part of their larger plan. Or disassociate himself from reality after all the leavings and leavings until he eventually said, "Who are you missioning about? Who is your mission about? What is your mission if I, your child, am to be sacrificed?"

When we moved to California, I had no desire to keep up any correspondence. I tried to completely forget about Justin as I began a new life in my own strange land. Every once in a while, though, my Central Baptist friends told me in letters about how bad he was doing. Some went to Ramsey High School with him, and what they reported wasn't good at all: he hung out with Ramsey's most fried class of burnouts; when he bothered to show up at school, he showed up stoned; when Central Baptist kids saw him in the hallway and said, "Hi Justin," he pretended not to recognize them.

Someone even told me that his girlfriend, his one true friend, drowned in the middle of Lake Johanna late one night after a party. The image that returns to my mind is that of a wasted girl floating on a little raft into the middle of a calm lake beneath a big midnight moon. The raft tips, she falls off, she sinks to the bottom of the lake, and no miracle of God revives her.

That set Justin more completely against his parents and the God that they believed in. Maybe he even saw himself as the cursed one, the Antichrist. And all he wanted was one true companion to help him find his way out of the foreign devil land and into the furlough without end amen.

california calls

Heeding the Call of God/Gordon

I sometimes ask myself the question that I've never asked my dad or mom: "What was the point of our move to California?"

To do God's will. That's one answer that I've heard.

Another: To heed God's calling to a new ministry.

I still don't understand. We all loved Minnesota, Central Baptist Church was thriving more than ever before, Dad and Mom were revered celebrities in that world, we had the best house we'd ever lived in, all five of us had many close friends, Marshall would be a senior at Murray High School, I'd be a junior, Marna would be in ninth grade. The reasons for not moving were compelling and convincing.

Still, the reasons for not moving were of this world, not from the unknowable mind of God. The calling of God, the will of God, dictated that we needed to be willing to abandon all, forsake all, leave all, flee the comforts of this here-and-now temporal world for the greater ministry.

Dad and Mom constantly reminded themselves of the parable of the rich young ruler who wanted salvation but wouldn't sacrifice all of his riches to follow Jesus. And so, he went empty away. The moral: You must lose your life to save it. If you save your life, you will lose it. Go ye therefore, or else you will go empty away.

It started with a here-and-now human phone call.

Gordon Rasmussen, the chairman of the La Crescenta First Baptist Church pulpit committee, first called Dad early in 1977. What I'm thinking now: the calling of God may be nothing more than the phone call from a man named Gordon Rasmussen, and God's will may be little more than Gordon's will. It is impossible to know how much is mystery and how much is choice and how much is destiny and what is the call of God and what is, simply, a man named Gordon Rasmussen dialing ten digits and getting a voice on the other line that happens to belong to my dad.

I've imagined the conversation. Gordon told Dad that his name had come up as a promising ministerial candidate, then asked Dad if he'd consider the possibility. Initially, Dad gave the matter no thought. He said no. Absolutely not. He wasn't interested, and he saw no signs that God was calling him to leave Central Baptist Church. Things at Central were going great: the new building plan he'd initiated had been completed only two years ago, the membership was growing, tithing was up, neighborhood outreach was expanding. Central was, Dad reminded Gordon, an inner-city church, and it was rare in 1977 to find an inner-city church that was in such a state of expansion. God was blessing Central, Dad felt effective and needed there, and it was not the time to move to a big church in California.

La Crescenta First Baptist had, Gordon told Dad, fifteen hundred members, twice as many as Central. Theirs was a growing church as well, and they needed leadership to match that growth. They needed leadership that would rise to their level of expansion. They'd talked to many people in the Baptist General Conference about experienced pastors worthy of the call, and John Anderson was the name that kept coming up. The name of the man God was leading to do great things. The name of the man God would call to bigger and better and greater things.

Dad: "It sounds like an exciting church and a great opportunity. But the time isn't right for me to leave Central Baptist."

Gordon: "God's sense of timing doesn't always match our sense of timing. Just give the matter some thought and prayer. God might have other plans."

And Dad couldn't deny those words: God's timing was different than human timing. God's plans were often different from the plans of His children. Who could truly know God's will? Yes, he should, at the very least, give the matter some thought and prayer. That's all God asked at that moment.

Mom told us about this man who called Dad from California and how Dad said no to him. Dad was so pleased with how things were going at Central that he wouldn't even consider leaving. We needed to know this: Dad was so pleased with how God was blessing Central that he wouldn't even consider the big church in California that wanted him more than anyone else.

"Well, unless it is God's will for John to go to California," Mom qualified. "If John felt strongly that it was God's will for him to go, he wouldn't say no. But he doesn't feel at all that way right now."

Right now. God's will. What could or would, I wondered, tilt things in the other direction? What would it take? How would Dad know?

I'd always wondered what God's will felt and sounded like. I'd asked Dad and Mom and youth pastors and Sunday school teachers, and no one could ever give a satisfying answer. Sure, it would be awesome, they said, if God always revealed His will through one distinctly and unmistakably heard voice, but God's will was, most often, merely a matter of praying constantly, reading the Bible daily for answers and guidance, and then following your heart. It was a matter of attending carefully to all of the ways in which God revealed Himself to us, and then doing the right thing.

Okay, but did God speak louder to some than to others, I wondered? Did different people have different volume controls?

And how much did God's will have to do with plain-and-simple repetition?

For example, Gordon kept calling and calling, and Dad started to feel like maybe, just maybe, God was calling him to leave Central Baptist and go to La Crescenta First Baptist. Is that how it happened? God called Gordon and told him to call Dad, Gordon called Dad again and again, Dad began to hear the call of Gordon as the call of God, and then Mom began to wonder if she was hearing things right.

And when Mom and Dad told me that the man from California kept calling and calling, I only said, "I don't want to move to California." When it came to God's will, I really didn't hear much of anything. How could I possibly hear God's will in the same spring that I heard and saw Led Zeppelin at the St. Paul Civic Center?

"We probably aren't going to move to California," Mom reassured.

"Good," I said. "Because I've been meaning to mention that I don't want to move to California. I wouldn't know anyone there. I would have to make all new friends."

"The chances of us moving to California are so slim that … it's just really unlikely."

That's when I knew: we're going to move to California. And I remember thinking, "Well, if we move to California, I'm going to get messed up. I'm going to mess myself up for good."

All through ninth and tenth grade I'd used my love for my parents, my desire not to hurt them, as an excuse for not partying harder, for not getting stoned nightly, for getting drunk only when I was certain that I wouldn't get caught. If we moved to California, that would be the end of that. I would mess myself up, because moving to California would mean that Mom and Dad didn't love their children anymore. Moving to California would mean the end of their love, and the end of their love would be the end of not wanting to hurt them. If we moved to California, I would become the prodigal son that I always knew I could become, the prodigal son that they feared I'd become. I'd hang out with the burnouts and get stoned every day and drunk every night. I'd try harder drugs than before: acid and cocaine. Not heroin. Well, maybe heroin, but only to try it.

I pictured myself on the airplane from Minnesota to California, singing the lyrics to one of my favorite Led Zeppelin songs, "Going to California." And if I met a love-eyed, flower-haired girl like the one in the song, I would follow her anywhere. And that would be the beginning of love.

The phone calls quit coming for a few months, and then Mom told me that the California church had set their sights on another pastor named Dennis Carlstrom, an acquaintance of Mom and Dad's. Dennis Carlstrom was a great preacher, they said, and a great minister in general.

Dennis Carlstrom was scheduled to candidate at La Crescenta First Baptist on Mother's Day, 1977. Candidating required the pastoral candidate to travel to the church, meet the congregation, and preach a sermon or two. The congregation would then vote on whether or not to officially "call" the pastor.

"He'll get the job," Mom said. "John and I are positive that they'll choose him."

All agreed: Dennis Carlstrom was a shoo-in.

The news spread quickly in Baptist General Conference circles: La Crescenta First Baptist Church voted not to call Dennis Carlstrom. The chemistry just wasn't right. The man for the job was not, after all, the man for the job. The word from the pews was that Dennis Carlstrom was cocky, overconfident, full of himself. And not very personable. This might have been enough to set the church against him, but he made their decision even easier by telling, at the beginning of the sermon, an inappropriate joke with a storyline that involved an affair between a married man and a married woman. Now, telling a loosen-the-crowd joke at the beginning of a sermon is standard procedure for a lot of pastors, and it wasn't this that the congregation objected to. It was the subject matter itself: a sexual affair between two married people. What was Dennis Carlstrom thinking? Mother's

Day, a Baptist congregation that would, that very evening, vote on calling him or not, and he tells a joke about sex outside of marriage? Loosen the congregation, sure, but not that much.

Gordon Rasmussen called Dad again later in the week. After the Dennis Carlstrom incident, Dad was now seen for who he was: the humble, gracious, personable man for the job, John Anderson. God was, Gordon must have told Dad, more clearly than ever telling the pulpit committee that John Anderson was the one. Yes, God was calling John Anderson to leave Central Baptist Church in St. Paul for La Crescenta First Baptist Church in California.

As Dad sensed that God was calling him to La Crescenta First Baptist Church, I started to think maybe Mom and Dad really were hearing the call—and if they were really hearing the call, I wouldn't mess myself up. When Dad and Mom asked again about how I felt about moving to California, I told them that my feelings were changing.

By midsummer I started hearing the call. Or something like it. It wasn't a voice in my ear or a quickening of the heart or a blinding light that appeared suddenly as I ran on the dirty pig path from one end of the Minnesota State Fairgrounds to the other. No, it was a simple coming to peace with the decision that my father had made. A blessed assurance that moving to California was what God wanted for our lives.

No, I wouldn't mess myself up as I'd initially planned. I'd begin life anew on the straight and narrow path to salvation. I was getting sick of living the double life, and Mom and Dad told me that most of my church friends in California would also go to my high school—because the high school was one block away from La Crescenta First Baptist Church. I would be able to live in one world and have one set of friends in that world. I'd never lived in one world like that before.

Sand, sun, surf, palm trees lining every street, California girls, a hot-and-not-lukewarm spiritual state: this would all feel so good that getting drunk, stoned, and naked would be completely unnecessary. I'd truly be able to live the Christian life more faithfully in California.

I was glad that we were moving, I told Mom and Dad in the middle of the summer. If God wanted us to move to California, then I wanted to move to California.

Results

Back to the initial question: what was the point of our move to California? It sometimes seems like the whole reason for the move to California in 1977 was for Marna and Jim to meet and, many years later, marry. Life is far more complex than that, of course, but if we're talking from the standpoint of sheer results, the 1995 marriage of Marna and Jim was the most apparent result of our move to California.

Worlds ago, back in the 1995 end-of-summer, back when I was still married to Julie, back when we were living in our house on Lafond Avenue in St. Paul, a few days before the wedding, my old La Crescenta friend Jon called.

"Hey Mark, it's Jon Ackerman. Remember me?"

My best friend in my final two years of high school, my most conservative born-again Christian years, wanted to know if I remembered him. I hadn't spoken to Jon in over a decade. I'd only written about him. Of course I remembered him. How would I forget him, I asked?

"I don't know," he said. "It's been so long. Hey, I'm coming to Marna and Jim's wedding. So are Stan and Mike."

Marna and Jim told me that they'd invited some of the old California friends to the wedding, but they assumed that none of them would come.

"Great," I heard myself say.

"It will be," Jon said, "a reunion of the old gang. Gosh, how long has it been since we've all been together? Ten years?"

"About that," I said. "Since Christmas '84—just before my mom and dad moved back to Minnesota. Yes, ten years."

I didn't say that as those years passed, I found it easier and easier to forget about my old California friends: Jon, Stan, and Mike. I assumed that those friendships had ended—as some friendships that were an essential part of a former world end without conscious decision or tidy closure. Those friendships were vital to me years ago, and it's hard to imagine how lonely my life in La Crescenta might have been without the "old gang" that Jon was so excited to see reunited. The six of us (Jon, Stan, Mike, Marshall, Jim, and me) were core members of the La Crescenta First Baptist accountability-discipleship group that I joined in my junior year of high school, and we spent countless California afternoons and evenings hanging out together.

Back in our high school years, Marna was, as far as Jim was concerned, little more than the little sister of Marshall and Mark. Some couples have to go through more to get together. In the relationship of Marna and Jim, it took a college semester together in a liberation theology–influenced San Francisco Urban Studies Program (through the Christian College Consortium that included Marna's Bethel College and Jim's Westmont College), a mutual interest in Central America, time spent working together in El Salvador, and many trips between California, El Salvador, and Minnesota. Jim had been working in El Salvador since 1985, and sometime between then and the 1995 wedding, they romanced and decided to marry.

The rest of the old gang willfully drifted apart in our early adult years. My own reasons for leaving those friendships behind mostly concern geography, faith, and politics. They still lived in California, I lived in Minnesota; they were still very conservative evangelical Christians, while I wasn't calling myself a Christian anymore; they were Republicans who'd all worked, at one time or another, in branches of the U.S. military, while I was a far-left-of-center-bleeding-heart who leaned toward pacifism. In the early eighties, at the height of the Reagan era, when Marshall, Jim, and I discovered lefty social justice politics, they (Jon, Stan, and Mike) began to seem like a "them," while we began to feel like an "us." We were, in other words, adults who would, in most situations, steer clear of each other.

Unless we had a past in common, as we did. We had a past in common: high school years of devout, zealous evangelical Christianity; jacuzzi parties under California moonlight; group dates; and a love for seventies progressive rock and fusion jazz (which I've mostly left behind). The ties that bind. It didn't take as much when we were sixteen, seventeen, eighteen. It would, we all knew, take more now that we were in our mid-thirties. And who among us really had faith that we could truly pull off the reunion? Certainly not Jim, Marshall, or I.

"Hey, I have a favor to ask," Jon said from his home in San Diego. "I was wondering if I could maybe stay with you for a few days during the wedding and everything. If it isn't too much of a hassle. If it's a hassle, feel free to say no. But it would be excellent to spend some time with you again. What do you think?"

What think? Think quick.

"Well," I said, "I'll have to ask my wife about that. I can't just make a decision like that without consulting my wife, Julie. If it was up to me, I'd say no problem."

"I know how that is. Totally. I'm married too, you know. You gotta talk about these things. Can you believe that? I have a wife and kids. I wish they could come. Yeah, I wish you could meet my wife and kids. It will be great to meet your wife. Got any kids?"

"No kids," I said, without mentioning that that was the issue of the year. Kids or no kids. I said no, Julie said yes. It was far more involved than that, with plenty of qualifying variables on both sides, but the essential disagreement came down to this: she wanted kids very soon; I didn't want kids anytime soon. Maybe I didn't want them ever.

"No kids," is how I put it to Jon.

"No kids? You gotta have kids. Kids are great, man!"

I'd heard that. About kids being great. I'd also heard about kids not being great. I only said to Jon, "Maybe someday," and that was, for the time being, the end of the kids discussion.

"This is going to be," Jon said, "so excellent! A reunion of the old gang."

A reunion. Not only were these old friends coming to the wedding, they were expecting a reunion. And I knew: the only way a reunion could possibly happen was if we (Marna, Jim, Marshall, and I) had remained in the faith, in the Lord, in the tie that binds. And we hadn't. Totally hadn't.

There was something uncanny, disturbing, and oddly fitting about this California revisitation, this unplanned-for time spent with three of my most rigidly Christian high school friends. I'd been writing about them, but I hadn't seen them for over a decade. Through the miracles of time and distance, they'd become my characters, my creations, my representations, my material. Now they were returning, in the flesh, as if to hold me accountable. As if I'd had free rein with them long enough, and now they wanted me to get them, and myself, right.

Property Values and Race Matters

The way I see it now, we Andersons never really belonged in La Crescenta, a suburb that rests in the foothills of Los Angeles County, a few miles from John Wayne's hometown, Glendale. We always felt like misfits, Minnesota Democrats misplaced in a bastion of serious Republicans. For example, no one I knew, besides my parents, opposed Howard Jarvis's legendary Proposition 13, the 1978 tax revolt that froze property taxes, gutted public spending, and set the stage for the 1980 Reagan landslide. Howard Jarvis has been called "the John the Baptist of Reaganism," and La Crescenta folks fully immersed themselves in his "I'm Mad as Hell" conservative populism.

La Crescenta was only twenty minutes, freeway time, from downtown Los Angeles, but it felt years away from the city. Though my St. Paul reality was far more WASP-y than I wanted to acknowledge, I thought of myself as a city kid. I didn't have any black friends in St. Paul, but I thought of myself as a friend to black people. When I heard racist jokes at Crescenta Valley High School, I said things like, "I don't think that's funny. I came from a high school that was fifteen percent black." That was the difference between St. Paul Murray High School (one of the whitest St. Paul high schools) and Crescenta Valley High School. Fifteen percent black: the difference that I repeated to bolster my city kid credentials.

I don't remember any blacks in La Crescenta, aside from Bubba, the music minister that my dad brought to La Crescenta First Baptist in 1980. I did hear a story that began, "A black family lived in La Crescenta a few years ago." The details are sketchy, but I remember that it was a high school basketball coach and his family, and that the coach's son was a basketball star.

Maybe I heard that story on the football team bus to Compton. In my junior year, back when I still played football, the Crescenta Valley Falcons faced the Compton Tar Babes (that really was the name of the team) in a 1977 playoff game. That's the first I'd heard of Compton.

"It's the Crescenta Valley Rocky Balboa Falcons versus the Compton Apollo Creed Tar Babes this week," Coach Gossard said to us before the playoff game. "Yes, men, we're the underdogs in this one. We're fighting for our lives. Our balls are on the line."

We all understood that Apollo Creed was the black antagonist in "Rocky," that we were white and they were black, and that, yes, Coach Gossard meant the game would be a battle between whites and blacks. The Compton Tar Babes promptly kicked the shit out of us on their home turf. I remember being told to load onto the bus right away. No postgame handshakes, no showers. It was the only football game in which the coaches wanted to get out of town and onto the freeway as quickly as possible.

Later that week, when our school sports journalists wrote about the game in the newspaper, they made up buffoonish names for Compton's star players, names that they knew would get a good laugh. "Compton halfback, Simpson Huckleberry, runs into the end zone for a touchdown," read a caption under a game photo.

I was not surprised when I found out years later that Lawrence Powell, one of the police officers who beat Rodney King, graduated in the Crescenta Valley High class of '80. My mom told me this as we discussed the L.A. riots that we'd been watching on the evening news, and when we got off the phone, I looked up the picture of scrawny, gap-toothed Larry in my 1979 Crescenta Valley Talon yearbook.

This brings me back to the story of the basketball coach and family. It ended, as I recall, with smashed windshields, slashed tires, burning crosses on the front lawn, "Niggers get out of town" spray-painted on the garage door, death threats, more death threats, and the words, "So they left La Crescenta after a year." And a moral: "You have to understand. People around here are really concerned about declining property values."

Degenerate-Speak

"Dude. Did you get the stuff?" Jon asked as he tossed his bags into the trunk of our red Toyota. He'd flown in from San Diego, and he'd be staying with us for three days and nights.

Same Jon that I remembered: dark brown wavy hair, very tanned, a touch of surfer in his talk. He still loved to caricature burnouts, the guys who most inspired our high school humor and disdain. Because we'd both stood on the fringes of what we called "degeneracy" before "rededicating our lives to Christ," we did extended parodies of stock-stoners. We got into the parts so much so that we'd cuss and fictionalize sexual adventures and all-night partying.

"Dude, I've got the worst fucking headache," he'd say, back then. "I don't know how much I drank last night. And then I was smoking this really awesome lumbo. I was so fuckin' wasted! But I'm pretty sure I got laid."

"Yeah, I smoked a few bowls of the lumbo too," I'd say. "That was some shit. But the chick I was with wouldn't let me get past first base. And I brought her to the party! I got her high!"

We'd banter back and forth for hours like this. At some point, Jon or I would say something like, "Can you believe that? There's actually guys who talk like that, seriously." We had to let each other know that these conversations existed in the realm of parody, mockery, satire, comic relief. They were our way of imagining and describing and role-playing the lives we'd left behind, the lives of the California guys our age who were having all the fun (as we tried to walk the straight and narrow path to salvation).

"Did you get the stuff?" That was Jon's cue that we were entering the old act.

I played along, initially, with Jon's nostalgic degenerate-speak as we rode home from the airport: "Are you kidding me? I got the stuff," I said. "If we don't get stopped by pigs on the way home, we'll be on our way to one very wasted night."

He laughed hard. I remembered. I remembered.

"One very wasted night," he said. "That's awesome."

Eventually, though, the old game only made me feel the distance between us. Because I sort of wished that I really did have the stuff. One very wasted night didn't sound at all bad to me.

The Story of Tim the Degenerate

Habitual adolescent backsliders annually repent of sins at camp, promise a return to the straight and narrow path, but usually stumble back into Satan's hands soon after school begins. That was my pattern, anyway. Ever since the bat flew out of the Trout Lake Camp chapel, though, I'd been living right.

And in California, in 1977, the Christian life was feeling a lot more livable. Even the peer pressure from my new California friends—Jon, Stan, Mike, and Jim—steered me back onto the path of the righteous and the good and the holy.

A lot of this new righteous peer pressure was encouraged and inspired by my California youth pastor, a charismatic man named Larry. Larry had seen the postcamp backsliding pattern unfold with too many teens, so he decided to take preventive action: a Friday morning "discipleship-accountability group" composed of all the high school guys who'd made camp decisions: Jon, Stan, Mike, Jim, Marshall, me, and about five other guys, including Tim.

Larry, a late-twenties man who wore shoulder-length blond hair and earth shoes, had two pet adages that gave us different impressions of God. God as jovial buddy: "Go ahead and laugh about it—God has a sense of humor too"; or, God as dictator: "Hey! When God says 'jump' all we can ask is, 'how high, Lord?'" No one thought to ask Larry, "What if God tells a joke that just isn't funny?" Or "What if God says 'jump' and we think 'He's gotta be joking'?"

Larry's accountability group met every Friday morning at six thirty, an hour and a half before school started. When we asked Larry to switch our meeting to the afternoon, he said, "It will mean more to you if you must sacrifice sleep to come." Larry knew: we couldn't argue with the word "sacrifice." If we tried, he'd counter with, "You mean to tell me that Jesus sacrificed His life on the cross for your sins, and you can't even sacrifice an hour of sleep for Him?"

So, we ambled, half-awake and dumbed-down, into a gray-carpeted second-floor Sunday school room and sat in a circle of folding chairs. For the next hour, we read favorite Bible verses, accounted for the state of our daily prayer and Bible study, shared commonplaces, and confessed any forays into the old ways of our backslider selves.

"I didn't do so hot this week," one of us might say. "I only read my Bible once, and then on Wednesday night I was with my old friends and they offered me a beer and I drank it. Before I knew it, I was wasted."

We'd gently chastise the stumbler, usually Tim: "Tim, man, you're blowing it. Next week you better do better, or you're going to end up where you were before camp."

Before camp. We all knew where that was: Sin City. It can swallow you in. Tim had recently reemerged from a long and busy spell in Sin City, and he was now trying again to walk that straight and narrow path to salvation.

As I started my new life in California, Tim's life became a parable with a distinct moral: "This is who you might become if you lose sight of the straight and narrow path." Even now as I tell Tim's story, I think of it as a way that I might have chosen to be—if I had followed through with my initial plan to mess myself up.

Tim was one of those church regulars who, with his mother, attended every Sunday morning, evening, and Wednesday night, from preschool through middle of seventh grade.

Around the time puberty hit, Tim fell in with a group of junior high burnouts and became another La Crescenta First Baptist adolescent backslider. For the next few years, Tim was long gone. He quit coming to church altogether, regularly dropped acid, and, when he bothered to show up at school, he got stoned before, during, and after. Somehow he wound up, in the summer of 1977, at Hume Lake Baptist Camp, a fundamentalist hotbed in the Sierra Nevada.

Other accountability group members retold Tim's rededication-to-Christ story. They didn't ever tell it when he was in the room, because they couldn't have done as good a job with the stoner voice. Though I wasn't there to witness, I pieced together a narrative from their accounts.

That year at Hume the white-haired camp pastor happened to be a self-proclaimed "End Times" expert. He'd spent the better part of his thirty-odd ministerial years studying Old Testament prophecy, the book of Revelation, wars, alignments and realignments of nations, Cold War dogma, and the history of the world's plagues and natural disasters.

"Coming again, coming again," he sang midsermon in his quivering baritone, "maybe morning, maybe noon, maybe evening, must be soon … Oh what a wonderful day that will be! Jesus is coming again!"

The grandfatherly evangelist repeatedly made eye contact with Tim, and Tim was certain that this prophecy-bearing sage knew everything he'd ever done. That's how Tim put it to the other guys. The man knew everything about him, and there was no place left to run or hide.

Tim felt the pressure, and it was too much to bear all alone: the growing-up years in the church he'd left behind, the years in the teenybop drug underworld, the hiding from God and the Devil, the gates of Heaven and the fires of Hell, this weeklong exile from his wide circle of stoner buddies, the dorky church kids trying to show him Christian love.

"And on the triumphant day of the Rapture, young people, I ask you tonight," the pastor said, "will you be lifted into the clouds with the believers, or will you get left behind with the unbelievers? Will you be left behind to go through the Tribulation on earth? If you don't want to be left behind on that day, I ask you right now to stand up and walk down the aisle to invite Jesus into your heart."

"I ain't getting left behind," Tim muttered as he shot out of his seat, down the aisle, and knelt at the foot of the stage to pray for the forgiveness of his sins.

"Welcome home," the pastor said as he embraced Tim and all of the other teens who, after him, repeated the prayer of salvation.

"Who wants to make a special point of checking up on Tim next week?" Larry asked. "Someone needs to call him a couple of times to see how he's doing with his quiet time and walk with the Lord. Like the Apostle Paul says in Galatians, we need to bear one another's burdens."

Whenever Larry asked for volunteers, he was really asking for help from the McDiffit brothers, lanky identical twins who always did the right thing simultaneously. The McDiffits or Marshall, the saintly seniors in our group. Those were the poles: Tim, nearest to Hell; the McDiffits and Marshall, nearest to Heaven. Larry feared that his more "at-risk" disciples, those of us nearest to Tim, would be pulled by Satan in the wrong direction if we tried to guide the course of his spiritual journey.

The three saints didn't have a history of backsliding, but they still found enough sin in their lives to walk the "rededication" aisle every summer at camp. While I repented getting stoned, getting drunk, and getting sexual, they repented (like born-again President Jimmy Carter) lusting in their hearts or thinking the word "shit" after slamming a finger in the door. Perfection was their unspoken goal. They couldn't come right out and say this, because only God was perfect, and the desire to become God was blasphemous. Hence, their relentless striving to become more and more "Christlike" became mighty confusing.

The McDiffits and Marshall were most-disciplined disciples who almost always had good things to share with the group. "I did really good this week," the saints would say. "I read my Bible and prayed every day and really felt close to the Lord. I'd like to share this verse from Philippians with you because it just really hit me right between the eyes … "

Every week, they introduced new challenges: "I'd just like to challenge you to go out of your way and say 'Hey, how's it goin?' to someone who looks lonely, like he just needs a friend or something." "I'd just like to challenge you to do the dishes for your mom one night this week." "I'd just like to challenge you to tell one of your teachers at school that he's doing a super job."

In the early months of his discipling, Tim wrote down every saintly challenge and dutifully reported his progress. "Well, I did the dishes for my mom twice this week and I told my math teacher that he's super and I said 'hey, how's it going' to three lonely looking dudes."

We all felt pleased with Tim's turnaround, despite his minor stumbles now and then. He was trying hard. He'd mostly stayed away from drugs and his old degenerate friends, kept up with his daily devotions, and attended all church services, Bible studies, social gatherings, and Friday morning meetings.

"You're really growing spiritually, Tim," Larry told him. "God is working in your life."

Tim had been obsessed with the book of Revelation since camp. At first, we didn't think much of this. It only made sense that he'd return to the place of his returning. Besides, he needed something to compensate for the secular rock concerts he'd forsworn—"They're avoidable stumbling blocks in your life," Larry told him—and the book of Revelation was, after all, a detailed description of the greatest rock show ever, one that Tim most definitely didn't want to miss.

"I feel like I need to begin at the end—however long that takes me—and then go back to the beginning. Read Revelation and then go straight to Genesis. Revelation is absolutely blowing my mind," he said.

While Larry was glad that Tim was still reading the Bible at all, he hoped that he'd eventually get to the gospels and epistles. New Testament meat and potatoes. That's what he encouraged us to read most.

"Well, I'll give you some advice, Tim," Larry said one morning. "Don't get so hung up on all the symbolic details—things that we can never really be certain about—to the point that you miss the main message: that Jesus Christ will prevail over evil in the end and His followers will spend eternity with Him in Heaven. In other words, don't get lost in the trees and miss the forest."

This sounded like reasonable advice. Tim was intelligent enough to get lost in his own thoughts, but not savvy enough to distinguish a great-while-stoned idea from a real possibility. He could make connections, but they might very well turn out to be all the wrong ones.

"But I feel like I'm understanding a lot of things that I never understood before," Tim responded, slightly hurt. "The forest and the trees and everything else. It's like, I read it and I see it all happening inside my head and I know why it's happening too. I'm making sense of everything, like God's speaking directly to me. I was just thinking the other day that maybe God put me here on the Earth to really understand the Revelation and tell people about it."

One Friday in mid-November, Tim showed up to the meeting sadder than we'd ever seen. His little oval face was sickly white, his long brown hair looked far greasier than usual, his red eyes had dark circles around them, and his wrinkled jeans and T-shirt stank, as if they'd been smoked and slept in all week.

"I kind of blew it this week," he told us when his turn came around. "My old best friend Ed calls me and asks me if I want to get a Coke and fries at Jack in the Box or something because he's feeling bored. I was feeling bored too, like there's nothing else to do. And it doesn't seem very Christian to just keep blowing off your best friend. So I walked over to his house and he asks me if I want to listen to the new Nugent record in his room and I figure, why not? He puts the record on and we're both digging it, and then he pulls out a bag of hash and his water bong and lights it up. I just start praying extra hard for Jesus to help me resist the temptation. I'm praying, 'Jesus, just help me say no.' And the first time he offered me a hit, I did say, 'No thanks.' But then he offered another and it smelled so good and I figured one hit won't hurt, so I broke down and took one. Then I kept taking hits every time he offered them to me, and I got so stoned I ended up crashing on Ed's floor and missing school the next day. We woke up in the afternoon, because we'd been up until about four in the morning. I felt so guilty about it, and then Ed said, 'Just get stoned and forget.' So I did, and that just made it worse. I kept thinking about it more and more—how much I let Jesus and all of you down. But I had my little New Testament in my back pocket, so last night I read some of the book of Revelation to Ed and he said it was cool. So maybe I planted a seed in his heart."

No one knew what to say—not even Larry. We silently waited and prayed for someone else to respond.

Finally, Jon, who'd gone through his burnout phase the year before, said, "Man, Tim, you're blowing it. You need to stay away from that Ed guy. He's bad news."

"But he's my best friend. We've been best friends since kindergarten."

"If he really was your best friend, wouldn't he respect the decision you've made to follow Jesus? Is he a better friend to you than Jesus?"

"No," Tim said.

"Then why did you disobey your real best friend? Just to impress your false best friend?"

"I wasn't trying to impress anyone. I was bored. Sometimes I feel like there's nothing to do. It was just something to do."

"Something to do," Larry broke in. "Something to do. How many wrong choices do we make in life just because we're looking for something to do? Yet, I can think of two things that God always would like for us to do: read our Bibles and pray. There's never nothing to do. Now Timothy, I know it might seem like a hard thing to do, but I think Jon is right: you need to stay away from Ed and his whole clan until you are a strong enough Christian to influence them, instead of vice versa. Because the road they're on leads straight to a place where there's nothing to do but burn—burn and weep and wail for eternity. And I'm telling you that because I love you, Tim, and I'll always be here for you. Every one of the guys in this room loves you and will always be here for you, and you need to remember that. But most of all you need to remember that God loves you."

"Yeah, Tim. We love you," we all echoed.

"I'll do better next week—I promise," Tim said.

"Who is going to call Tim a couple of times this week to see how he's doing in his walk with the Lord?"

The McDiffits and Marshall raised their hands.

Tim's next binge started on Monday and lasted until Friday, and by Christmas he stopped coming to the accountability group and all other church activities. None of us were too surprised or, truth be told, upset. We'd pretty much written him off as a worthy but lost cause. Damaged goods. The three saints and Larry eventually gave up on him too.

I can only imagine Tim's strange and lonely days, the strange and lonely days that led to his greatest revelation. I picture him stoned alone in his bedroom, Black Sabbath *Paranoid* blasting, black lights shining on his fluorescent poster of Jesus wearing the crown of thorns, next to Farrah Fawcett in a red bikini.

Time has slowed enough for him to really read and understand every syllable of Revelation 13, and when he gets to verse 7, he sees for the first time the missing piece that makes sense of everything. He knows it's perfect, the 13 minus the 7: "And it was given unto him to make war with the saints and overcome them: and power was given him over all kindreds, and tongues, and nations." He reads it again with emphasis on the words "make war with the saints."

Saints and sinners. Saints are for God and sinners are against Him. He tried to become a saint, but in his heart he was a sinner. He couldn't make peace with the saints, but he could make war with them. That could only mean one thing.

"I am," he shouts, "the beast rising from the sea. I am the Antichrist."

He's no longer the weak-willed backslider. He's a strong and powerful warrior—at least until he falls asleep. When he wakes the next morning, the strength is gone, but the thought remains: "I must be the Antichrist."

Or was he at a weekend party in the yucca plant foothills?

His friends are as sick of hearing about his Christian guilt as they are of hearing about his stoned insights into the book of Revelation, the book he can't leave in the past with his guilt. It's starting to, quite simply, bum everyone out. So, comrade Ed decides to play a little trick on him as they sit in a circle around a two A.M. campfire.

"Watch this," he whispers to the guy next to him.

"You know what I think, Tim? I think you're so into this Revelations shit because you are the Antichrist."

"Shut up," Tim says.

"I'm serious. Think about it. You don't belong with those dorks at that church. You tried to become one of them, but you couldn't. You were put down there for a reason: to find out what they're saying, so you can win them over to your side later. They're your enemies, but you're acting like they're your friends. The reason you're interested in all that battle of Armageddon shit is because you know deep down it's about you. Dude, I'm behind you all the way. Your number is up," Ed says, as he draws 666 in the dirt.

Ed raises his bottle of beer. "Here's a toast to the Antichrist."

Tim's beaming as they raise bottles. He'd never thought of it that way before. He clinks his bottle against Ed's.

"What a dumbfuck," Ed whispers to the guy next to him.

As the thought went from a certainty to a possibility to a doubt and back to a certainty, Tim needed to test-market it with a different audience.

Marshall was the first to receive Tim's news.

One April afternoon, Marshall picked Tim up as he was hitchhiking on Foothill Boulevard. Tim had dropped out of school, hadn't been to church in months, and Marshall, ever-striving to be more Christlike, felt guilty that he hadn't bothered calling him recently.

"Tim, I haven't seen you around for a while. What have you been up to lately?" Marshall asked.

"I'm actually coming home from a party right now," Tim said.

"On a Monday afternoon?"

"It started on Friday night."

"Tim, man, I'm worried about you. I really thought you were going to turn your life around."

"I wanted to before, but you know what I figured out?"

"What?"

"I'm the Antichrist."

"Tim, you're not the Antichrist."

"I swear I am. Listen. Since I realized it, I've been seeing sixes everywhere. On car license plates, on buildings, on uniforms, on TV commercials. The other day I went to the grocery store and bought a big bottle of Coke and the lady rings it up, and there on the cash register I see the numbers sixty six."

"But that's how much it costs for everyone, not just you. There's nothing strange about that. I could have bought a bottle of pop and got the same numbers."

"But the thing is, you didn't. I did. And then the next day I was in line for a cone at Baskin Robbins and I pick my number, and you know what it is?"

"Sixty six?"

"No, *thirty*-six. Whoooah."

Marshall didn't know what to say. Any response seemed pointless.

"I still wish you'd come to church again," Marshall said, as he pulled the green Plymouth into Tim's driveway.

"I won't be at church. But I'm coming to camp again next August. You gonna be at Hume Lake next summer?"

"I'm graduating in June, so I'll be too old."

"Well, you can tell the rest of your disciple buddies that they'll have the Antichrist in their cabin, so they better be ready."

Marshall just shook his head.

As he'd warned, Tim showed up at La Crescenta First Baptist on the morning the church bus left for Hume Lake. His matted brown hair twisted down his back, he'd grown a scraggly mustache and beard, his pot-scented clothes hung loose on his skinny body, and he wore mirror shades to hide his red eyes.

Tim walked on the bus and looked for an empty seat.

"Don't sit by me don't sit by me don't sit by me," I whispered.

I felt grateful when Jennifer, a zealous junior who was unconditionally nice to everyone, invited Tim to sit with her. Jennifer regularly attended the high school girls' accountability group meeting, and she was to that group what Marshall and the McDiffits were to the guys' group. Jennifer spoke often during Bible study "share time" about the importance of loving the unlovely and seeing Jesus Christ in every human being. She'd been told of Tim's Antichrist claim, and she threw everyone in the youth group for a loop when she said, "If the Devil can come disguised as an angel of light, we as Christians should be able to see Christ in the Antichrist."

The authority of her "we as Christians" rattled me.

"Is that true?" someone asked Larry.

Larry avoided a direct answer and went into a long monologue about the mystery and majesty of God, the errant ways of men, the danger of being blown about by every wind of doctrine, and the importance of unwavering submission to the will of God (which meant, of course, if you were a woman, "unwavering submission to the will of men").

"Hey, the thing we need to remember," he said, eventually, "is that when God says 'jump' the only thing we should ask is, 'how high, Lord?'"

And when Jennifer saw Christ in Tim that morning on the bus, God said to her, "Offer Christ a seat next to you."

Jennifer asked one question only: "Would you like the window or the aisle?"

"I want a window seat so I can rest my head somewhere," Tim said. "I'm going to be crashing pretty damn quick."

Tim was sound asleep before the bus started rolling. He only woke up once, south of Bakersfield, when the bus hit a bump and his head bounced hard against the window.

Jennifer asked one more question: "Would you like to use my pillow?"

Redwood and pine trees surrounded Hume Lake, a lake small enough that a good swimmer could glide across and back without tiring. Paths through the woods led to cliffs low enough to dive off and to a cold stream with natural whirlpool baths.

Tim wound up in the cabin "Jericho" with all of the other La Crescenta guys, but we didn't see much of him. He spent most of the week climbing cliffs and wandering worn paths beneath the redwoods, trees that were far too big to miss. He skipped most of the planned camp activities: medicine ball, the water balloon and egg tosses, track and field contests, skit night, morning and evening chapel.

Our Jericho cabin counselor, Rick, didn't seem to care what Tim was up to—as long as he made it back to the cabin before the final bedtime bell rang. While Tim was off in the woods, Rick—a thin and athletic La Crescenta First Baptist college guy who'd heard rumors of Tim—advised us to ignore him instead of arguing about his Antichrist claim.

"I don't think he really believes it himself," he said. "He just wants a reaction."

Still, Rick was the least likely to resist Tim and the most likely to react. I sensed that he was itching for a confrontation, and telling us to ignore Tim was his way of getting us to bow out of the coming battle. Rick wasn't one to let an evangelistic opportunity like this slip by. He'd attended a Southern California Bible college for a year and thought of himself as an "End Times" expert. The end of the world was imminent, he was certain: born-again Christians should save as many souls as possible before the Rapture but do nothing to prevent prophesied world destruction. Believers would be spared, so why worry about the inevitable?

My dad once got into a conflict with Rick about this in the early eighties, soon after Reagan became president and escalated the nuclear arms race. One of about seven Democrats in La Crescenta, Dad scheduled some "life issues" seminars: Christians and capital punishment, Christians and abortion, Christians and the arms race, Christians and world hunger. At the arms race seminar, Dad raised this question: was a pro-life stance consistent with a pro–arms buildup stance? The only person who vigorously challenged him was Rick.

"Nuclear holocaust is prophesied in the book of Revelation," Rick argued later in Dad's office. "Christians should do nothing to keep the prophesy from coming true. Instead of wasting time with these 'life issues,' you should be preparing people for the Rapture. Why don't we ever have seminars on Biblical prophecies that are coming true? Why don't you spend more time preaching about the book of Revelation?"

"Because, Rick," Dad said, "that's exactly what people here would love to hear me preach about."

In Rick's world, Tim wasn't merely a drug-addled teen in search of attention, a screwed up kid trying to mess with the minds of the church kids: Tim was an agent of the Devil, a challenge to the camp order, a force that needed to be brought down low, an antichrist. Not *the* Antichrist, but an antichrist fomenting anarchy.

Rick's inevitable showdown with Tim finally came on Friday night, our last night at Hume.

After reading a passage in Ephesians, Rick switched off the reading lamp next to his bed and hoped to engage us in a lights-out discussion of "faith versus works."

"Do you guys have any thoughts on this?" Rick asked. "I know it's tough to understand how we're saved by grace through faith and not by works."

If we weren't up for a theological discussion, we could always fall back on the teen camp lights-out standby: in a caring, committed, Holy Spirit-driven, boyfriend-girlfriend relationship, how close can you come to having sexual intercourse before you're sinning? In general, the California counselors and youth ministers granted more leeway than the Minnesota ones. I was always looking for someone else to give me new permission.

Before anyone had a chance to respond to the faith versus works question, Tim said matter-of-factly, "Did I tell you guys that I'm the Antichrist?"

Rick became, at that moment, the first grade teacher whose reading lesson was disrupted by the boy who said, "We went to Disney World last summer."

"We're not talking about that right now, Tim," he said. "Does anyone have anything to add about the faith and works question?"

"You're ignoring me, Rick," Tim said impatiently. "I said that I'm the Antichrist."

"I heard you. That has nothing to do with what we're talking about. I won't even discuss it."

"Why? Are you afraid that I might prove to you that I really am?"

"No, Tim—I just think it's the most ridiculous thing I've ever heard and I won't waste a minute discussing it. You're not the Antichrist and you know it. We all know it, so quit playing your little game."

"What game? I'm serious about this, and you better take me seriously because Satan's behind me all the way. I've got more power than you realize."

The word "power" prompted Rick into a different approach.

"Well Tim, if you're the Antichrist, what are you doing here in California? According to Biblical prophecy, the Antichrist is going to establish his empire—a ten-nation confederacy—in Rome. You're a long way from Rome."

I was content to listen to the battle from my bunk and let well-armed Rick launch the intercepting missiles. He was the expert.

"I've got," Tim said, "plenty of time to move to Rome. I'm seventeen now. I'll come into power in about twenty years—soon after the year 2000. I'll start in America, then move to Rome."

"Okay Tim, so you're going to move to Rome after starting here. But how are you going to come into power in the first place? The Antichrist will be the most important and powerful person on Earth. He'll be the greatest politician ever. You're going to have to run a political campaign at some point."

"Well, I'm going to start by becoming governor of California. That seems to be as good a place as any. Look at Ronald Reagan and Jerry Brown. That's where they both started, and now they're presidential candidates."

"But Tim, who would actually vote for you? How would you win the election? You need money and a platform to run on. If you don't get your act together you probably won't even graduate from high school. Do you think people would actually vote for a high school dropout?"

"Hey, all I'll have to do to get people to vote for me is say, 'If you elect me to be your governor, I'll legalize marijuana.' I know lots of people who will vote for me. I have more friends than you realize. They'll vote for me, they'll get their friends to vote for me, those friends will get their friends to vote for me, those friends will get their friends ... there are a lot of heads out there. Plus, I'll get a good chunk of the Jerry Brown crowd, because most of them would like for someone to legalize pot. Don't tell me that Governor Moonbeam doesn't imbibe on occasion."

"But money, Tim, where's the money going to come from?"

Rick was starting to sound like Tim's campaign manager.

"Where do you think it will come from? From the same people who help Jerry Brown. All of those rich California rock and rollers: The Eagles, Linda Ronstadt, Jackson Browne, and all of their friends. Benefits and festivals. You didn't think I thought this out, but I did."

Rick was getting frustrated because, as hard as he tried, he couldn't stump Tim. I was worried. Tim, the youth group burnout, had his next twenty-two years planned, while I still couldn't answer the question, "What do you think your college major will be?"

"Okay Tim, you're established as the Antichrist, people love you, you've got your ten-nation confederacy. What's your first major act going to be? What are you going to do to get the world behind you?"

"I'm going to attack and conquer Russia. Once I've got Russia, the rest of the world will be a piece of cake."

"Ah, but that's not how careful interpretations of Biblical prophecy tell the story. According to careful interpretations, you'll first win the Israelis to your side and bring peace to the Mideast. The rest of the western world will be so impressed that they'll be ready to follow you. You won't attack Russia until Russia makes the mistake of attacking Israel."

I breathed a sigh of relief, as did the rest of the guys in cabin Jericho.

Tim started laughing and said, "What are you talking about?"

"I'm talking about what's been foretold—Biblical prophecy that must be fulfilled."

"Yeah, but I'm the Antichrist. Don't you get it? I don't have to follow what's been prophesied in the Bible. Why would I bother with that? I can do whatever the hell I want."

Rick didn't know what to say. He'd been had. All those years of studying the Last Days and here he couldn't convince a seventeen-year-old stoner that the kid wasn't the Antichrist. Nothing he said mattered anymore.

"I'm the Antichrist! I'm the Antichrist! Yeah!" Tim shouted triumphantly. "I'm the Antichrist! I'm the Antichrist! I'm the Antichrist! Yeeeah!"

"Tim, just shut up," Rick yelled. "Just shut up."

At this point, the rest of us felt comfortable entering the discussion.

"Yeah, Tim just shut up! Just shut up," we yelled.

"I'm the Antichrist I'm the Antichrist," Tim sang merrily, "I'm the Antichrist I'm the Antichrist I'm the Antichrist …"

"Shut up!!"

"I'm the Antichrist I'm the Antichrist …" Tim muttered, then whispered, then mouthed silently, until the cabin got quiet enough for us to drift into sleep.

I heard snores and steady breathing. I felt alone again.

Then, from the bottom bunk across the room I heard Tim's barely audible voice say, "I still know that I'm the Antichrist."

"Shut up Tim," I yelled one last time.

The last time I saw Tim was the summer after my freshman year of college—at a church potluck. I don't remember what we talked about or what, if anything, he brought. Where is he now? What is he doing? Will he ever be the governor of California?

Hear-Hear

The night before the wedding, the night Jon arrived, some friends had a pre-wedding party at a house in the Frogtown area of St. Paul. Frogtown: an ethnically rich neighborhood of stucco and tarpaper houses, rusty Monte Carlos, elm trees, and fishing boats on back lawns.

We walked to the backyard patio where about twenty friends sat beneath mosquito-repelling lamps, smoking cigarettes, sipping beer, and barbequing chicken. Most of the friends were Bethel College alums who'd abandoned their evangelical Christian ways and were attempting to find their places in the secular world that, years before, they had attempted to be in but not of.

I grabbed a beer from a cooler, Jon grabbed a Coke. Jon tried to engage me in more degenerate-banter: "Oh man, I'm starting to feel wasted. I hope I don't get sick."

I tried to ignore him. Did he think we were degenerates? Did he think that this was degeneracy? Did he think that I had become Tim in Minnesota? I didn't know for sure, but I could tell that he felt misplaced. This wasn't the type of party where he wanted to find himself, and he could only hope that I felt uncomfortable too.

"One very wasted night," he said. "That was an awesome line."

My face made a tiny smile.

A few minutes after we got there, another California friend showed up: mild-mannered, soft-spoken Mike, Crescenta Valley High Class of '78 valedictorian, West Point graduate. I always liked Mike, one of our kinder and gentler California friends. The last I heard, Mike was in Panama. Or was it Honduras? What was he doing? Playing war games? Preparing to topple the Sandinistas? Clear-cutting forests into airstrips? Training Contras? Plotting the ouster of Noriega? Or just building roads? I didn't know and I didn't ask.

We saw each other and hugged. Marshall and Jim saw Mike and walked over.

"Look at this," Jon said. "It's a reunion of the old gang: Mike, Jim, Marshall, Mark, me—only Stan is missing, and he'll be here tomorrow."

A reunion. We tried our best to reunite. I asked the given questions about jobs, wives, kids, geography—the topics left after I ruled out religion, politics, the arts, and anything substantial that would require more effort than I was willing to invest in the situation.

As the party wore on, I sensed Jon and Mike's growing disappointment. Who were we anymore? What was this Minnesota? Beer, cigarettes, mosquitoes, fishing boats, rusty Monte Carlos, stucco and tarpaper, degenerating oak trees, Prince 1999 playing on the stereo. Not a palm tree, beach, surfboard, or Bible in sight. Did it look, to them, like Hell? Hell beneath mosquito lamps?

"So Mark, where are you going to church these days," Mike asked.

I wondered how long it would take for Jon or Mike to pop the question. Not "Are you going to church?" but "Where are you going to church?" Their assumption was that I'd remained in the fold.

The last time Julie and I went regularly was around '88. It was a Mennonite church. We went there because we thought we should be going to church, and the Mennonites tend to emphasize peace and justice over soul-saving.

I only said to Mike and Jon, "Julie and I were going to a Mennonite church a while ago, but we don't go anywhere anymore."

I didn't tell them how we decided to no longer be churchgoers: we woke up one Sunday morning, and one or the other of us said, "I don't really want to go to church today. I don't really want to go to church anymore, do you?" She'd been thinking that I wanted to, I'd been thinking that she wanted to, and that morning we realized that neither of us wanted to. This made our decision easy.

"What do Mennonites believe?" Mike asked. "Are they Christians?"

"Sure," I said, "they're Christians. The most distinctive thing about Mennonites, I suppose, is that they're absolute pacifists."

"Pacifists?"

"Very much so," I said. "A lot of Mennonites are deeply involved in social justice issues."

"So," Mike said, "they preach a social gospel?"

Social gospel: a pejorative term in many evangelical Christian circles. Social gospel implies an emphasis on good works over faith. Good works over a personal relationship with Jesus Christ. What's most offensive to many evangelical Christians is the very notion that

Jesus Christ was a socialist, or, for that matter, a social anything. A social gospel emphasizes the here-and-now over Heaven. And in that here-and-now wedding party reality, we veered sharply into both religion and politics, two of my forbidden conversation topics. It was, I suppose, unavoidable.

"Would you describe yourself as a Mennonite?" Mike asked.

"No, no, that was seven or eight years ago. I wouldn't describe myself as anything now."

I decided to shift the direction of the conversation.

"Where are you stationed these days, Mike?"

Before he had a chance to answer, someone said "Hear-hear" to get everyone's attention. Saved by the hear-hear. That's one thing I've always loved and hated about parties: the hear-hear keeps most everyone from conversing about or dealing with anything substantial.

The hear-hear person suggested that we take some time to share good memories of Marna and Jim, alone and together. One by one, friends stood up and gave testimonies of Jim and Marna. This is a sincere but goofy pre-wedding tradition that binds and reminds all present of how the union began, why the two should become one. The relationship is pieced together with stories.

This must have gone on with much hearty laughter and merriment, but I was distracted. I don't remember the stories. Maybe one was about how Jim hated to study, how he hated to do any kind of homework, and how Marshall had to drag him, literally drag him, to the Glendale Community College library. If my dad was there, he would have told his earliest memory of Jim, skateboarding down Montrose Avenue, onto Foothill Boulevard, and into the parking lot of La Crescenta First Baptist Church.

I'm remembering a different story. This same Jim had just come home from El Salvador, after remaining there for a decade, from 1985 to 1995. He'd built compost latrines, farmed peanuts, manufactured peanut butter organically with local campesinos, absorbed liberation theology, built his own house, baked his own bread, rode a motorcycle from village to village—in a war-torn country, in a country of U.S.-backed government death squads, a country where whole villages were destroyed, all villagers massacred, a country where union headquarters were routinely bombed. Jim knew in advance about the 1989 FMLN uprising. He attended the funeral of the six Jesuit priests who were murdered by government forces, stayed until it got too dangerous (winter '89), and went back when it seemed safe enough (summer '90).

Long before this, Jim was the happy-go-lucky guy from La Crescenta who loved to surf, loved to skateboard, loved the Lord, lived to play volleyball, and hated to study. That's the Jim that our old friend Mike knew, the Jim who Mike wanted to tell about. Mike's is the only testimony that I remember from that night.

"I've got something to share," Mike said. "I remember back in high school when I first started getting to know Jim. We sealed the bond of our friendship with some great surfing outings together. I can remember sitting on our boards out in Newport, waiting for waves to ride, and sharing with each other our walk with the Lord. We'd share verses we'd read, struggles we were having, ways in which we were growing spiritually. And then we'd pray to Jesus, together, out there on the Pacific. Jim, I just want to tell you."

Mike's voice started to crack. He was on the verge of tears.

"I just want to tell you that I'll always remember and cherish the Christian fellowship that I had with you on those surfing trips. Those are some of my best memories of growing up in California."

The circle got quiet. I felt touched and disgusted at the same time. Mike was using this moment to publicly hold Jim accountable to the past he'd left behind: that was you then; just look at you now.

"People change," I wanted to shout. "Get over it, Mr. West Point."

Still, it's sad that people change. I could acknowledge that much. It's sad to be among the left behind.

Jim nodded his head and quietly thanked Mike.

"All right Mike," Jon said. "That was totally cool what you said. Yeah, fellowship. Fellowship. We had some great fellowship back then, didn't we?"

The Presence of Satan

In the afternoon before the wedding, relatives and friends of the bride and groom lounged and chatted by the swimming pool of the Hopkins House, a motel near the Excelsior mansion where the wedding and reception would be held. Mom got into conversation with Mike that she told me about a few days later.

She asked him if he went to the pre-wedding party, and he said yes he did, he sure did. And he had to say that he was disturbed by what he saw.

"Disturbed?" Mom asked.

"Very disturbed," Mike said.

Mom asked what he meant, and Mike told her that it was a dark scene.

"A dark scene?"

"A very dark scene. People getting drunk and smoking and using profane language. I left that party with a very bad feeling. I did not enjoy spending time with those people."

"Those people happen to be," Mom said, "the friends of my children. It bothers me to hear you talk that way about the friends of my children. I know most of them, and I think they are nice people."

Over the years, from the seventies through the nineties, through much difficult conversation and many tears, Mom and Dad gradually became more tolerant of and open-minded about the friends and paths that we, their three children, chose. Age and experience humbled and changed them. They've never abandoned their Christian faith, they still believe much that I no longer believe, Dad is still a Baptist minister, Mom still sends me cards and letters with handwritten Bible verses, but they've changed far more than I can fathom. I began to give my parents more credit after listening to many formerly evangelical friends tell about the hardening and narrowing of their parents.

I mean, Mom stood up for my drinking, smoking, and cussing friends. That's a long long way from the old world of no jazzy music.

"They may be nice people," Mike said. "They may be good people. But are they believers?"

"I don't think it's my place to decide that," Mom said. "Some are believers. Some believe differently than you do. I can't generalize about the whole group."

"Well, all I can say," Mike said, "is that I felt the presence of Satan so strongly at that party. Those people just seem so lost in sin. I saw so much darkness at the party. Yes, I strongly sensed Satan's presence at that party."

Mom didn't know how to respond to the presence of Satan, so she decided to shift the direction of the conversation.

"Where are you stationed these days, Mike?"

Darkness on the Edge of Town

I was broke on that Saturday in 1978, and I needed record money. Jon suggested that I thumb through my collection to find stuff to sell. I could get up to a dollar-fifty for each LP, and Poo Bah Records in Pasadena, our weekly stop, had used records for as low as a quarter.

"Here, I'll just go through your records and find ones to get rid of because you're probably hanging on to some that you don't need."

I let Jon have his way for two reasons: I considered him my best friend, and I felt horribly intimidated by him. I was the new guy in our California suburb, he was the popular native. Why wouldn't I let him decide what music I should get rid of? That was just the price I had to pay to keep the cool friend I didn't think I measured up to. As Jon scrutinized my collection, every record became a testament of who I was, what I valued, what I was willing to pay for, what I was willing to part with, and what I had to keep.

"Let's see, you can get rid of these Chicago records," he said as he started a pile on the floor. "I always hated that band. Horns. Get rid of these Elton John records. And The James Gang. And these Aerosmith records. No way! You actually bought three Aerosmith records! Oh man, this is worse than I thought: you've got the whole Led Zeppelin catalog. Get those out of my sight! We're doing pretty good here, though. You've probably got about ten dollars' worth of stuff to sell so far. They'll definitely buy the Zeppelin records, even if they're in lousy shape. They know that degenerates don't pay any attention to the shape of their records. What else? Get rid of this Bruce Springsteen *Born to Run.*"

"No. I'm keeping that one," I said.

"What?"

"I don't want to get rid of that one. I can part with the rest of them, but *Born to Run* is a great album."

"I've heard it. I don't see what's so great about it. The guy can't sing. There are no synthesizers or long guitar solos. The lyrics are stupid. Oh, what's that one line in the song 'Born to Run'? Here it is: 'Just wrap your legs round these velvet rims / and strap your hands across my engines.' You know what he's talking about don't you?"

"You're making it sound dirty. It's just about a motorcycle ride out of town."

"I can't believe you really think that. C'mon—just get rid of this record. You won't miss it."

"No! I want to keep it. I'm not getting rid of it!"

I'd never stood up to Jon before.

"Hey. Whatever, man. Get off on it, then," he said, and laughed.

As far as my La Crescenta, California, friends and I were concerned, two things separated us from our high school peers: our Christianity and our musical taste. To be part of our tribe—Jon, Stan, Jim, Mike, Marshall, and me—you had to be a born-again Christian and a seventies progressive rock lover. Girlfriends got special exemptions, but no guys got invited to Jon's jacuzzi gatherings if they didn't profess a love for both Jesus and the band Yes.

Progressive rock bands such as Yes, Genesis, Emerson Lake and Palmer, Camel, and Utopia defined our reigning aesthetic: long songs, extended instrumental solos, unusual time signatures, synthesizers (the more the better), and spacey lyrics that we couldn't understand enough to condemn. While the Bee Gees, Peter Frampton, and Fleetwood Mac took over AM radio and set records for most albums sold, and hard-rock/metal bands such as Aerosmith, Foreigner, Van Halen, and Ted Nugent dominated the FM album-oriented-radio format, we developed a healthy mistrust of any music that got steady radio airplay. We were drawn to Yes's *Tales from Topographic Oceans* (a two-record set that included four songs, each clocking in at about twenty minutes) because song length alone kept it off the radio.

We viewed our carnal, metal-listening, unbelieving male peers as sinners, reprobates, and degenerates. Their music celebrated sex and nonstop partying, the world we'd left behind. Progressive rock lyrics, on the other hand, were usually too cryptic to be sinful, and they were sandwiched between so much instrumental fodder that they seemed inconsequential. Sure, bands such as Yes and Utopia occasionally strayed into Eastern religion and new-age mysticism, but our Christ-conscious ears could tolerate these misguided attempts at transcendence more than, say, odes to oral sex (such as Aerosmith's "Walk This Way").

Most rock critics roundly dismissed progressive rock as pretentious and elitist. They were trying to push punk rock on us. We wouldn't come near that stuff. Words couldn't possibly express our contempt for punk. Progressive rock celebrated instrumental virtuosity, heavy metal celebrated sin, but punk rock celebrated incomprehensible evil. Evidence: the king of punk, Johnny Rotten of the Sex Pistols, called himself "an antichrist"; Patti Smith, dubbed "the high-priestess of punk," blatantly declared that Jesus didn't die for *her* sins, and recorded a song that included the Twenty-third Psalm followed by a litany of goddamns; the only two guys at our school who were into punk wore their short hair uncombed, safety pins through their ears and noses, and buttons that read "Save Our Children from Anita Bryant." Punk rock was anti-Christian, pro-homosexuality, sadomasochistic, and far beyond any sense of decency and good taste. We could at least identify with the heavy metal impulse to get wasted and have wild sex with young women our age, temptations we tried our best to resist. But punk—punk didn't even celebrate the carnal realm.

It bugged my California friends tremendously, then, that I liked the music of Bruce Springsteen. Our collective musical identity was our secular denomination, and nothing about the music of

Springsteen fit into it. He was a rock-and-roller in the tradition of Elvis Presley, Buddy Holly, Little Richard, Chuck Berry, The Beatles, the Rolling Stones, the Band, Bob Dylan…; his voice was guttural, earthy, and crude; his song arrangements were simple, uncluttered; his lyrics were about cars, girls, the road, gas stations, city landscapes, making love in the dirt, unfulfilled dreams, working in factories, and darkness.

Because I'd spent my pre-California adolescence in St. Paul, a very blue-collar and Catholic midwestern city, I knew something about the world that Springsteen sang about. I went to school and hung out with guys who reminded me of characters in his songs. At St. Paul Murray High School, they were the Southsiders, the kids who lived on the other side of the railroad bridge.

Springsteen's world didn't look anything like La Crescenta. My La Crescenta friends were sons of JPL, NASA, and Lockheed engineers. The significant exception: my friend and future brother-in-law Jim (the guy who sought my support when he grew to like Springsteen) was the son of a policeman who later became a truck driver. The sons of the space-age engineers thought of Springsteen as a loud commercial radio belch, hyped a few years earlier on the covers of *Time* and *Newsweek.* They also repeated a guilt-by-association charge: Springsteen wrote "Because the Night" with Patti Smith.

"Not only is his music bad," Jon said, "but he's also friends with punks who blaspheme the name of Christ. He's probably a punk himself. Doesn't that bother you?"

The punk connection did bother me, although I secretly liked what I'd heard of Patti Smith.

We sat in silence as Jon drove to Poo Bah in Pasadena, fifteen minutes from La Crescenta. Jon broke the silence as we pulled off the freeway.

"Tramps like us. Baby, we were born to run," he sang in a beefy, Neanderthal voice. "Oh, man, you actually like that."

Jon got peculiar satisfaction out of finding obscure European import records for a dollar or less in the Poo Bah bargain bins. The more unknown the artist, the higher Jon valued the record; he'd then brag to us about his discoveries and maintain his reputation as the foremost Crescenta Valley progressive rock aficionado.

"Excellent!" Jon would exclaim after we'd been browsing for forty-five minutes. "Look at this! Happy The Man's first album as an import—for fifty cents! And I also found Camel 'Moonmadness' for a dollar."

"How do you know which bargain records to buy?" I asked him once.

"Well, I've got a system worked out for recognizing great progressive rock records," he said. "First of all, I look at the cover. If it's got, like, spaceships or distant planets or if it just looks kind of surreal, I give it a closer look. Most records with real pictures of the musicians on the cover are bad. Next, I look at the credits and see if any of the musicians are on other albums I own. That's an easy one to get fooled by, though, because they might just be studio guys who play on anything that pays enough. So, I look at the instrument listings. The more synthesizers, the better. If one of the musicians plays something weird like a stick, then it's a pretty safe bet, because only real cool bands have stick players.* Next I look at the label. Passport and Charisma are pretty reliable; Casablanca's one to stay away from. Oh, I almost forgot one of the most important features: song length. If most of the songs are longer than seven minutes, you can bet there will be some great jams."

I often tried to out-Jon Jon by finding a progressive artist that he'd never heard of, but even when I did, he wouldn't acknowledge the debt.

"The keyboard player on that record," he'd say, "is on Nektar's second album, and I turned you on to them."

I eventually gave up on Jon's progressive rock system and got into jazz to fill the void. Jon liked fusion jazz, but nothing straight-ahead. When I'd play Miles Davis, Charlie Parker, or Charles Mingus for him, he'd nod indifferently. He gave the music his blessing and knew that, according to his standards, he ought to like it. There were two

*A stick is a fretless cross between a bass, an electric guitar, and a synthesizer.

problems, though: it swung and it had horns. Still, it wasn't punk, metal, or Springsteen.

Jon's other love was surfing. If only someone would have invented a waterproof stereo headset that would stay attached and keep pumping music through a ten-foot swell … I picture Jon: "Man, I just got tubed during the synthesizer intro to 'Communion with the Sun,' and it was so excellent! I just kept saying, 'Thank you Jesus thank you Jesus,' as I was surrounded by wall-to-wall wave and total stereophonic sound."†

I went on a lot of Saturday surfing outings with Jon, but I never got the hang of the sport.

Once, Jon and I went to Newport Beach on Memorial Day weekend. The waves averaged eight feet, the sun shone hot, the temperature climbed to the eighties, and by noon a wall of surfers lined the coast. I learned quickly that surfers don't have much patience for beginners, especially on days when the swell is high. Beginners aren't natives, and non-natives aren't welcome. "My wave, my beach" has become, for many, a personal and political philosophy.

Jon and I paddled out together at the beginning of the day, but each time he caught and rode a wave, he drifted further away. We got in the water at six o'clock, and Jon lost me by seven.

Strangers surrounded me. Every time I got up the courage to ride a wave, someone beat me to it.

"My wave," they'd shout, and there was no room for argument.

Finally, I decided to go for one. I shouted, "My wave," as though it had always been mine. I rode and owned it for about five feet, then fell off my board, bungee-cord leash attached to my right ankle. I dropped into the Pacific, felt a pull on my leg, then a snap forward. The board, surfing without me, dragged me along, spun me around and around, as I swallowed salt water and ate sand.

Then the ride ended. Dizzy and nauseous, I looked for a hole in the surface to pop my head through.

"So you're the prick who owns this fuckin board!" a thick-necked

†"Tubed" is surfer slang for being completely inside a wave.

surfer with huge biceps and a mustache yelled at me. "Your fuckin board hit me in the fuckin stomach, motherfucker. See this red mark here?" he asked, pointing to his stomach.

I nodded.

"That's where your fuckin board hit me. You think that felt good, motherfucker?"

He walked toward me. I was sure that he wanted to snap my neck and toss my board to Santa Barbara; my limp body, still attached to the leash, would be a banner of warning to all novice surfers along the Southern California coast.

I shook my head, but couldn't eek out a "No."

"You better fuckin believe it didn't feel good. Want me to show you how it felt?"

"No," I muttered.

"Well then I have some advice for you: get the fuck out of the water before I beat the shit out of you—and don't come back in the water until you learn how to surf!"

I found my beach towel and slept in the sun, until Jon found me late in the afternoon.

"The waves are soo excellent today! I got tubed twice!" he reported. "Getting tubed is so so, oh man, I don't have words for it—shooting on through the wave as it cascades over you. I wish just once you could get tubed—you'd understand why I love surfing so much. It's, like, that's when I feel closest to Jesus, man. Right there in the wave. That's the closest I'll probably ever come to walking on water. I just had a weird thought. Wouldn't it be awesome to go surfing with Jesus and Peter and all of the disciples?"

"Sure," I said.

"So how was your day in the water?"

I told Jon about my ride on the ocean floor and the angry guy with a mustache.

"Yeah, surfing can really suck when you're just learning," he said. "It's pretty competitive out there today. C'mon—let's head over to my uncle's place. You'll love it there. He's got the coolest records of anyone. We can listen to tunes and crash on his floor."

Jon's uncle was a lanky, malnourished keyboard player in his late twenties who lived in a tiny second-floor apartment a couple of miles from the beach. The apartment, Jon thought, had all anyone really needed: bamboo shades, gold shag carpeting, macramé wall hangings, a brown vinyl couch and matching La-Z-Boy chair, a Coleman camping stove, a Bible on a card table, an electric piano, a mini-refrigerator (flour tortillas, jack cheese, refried beans, salsa, and a pitcher of water), and wall-to-wall progressive-rock and fusion jazz records. The place smelled like salt water and sun-dried seaweed. Someday, Jon imagined, he'd get a place like this, he'd become a marine biologist, he'd meet a God-fearing blonde beauty at a local Baptist church, and he'd be set.

I liked the place long enough to eat a burrito, listen to a record, take a nap on the shag, wake up, and notice that the salt water and seaweed scent had settled and become a stench. I was getting claustrophobic.

Jon's uncle put the Mahavishnu Orchestra's *Birds of Fire* on the turntable.

I drifted in and out of sleep.

"McLaughlin really outdid himself with this one," I heard Jon's uncle say in a low, thick voice.

"It's so good that it doesn't seem possible," Jon said as the mood shifted from acoustic Eastern mysticism to electronic pyrotechnics. "It's like parts of this are total blazing energy and other parts are sheer beauty."

"He really outdid himself with this one."

That's all I remember Jon's uncle saying.

Jon was still talking about the Mahavishnu Orchestra album as we drove home from Newport in his VW hatchback. We had the radio tuned to an FM pop station. The DJ announced, "Here's a brand new Bruce Springsteen single, 'Prove It All Night,' from his much-awaited album *Darkness on the Edge of Town,* which is scheduled for release sometime in June."

"Hey—your buddy Bruce!" Jon said. "I'm turning the volume way up! I've got to hear this."

I hoped that he'd find something redeeming in the song. I wanted to buy the album without fear of damnation.

"I've been working real hard trying to get my hands clean," Springsteen growled above the swampy groove. Gone was the *Born to Run* wall-of-sound majesty. The desperate punk in the song invited a girl to meet him "in the fields behind the dynamo" where they'd "prove it all night." I cringed at Bruce's blatant display of carnal desire, this sleazy song of seduction. "Prove it All Night" put me in a moral quandary—as no song had before, as no song has since.

"Aw man, this is awful!" Jon said. "Yeah, get down in the dirt and spread those legs for Bruce baby! Do you see what I mean about Springsteen now? You don't actually like this, do you?"

"No," I said. "This sounds a lot different than *Born to Run.* I hope the rest of the album isn't like this."

"What do you care about the rest of the album? You mean you still might buy it?"

Our friendship was being put to the test.

"If the rest of the album is anything like *Born to Run,* I'm going to buy it."

"Mark, I'm really disappointed in you, man. I mean, you heard that song. It's about screwing a girl in a field all night. That's just degenerate music. Degenerate music. Music for degenerates."

Prime examples of degenerate music as Jon knew it: Ted Nugent's "Free For All"; Van Halen's "Ain't Talkin' about Love"; Aerosmith's "Walk This Way"; Kiss's "Rock 'N Roll All Night"; and now, Bruce Springsteen's "Prove It All Night."

I still bought the album the day it came out, so what did that make me?

Why did buying that album mean so much? Why do these little things become so important?

Sometimes I listen to *Darkness on the Edge of Town* and I try to remember what I heard and saw when I was sixteen going on seventeen. It has remained my favorite Bruce Springsteen album through the years. Its cost was greater, its darkness most relentless, and its tone of despair is still resonant: "I'm caught in a crossfire that I don't understand"; "You wake up in the night with a fear so real"; "Nothing is forgotten or forgiven when its your last time around"; "When we found the things we loved, they were crushed and dying in the dirt"; "She stares off alone into the night with the eyes of one who hates for just being born"; "I lost my money and I lost my wife"; "I live now only with strangers." The characters search deep in the darkness for some sort of redemption—anything to keep them from succumbing to despair: "We'll keep pushin' till it's understood, and these badlands start treating us good"; "I believe in a promised land"; "I'll be on that hill with everything I got"; "It ain't no sin to be glad you're alive."

Church taught me about a darkness called sin that originated with Satan, the King of Darkness. The one way to overcome darkness: become born again by asking for forgiveness of sin, by accepting Jesus Christ as personal Lord and Savior. As I listened to *Darkness on the Edge of Town,* though, I couldn't call this darkness "sin," I couldn't call the people who lived in the darkness "sinners" or "degenerates," and I couldn't positively say that they needed Jesus. I hadn't yet lost my desire to proselytize, but I knew that I didn't have the words to save these people, and they didn't need anything that I had to offer.

I couldn't find anyone to go with me to Springsteen's July 5, 1978, show at the L.A. Forum, so I drove there alone, a day after my seventeenth birthday.

Here's the concert image I've kept: Springsteen jumps into the audience and is hoisted onto the shoulders of fans on the song "Tenth Avenue Freeze Out"; he sings, "And I'm all alone ... I'm on my own ... And I can't go home," as the hands of strangers hold him up and reach out to shake his hand. That's the one time I saw arena-rock's best promise kept: the shared loneliness of thousands became one giant cathartic communal loneliness. We hoisted it on our shoulders and celebrated it.

As I drove home on the freeway after midnight, I went through a bright tunnel, a tunnel I'd driven through many times before. I knew that I needed to be in the left lane that led to the ramp back to La Crescenta, but this time, still stunned by the concert, I kept going straight. I found myself exiting onto a boulevard that I couldn't name in a part of Los Angeles that I didn't recognize. All it takes in L.A. is one false move, and you aren't just in another suburb or section of the city: you're in another world.

Boarded-up stucco houses and apartment buildings, warehouses, closed gas stations, vacant "for sale" fast food restaurants, and ever-present palm trees lined the deserted street. Where was I? I still don't know. Somewhere in the darkness on the edge of town. How long had I been there? Where were the signs that led back to the freeway?

I drove up and down the same stretch of road for an hour, maybe longer, afraid that I'd drive off the map if I ventured too far in any one direction. Along with the fear came a feeling more terrifying: a desire to remain lost forever. As long as I remained on that lost stretch of road, I could be anyone, but as soon as I saw the sign pointing me back in the right direction, I'd have to return to what I knew.

Fellowship Is Important

The Sunday morning after the wedding, Stan, Mike, Jon, Julie, and I met for breakfast at a St. Paul Perkins restaurant. After an hour or so of harmless catching-up and avoidance of conversation topics, I had to go work at the Electric Fetus. My shift was starting at eleven. Julie was going to drop me off, but Stan offered to drive me there in his rental car. He said he wanted to see the store, and Jon wanted to see it too, so he came along.

Before we'd even merged onto the freeway, Stan asked the question that I most dreaded: was I going to church anywhere? I should have expected it. It was a Sunday morning, I was going to work and not church, and he'd want to know if this was normally how I spent my Sunday mornings and afternoons. In a record store called the Electric Fetus?

I told him what I told Mike at the party: Julie and I were going to a Mennonite church years ago; then, one Sunday morning we woke up, and we both agreed that we didn't want to go to church at all anymore. And that was the end of that.

"You should be going to church somewhere," he said. "Fellowship is important."

He kept repeating that: fellowship is important. And there we were, three fellows in a car on the freeway.

"Julie and I have been talking about going to a Unitarian church," I said. Yes, we had talked about it, but I really didn't attach much significance to the Unitarian possibility. I only wanted to tiptoe out of the church question. Offer a placebo and move on.

"A Unitarian church?" he asked.

He'd heard about the humanist Unitarians.

"You need to go to a church," he said, "that preaches the Gospel. A Unitarian church is not a place for a believer in Jesus Christ to find fellowship."

A believer in Jesus Christ. How could he assume that I still called myself a believer in Jesus Christ? I didn't, and I didn't want to be having the conversation. I wanted an uneventful ride to work, a ride to work without incident.

Despite my past experience with Stan, despite what I saw and learned in my years as an evangelical Christian, I felt surprised by his complete dismissal of the Unitarian possibility. It reminded me of a time when a bunch of us former Bethelites, friends who'd stopped going to church, went to the St. Paul Cathedral for their Christmas Eve service. Less than a half block away from the cathedral, a small group of fundamentalist Christian protestors were heckling people as they walked by. They had signs and banners, and they were yelling things like, "You're all going to Hell! Catholics are going to Hell!" People who called themselves Christians were actually protesting people going to the wrong Christian church. One of my friends turned around and yelled back, "Hey, this is the first time I've been to church in years, and you're telling me that I'm going to Hell for going to the wrong one?"

I didn't know how to respond to Stan's church dismissal, it was five till eleven, and I needed to get to the Electric Fetus as soon as possible.

"You can stay in this lane for a few miles," I said, "but you'll eventually need to get in the right lane again."

Stan asked what I thought of Jim and Marna's wedding, and I said that I thought it was a very nice wedding. As weddings go, it was one of the nicest weddings that I've ever been to. Maybe it was a little short, but many weddings are too long.

"Well, that says a lot," Stan said. "That says a lot. Personally, I was very disturbed by the wedding. Very disturbed. It wasn't Christ-centered at all."

The Wedding

Marna and Jim celebrated their marriage at a big white Victorian house on a hill that overlooked Excelsior's Minnetonka Bay, a boat-congested water body in the affluent southwestern suburb of Minneapolis. With its wrap-around porch, spiraling staircases, and crystal chandeliers, the wedding house looked like a turn-of-the-century high society gathering place. Compared to Marna and Jim's generally unpretentious manner, the place seemed a bit posh, but the green and sunny beauty of the setting was undeniable.

Most weddings draw unlikely assortments of individuals, but Marna and Jim's brought together the most ideology- and lifestyle-diverse wedding crowd that I've ever been among: Jim's parents, the friendly and eminently huggable Bob and Barbara Morgan (conservative blue-collar Baptists from Oregon); Dad and Mom, the Reverend Dr. John Anderson and his wife Barbara (moderately liberal Baptists); a cadre of Marna's friends from WHISPER and the Sexual Violence Center (lesbian couples, radical feminists); a large contingent of Bethel alumni (former evangelical Christians, most married, many with kids, many smokers, most drinkers); aunts, uncles, cousins, (churchgoing midwesterners, including some Promise Keepers); the group of California high school friends (military-connected Christian rightists); a posse of Jim and Marna's friends from El Salvador (leftists, liberation theologians, FMLN supporters).

If not for Jim and Marna, there would be no reason for these people to spend an evening together in the same place. I happened to see this as a beautiful thing. Both of the wedding ministers—Dave Batstone, a professor who'd worked with Jim and Marna in El Salvador, and Dad Anderson—mentioned the beauty in diversity of the gathered.

"These people represent a coming together of the stories in your lives. They are a manifestation of your various histories; they embody who you've been and who you've become."

Did Dad or did Dave say that? Does it matter? Not to me. Both pastors understood one meaning of the wedding ceremony: it wasn't simply "the two becoming one flesh," a troublesome metaphor that I've heard too many times. It was the marriage of many stories that came together from many places.

"Look around you," Dad (or Dave) said. "See who is here for you," Dave (or Dad) said. "See the body of people who love you."

Dave read a Buddhist proverb, Dad read Paul's Love Chapter (1st Corinthians 13), someone sang, Marna and Jim repeated vows they'd composed, exchanged rings, kissed. Max and Rochelle, saxophone-playing friends, blew the opening of the "Theme from Rocky" into the traditional wedding recessional (and it worked surprisingly well).

Christ-Centered

Christ-centered. What does that even mean? Granted, I was guilty of saying things like "Christ-centered" back in the day. It's one of those evangelical Christian constructions that someone, I believe, wrote on an old overhead transparency, and so many people copied versions of it in notebooks that it began to look like a real and living thing: The Christ-Centered Life. Then came the "Christ-centered" books and seminars and sermons and Bible study series and seminary courses, and, late in the twentieth century, a guy driving you to work is telling you that your sister's wedding was deficient because it wasn't Christ-centered enough.

"It's very clear to me," Stan went on to say, "that Marna and Jim don't want Christ to be the center of their marriage."

I wanted to say, "Well, they talked to other people who'd made Christ the center, and he just wasn't working out there. He couldn't snap the ball to quarterbacks quick enough. So they decided to just put him on special teams."

In real life, though, in the car on the way to a place called the Electric Fetus, I told Stan that I thought it was a bit presumptuous of him to say what Jim and Marna's wedding should have been. I said that he didn't know Jim and Marna anymore, and he didn't know anything about what they wanted their lives to become. He saw a ceremony that couldn't have been much longer than half an hour, and he was ready to say what they did want or didn't want or ought to want from their marriage?

Jon just sat there listening, waiting for the right moment to leap in. He was more on Stan's side, but he seemed uncomfortable with this heated battle between friends who were reuniting for the first time in ten years.

"Well, it is very clear to me," Stan said, "that none of you—Marna, Jim, Marshall, you, that whole ex-Bethel crowd—none of you want Christ in the center of your lives anymore. And I'm very disturbed and concerned about it. It makes me very sad."

Very sad: that's another way of putting it. Believer or unbeliever, very sad is very sad. That's the only way I can keep from getting more angry at Stan when I remember this conversation. I can say to myself, "He said that it made him very sad. He must have really been sad." Not only did he lose some of his best friends. He lost some of his best friends, and one day he would be separated forever from them, as he made his home in Heaven, and they burned without ceasing in Hell. I don't have to believe in Heaven and Hell to believe that Stan was disturbed and concerned and very sad about this eternal separation.

"What happened to your faith? Was there one event," he asked, "one thing that led you away from the Lord?"

I couldn't quite place that "you," the subject of his question. Was it singular or collective? It wasn't clear to me whether he meant the one thing that led me away, or the one event that led all of us away together. I could have asked, but I didn't want to ask anything that would lead to more and more and more of this ride-to-work conversation. Stan wanted something more than I could offer. A moment in time that set us on the different road. Like the time Satan appeared before all of us on that one camping trip. Maybe we were all sitting by the campfire, and Satan's face shone through the flames. "Leave your Jesus and come follow me," he said. Something like that. A blinding light in our eyes, like Saul on the road to Damascus, but the opposite messenger and result.

Maybe Stan even wondered if he'd missed that one thing, and that was why he'd stayed the same, while so many around him had changed. Probably not, but I'd like to believe that his sadness made him wonder for a moment. More than likely, Stan only wanted to fly back to California with something concrete that he could share with the people at his church: one more thing that leads believers away from the Lord. Better still, the one thing that leads believers away from the Lord.

I wanted to say, "Yes, there's one major thing that, more than anything else, led me away from the faith that I grew up with: the faith that I grew up with."

I would have said that, but I thought of the line later in the day: my faith led me away from my faith.

Maybe I said, "No, it wasn't one thing. It was a lot of things."

People are led to truths in more mysterious ways than Stan was willing to acknowledge, but I couldn't talk about the mystery of truth with him. His truth would eliminate all mystery that wasn't of it.

More than likely, I only said, "Get in the right lane. You need to get off at the next exit."

A Revival

I stood in the dark behind the stage curtain, waiting and praying for someone to walk down the aisle and up the steps, part the velvet, find me, and repeat my prayer of salvation. My life had come down to that very moment of waiting.

"Is there anyone here tonight who would like to receive Jesus

Christ as his personal savior?" the hired evangelist asked as the Jesus rock star Randy Stonehill walked off the stage after his final encore. "Backstage and up front we have counselors waiting to talk to you."

Hoping for multitudes, I, a counselor, listened for footsteps and then peeked out to see the aisles empty, everyone seated. They'd come. One or two would lead the way and the rest would follow.

I'd been planning this moment since the beginning of the 1979 school year, my senior year at Crescenta Valley High. Jon, Stan, Jim, and I came home from Hume Lake Bible Camp fired up, inspired by pastor Bob Williams's challenge to lead everyone at our school to the Lord. The man was a master motivator. Only the most heart-hardened reprobate could sit unmoved through his sermon that, detail by torturous detail, punishment by horrific punishment, catalogued the horrors of Hell. I don't know where he got the information, but he was more on the inside track than I, so I didn't question it.

He'd perfected one rhetorical specialty, an empathetic spin on the usual hellfire-and-brimstone message: depicting, image by repellent image, what Hell would be like for the lost school friends who we didn't love enough to convert. It was Paradise Lost with a sixties "He Ain't Heavy, He's My Brother" twist.

"As the worms eat away at their flesh," he said, "and the fire burns but does not consume, your friends will remember how you once ashamedly mentioned that you were a Christian, but didn't ever attempt to share your secret message of salvation. And they'll curse your name forever! Young people, how can you let your friends spend eternity like this?"

How could we do this to our friends, to our school, to our world? As my Grandpa Curt was fond of saying, with friends like that, who needs enemies? And with the eternal cursing of our names multiplied by billions, would we ever be able to hear Heaven's angels harping? Some of the curses would surely bleed through the walls. I couldn't imagine a Heaven that didn't care about its very own Hell—or, for that matter, a Heaven in which Hell could be heard.

These quandaries didn't make me lose trust in Pastor Williams. Instead, they led me to grant him the suspension of disbelief that I granted to God: I don't know, therefore He must.

To his credit, the next night Pastor Williams reveled in the glory of Heaven, and reminded us that, since the beginning of time, God has been preparing individual mansions for each and every one of His followers. Since the beginning of creation. That's a long time to be working on a house—but if anyone had the space and time to work that hard and long on this heavenly housing project, God did.

"Young people," he said, "can you even imagine what your heavenly home looks like by now?"

Well, I could and I couldn't, but Pastor Williams ran wild with that one.

It would be, he said, rooms upon rooms upon rooms, all with gold floors and walls and ceilings, adorned with diamonds and rubies, diamonds and rubies. In each room, the sweetest sounding stereo system would play, nonstop, the latest angel harp hits, songs so cool that they couldn't possibly be fathomed with our puny earthly minds. Every mansion would be well equipped with swimming pools and jacuzzis, inside and outside, take your pick, and the heavenly music would be heard on the sweetest sounding underwater stereos.

"What kind of a Christian," he asked, "wouldn't want to shout to the whole world about the eternal rewards of following Christ on earth? What kind of a Christian friend would keep these glorious promises from a friend who is doomed to spend eternity in Hell?"

It didn't take a wild imagination to answer these questions: not a very good friend—not a very good Christian friend at all. That's the kind that would selfishly horde these glories, as I had. I was that kind who would.

By the time he got to his call for action, I was well primed, more ready than ever to lead the Christian parade into the new millennium.

"Don't hesitate," he said, "to proclaim the name of Christ whenever and wherever you can: in school assemblies, at sporting events, in the classroom. Make signs, banners, posters that shout the message of salvation."

I would do these things. I would do all that he advised: organize before- and after-school Bible study groups, get elected to a high school student government position, use the leadership platform to win souls, recruit Christian rock stars to perform concerts in the school auditorium, host school-ground revivals, push it all to the limit, to the end. Let the teachers and principals sweat over the separation of church and state.

"You've got," he said, "no time to waste!"

After hearing Pastor Williams, I wholeheartedly believed that it was both possible and desirable to lead most of Crescenta Valley High, the state of California, America, and the world to Jesus before the year 2000. With faith, prayer, zeal, and fittingly timed tactics, we as Christians could make anything happen. Ever since the early-seventies Jesus Movement days, I'd heard predictions (repeated every year at camp) of a great evangelical revival that would sweep across America in the 1980s. It would be a third Great Awakening, the greatest one of all. The latest sign of the times: Bob Dylan, rumor had it, was now a born-again Christian. The Voice of A Generation was now speaking for The Jesus Generation. All we needed was another Jesus Christ Superstar—a converted Springsteen or Lennon—and the real Jesus Revolution would commence. It was in the air.

I imagined this born-again Christian utopia: I'd be surrounded everywhere by like-minded believers, and instead of saying "Hello" we'd say "Praise the Lord"; we'd all listen to the same music, read the same book, have the same heroes and reference points; we'd send our children to public schools where all the teachers would be Christians, and they'd be instructed in the ways of the righteous; we'd share food, money, housing, all our possessions—there would be no poverty, no starvation; we wouldn't know the loneliness of having to be in the world but not of it because we'd be the world and the world would be us; arms around shoulders in a giant circle from where in the world to where in the world, one great choir singing, "We are one in the spirit, we are one in the Lord ... and we pray that all unity will one day be restored, and they'll know we are Christians by our love." One World, Our World.

My best friends from La Crescenta First Baptist took Pastor Williams up on the student government infiltration idea, and we won the four highest offices: Jim became the student body president, Stan became the vice president, Jon became the treasurer, and I became the boys' representative (an ill-defined position that involved filling the pop machine in the school courtyard and organizing the annual student versus faculty basketball game).

To signal the changing of the guard, the move into theocracy, Jim said in his inaugural speech, "Jesus Christ is my personal Lord and Savior and, in the year that I'll be your servant in Him, I hope to share His message of love and salvation with all of you." Some students (secular humanists, every one of them) called for his impeachment on grounds that he'd violated the separation of church and state, but our principal, Dr. Thomas, was a member of La Crescenta First Baptist, and he happened to appreciate Jim's moving testimony of faith.

With Dr. Thomas's support, we planned an end-of-the-year revival that would bring everyone at our school together for one night of evangelism. It would, we knew, have to use a musical event as its catalyst. Teens wouldn't go out of the way to see a preacher, but, if the hype was right, they'd go to a concert. So, we recruited our favorite Jesus rock star, Randy Stonehill, a charmingly charismatic performer who sounded like Todd Rundgren, James Taylor, and his mentor, Larry Norman. Randy would perform a daytime assembly and evening concert in our high school auditorium. He couldn't mention Jesus in the required-attendance assembly, but it would serve as a commercial for the evening concert, the concert in which he'd be free to say anything.

When I now look back at our caper, our coup, I'm struck by our enthusiastic audacity, and I shudder at how easy it was to pull off.

"The love of Jesus Christ is so real, so real, man," Randy said in closing to the five hundred or so high school students gathered in the auditorium that night. Each time he said the word "real," he waved his curly brown locks for emphasis. "But, like, you know, you're on a sinking ship and the water's rushing in and the ship's going down and you're, like, saying, 'I can swim—I don't need a lifeboat.' But just, like, reach out your hands, my friends: the lifeboat is right there. I reached out and Jesus saved me. Reach out. Jesus is real. He'll save you. Goodnight."

He walked off the stage in his quilt-patch big-bell Levis, gleaming acoustic guitar on his shoulder.

He'd given, I was convinced, the performance of his life. The audience hung with him the whole way: from the rockers to the Jesus ballads to the between-stage banter to the personal testimonies to the sing-alongs. We all felt the Holy Spirit binding us.

I headed backstage and positioned myself by the curtain as the postconcert evangelist gave the altar call.

"Is there anyone who was moved tonight by the words and music of Christ's talented messenger, Randy Stonehill?" he asked. "If anyone would this very night like to receive Jesus Christ as personal Lord and Savior, please step on forward and talk to one of our counselors backstage."

I gazed out and saw the faces of notorious unbelievers: tobacco road burnouts, wild jacuzzi partiers, all-conference jocks, and backslidden Mormons. Soon we'd all be one in the spirit. One or two would walk forward, and hundreds would follow.

A skinny man with black horn-rimmed glasses, wallaby boots, and navy blue slacks walked forward down the aisle, up the stageside stairs, through the curtain, and up to me.

"May I help you?" I asked. I'd started a job as a grocery store clerk the week before.

"Yes," he answered. "I'm Alex and I'd like to hear more about what Randy was talking about. I might want to accept Jesus, but I'm still not sure. Can I talk to you about it?"

"Sure. That's what I'm here for. My name is Mark."

We walked past an artificial Christmas tree to some folding chairs. I turned on a living-room lamp, a prop left from *The Man Who Came to Dinner*, and got out my copy of *The Four Spiritual Laws.* This was a step-by-step guide, a script, that I was taught to use when converting strangers. It handily provided the words to say and scripture to read, and, as best it could, codified the conversion experience. Some were better at extemporaneous proselytizing than others, and *The Four Spiritual Laws* was designed to avoid any major screwups.

The final destination was Law Four, which invited the unbeliever to accept Jesus Christ as personal Lord and Savior. Drawings of an "S" and a cross on separate chairs (called "thrones" in the pamphlet) represented, respectively, the life controlled by Self and the life controlled by Jesus Christ. The goal was to knock the Self off the throne so that Christ could sit there.

Uneasy about converting strangers, and convinced that this was a discomfort, a shyness, that I had to overcome, I tried to memorize *The Four Spiritual Laws*, and I prayed that the Holy Spirit would help me stop the gaps. If I asked the Holy Spirit for guidance, I was told, I would find the right words to say.

"Are you familiar with *The Four Spiritual Laws*, Alex?" I asked. I had no time to waste on friendly preconversion banter.

"No, I don't believe I am. Tell me about them."

I read the introduction to Law One that the pamphlet provided. It compared *The Four Spiritual Laws* to laws of physics: while laws of physics rule the cosmos, *The Four Spiritual Laws*, it claimed, rule relationships between God and us.

"How do you know that," Alex asked.

How did I know that? How did I know that? Did I know that? This guy, I sensed, was going to play hard-to-convert.

"It's in the Bible," I said, hoping that he didn't ask where. "And I believe the Bible."

"Do you believe everything in the Bible?" Alex asked.

I hadn't read the whole Bible from cover to cover, but I wasn't about to tell him that. Maybe he'd read more of the Bible than me. He looked about thirty, so I assumed that he was more well-read.

"I believe," I said, "that the Bible is the Word of God."

"What if the Bible said," he asked, "that human beings have petunias for brains? Would you believe that?"

The Bible didn't, as far as I knew, say that—although the Old Testament did say some pretty off-the-wall things. I'd been meaning to read some of the obscure and oddly named books that I'd stumbled upon on my way to the New Testament: Habakkuk, Zephaniah, Haggai, Zechariah. Petunias for brains. If it was anywhere in the Bible, it would be in one of those books.

"It doesn't say that, so I don't have to believe it," I fired back.

"Do you believe that God created man on the sixth day of a literal twenty-four hour day?"

This was a trick question that I had to think hard about. Yes, I believed that God created man. Yes, I believed that God created man on the sixth day. But was it a literal twenty-four hour day?

"God created man," I said, "on the sixth day."

"On the sixth day of a literal twenty-four hour day? Was it a literal twenty-four hour day? That's what I'm asking."

"It doesn't say 'twenty-four hours,' but it says it was a day, and a day is twenty-four hours."

"Well," he asked, "how can that be, since science shows that man evolved over millions of years?"

I didn't know whether or not I believed in evolution, but I knew that I wasn't supposed to believe in it. And I'd never been good in science. When evangelists pitted the Bible against "atheist" scientists, as they so often did, I went along with their line of thinking because the scientific perspective never made sense to me in the first place. Evolution was easy enough to faith away at church, but I didn't know what to say to this man, my potential convert.

I thought long and hard, looked around the room, but the Holy Spirit wasn't holding up the cue card. I had to take control of the situation, get back to the script.

"Let's just get back to the Laws," I said. "We need to get back to the Laws. I mean, I don't have answers for everything. A lot of this stuff you just have to accept on faith."

"You aren't answering my questions, but, okay, we can move back to those laws. Even though I'd still like to know why they're laws and who invented them."

Just then, the star of the night, Randy Stonehill, walked by us, nodded, smiled, said, "Hey guys," and headed out a backstage door where a throng of church kids and friends waited to meet him and get their records autographed. I wanted to be out there. I wanted to be a star-worshiping teen again.

Randy didn't shut the door behind him, and I considered yelling, "Randy! Randy! Come back! This man won't convert! Help me!"

Randy would see this as a lack of faith, though, and I wanted more than anything to introduce my new convert to him: "Randy, this is Alex. He discovered this very night that Jesus is real—with the help of the Holy Spirit, you, and me!"

I returned to *The Four Spiritual Laws.*

Law One proclaimed God's love and told of a "wonderful plan" that God has for the life of the potential convert. I read aloud the quoted Bible verses.

"John 3:16 says 'For God so loved the world that he gave his only begotten son, that whosoever believes in Him should not perish, but have eternal life.' And in John 10:10, Christ says, 'I have come that they might have life, and might have it abundantly.'"

"Why do you think so many people in the world don't live abundant lives," I asked Alex.

"I don't know," Alex said, without concealing his irritation. "What's abundant life anyway? What does that mean? What's abundant life to you?"

He'd done it again: turned the questions back onto me.

I could see my friends outside, chatting and joking around with Randy. I still had three laws to go. Somehow, I had to knock Alex off his high and mighty throne so that Christ could sit on it, get him to repeat the sinner's prayer, and then give him the pamphlet's advice about how to proceed as a new Christian. But there we were, stuck in no-man's-land, between Law One and Law Two, the answer to the question I'd asked him about why people weren't living abundantly: human beings are divorced from God and filled with sin.

"Abundant life," I said, "means that you're living in Christ and doing His will, and you're happy in the joy of the Lord."

This wasn't in the script. I was winging it. Or maybe the Holy Spirit was finally putting words into my mouth.

"All right," Alex said. "So, does that mean that I'll have a mansion in Malibu, a yacht, a beautiful movie star wife, a Porsche, and millions of dollars? That's what I want in my abundant life."

"Christ is talking more about spiritual abundance than material abundance. You'll have the Bible, prayer, God's promises, the fruits of the spirit. Those are just some of the spiritual riches that you'll get with this abundant life."

"Well, you know, Mark," Alex said slowly, accenting each word and laughing, "that just doesn't sound very abundant to me. That really sounds pretty boring. I mean, c'mon, is that all that abundant life is to you?"

I couldn't say anything. The life I was describing didn't, when I thought about it, sound abundant. I glanced out the door again.

"You wish you were out there, don't you?" Alex said.

"No," I lied.

"Yes you do. I can tell by the way you keep looking. I won't keep you any longer."

"No, don't leave yet."

I thought that maybe I could get him to stay longer if I put more of what he liked in my description of the abundant life.

"Christians can," I said, "have fun too."

"I know. I know. You don't need to keep this up, though. This isn't what you think."

He paused.

"Listen, Mark. I have something to tell you. I hope this doesn't upset you. I'm really a Christian myself. I'm a believer. I've been one since I was ten years old. The Lord sent me back here to give you a few pointers—to test you, and see how you presented the gospel message to me. So if you don't mind, let me share some tips with you. Now, when you told me about the abundant life, what you could have said was … "

The rest was a blackout. I didn't hear a word he said. Who was this man? The Devil? An angel of light? A wayward messenger of the Holy Spirit? Marshall in ten years? Myself in ten years?

If this man wasn't who I thought he was, then who was I anymore?

He continued to speak rapidly, flipping through his Bible, and quoting passages that would have bolstered my timid answers.

I wouldn't even make eye contact with him.

"I've got to get out of here. I've gotta get away from you," I said.

"Hey, I hope I didn't upset you," he said.

When I told the story to my parents later that evening, they kept saying, "What a jerk! He was nothing but a big jerk!" Over the years the story has come to represent to them the beginning of an end: if only I hadn't met up with the jerk, I'd still be in the faith.

I know differently. The man was a jerk with a message: "Find out about the abundant life!"

He was, by the way, the only person who accepted the invitation to come forward that night.

When Marshall Got off the Plane Crying

It wasn't, as I told Stan in the car, one thing that led me away from the faith: it was many things. High on the list of many was Marshall's first depression in the summer of 1980, the summer after my freshman year at Bethel College. Nothing in my faith had prepared me for this one thing. Sometimes it even seems like it was The One Thing.

Marshall was twenty and in his sophomore year at Glendale Community College. His plan was to finish his freshman and sophomore years at Glendale and then spend his junior and senior years at Bethel. Because we'd moved to California the summer before his senior year of high school, he wanted to stay there for a couple more years. He thought he needed to settle briefly before moving back to Minnesota. As I was adjusting to dorm life, he was living in the bedroom that we'd shared at our parents' home in La Crescenta.

The depression hit in the spring of his sophomore year, and absolutely nothing had prepared him for it. Nothing in the theology, nothing in the scripture we'd memorized and absorbed, nothing in our understanding of faith could account for the severe depression of a God-fearing young Christian man who'd tried all of his life to do everything right.

Some Christians would blame the depression (*all* depression) on sin or Satan, but that explanation didn't fit Marshall. Not that I didn't, at the time, believe in the harsh consequences of sin. I sometimes wondered, for example, if the Randy Stonehill concert weirdo who jerked me around the year before was sent as a punishment for the excessive heavy petting that I'd done with my girlfriend. That sounded as likely as anything else. But Marshall didn't have enough sin in his life (as far as I knew) to punish with something so severe. Why would Marshall, of all people, be punished with something that, for months, took away his joy in life? Why would Marshall be punished with something that, in the harshest nights and days, looked like it might lead him to take his very life?

Unlike me, Marshall had never been drunk, he'd read his Bible and prayed daily, he'd never been stoned, he'd witnessed to unbelievers, he went to every church function, he regularly prayed out loud in public, he periodically stood up in Sunday evening church to give his testimony, he'd remained a church star child, and he was still a virgin. He *claims* that he'd never even masturbated. As far as I could tell at the time, he had his shit together.

He was strong, I was weak, that was that. That's how I'd always known the major difference between Marshall and me. Being good was natural for him, a struggle for me. But there he was, going through something more awful than I'd ever gone through. More awful than anything my imagination had made room for. There was no room for whatever this was. What was this? What was the justice in this?

And what, then, was I?

Is there a good way to write about the clinical depression of a family member? I'm not interested in telling a good story about it. How would it proceed? Marshall got severely depressed, the depression lasted for months, he got better, he was never the same Marshall again (he left his faith behind), and he's struggled with depression ever since (and no, it isn't because he left his faith behind).

There is no real beginning or ending to this story. I can only give impressions.

Marshall flew to Minnesota during spring break in 1980, spent time with Jill, his Minnesota girlfriend, hung out with old Central Baptist friends, flew back to California, and got off the plane crying. That was always the beginning of the story when Mom told it: Marshall got off the plane crying.

"I don't know," she said when I first asked what was wrong with Marshall. "It started last April when he got off the plane from Minnesota crying. He couldn't explain why he was crying. He said that it wasn't because of anything that happened with Jill. We didn't know what was going on. We still don't. He just couldn't stop crying. He cries less now, but he can't sleep at all."

Mom added one last comment: "He just hasn't been the same since he got off the plane."

First the crying, then the sleepless nights, then the dropping-out of school (all of his teachers told Mom that he had, when he dropped out midquarter, the highest A in the class), then the dropping-out of all church activities, then the unreturned phone calls, then the speechless days.

"It must be a shock to see him again," Mom said to me. "Marshall's always been the talker. Now he hardly says a word. We're lucky if we can get him to answer a 'yes' or 'no' question. Has he asked you anything about your first year at Bethel?"

"He asked if I had a good year. I said 'pretty good,' and he didn't ask anything else about it. It looked like he was trying to think of something else to ask. But he couldn't think of anything else."

It was mid-July. I was in the living room reading *Rolling Stone* when I heard Marshall sobbing outside. I went out to the side of the house. He was weeping with his arm on the brick wall, his head in his arm.

"I'm never going to get better. I'm going to be depressed forever."

I hugged him and said, "You'll get better. You'll get through this." I almost believed my words. It was the first time in my life that I felt stronger than Marshall. Like his big brother.

He couldn't sit still. He couldn't concentrate enough to read. He couldn't sleep.

We still shared the bedroom. He'd roll around in his bed long past midnight. I'd doze off for an hour or more and then wake up to the sound of him dressing.

"Where are you going?" I'd ask.

"To the beach."

The beach was a forty-five minute drive.

"What time is it?" I'd ask.

"Late."

"It's two-thirty."

"I can't sleep. I need to go somewhere."

He'd walk out the door, start up my parents' VW bug, head down Briggs, onto Foothill Boulevard, and take the Harbor Freeway to Hermosa Beach. He'd walk, sit, and stare, walk, sit, and stare until dawn.

That was the scariest sound of the summer: the Volkswagen starting after midnight. He'd been driving recklessly and erratically all summer (he couldn't keep his mind on the present, and he felt like dying), so I feared that he'd die in a car wreck, drive off the road, or drown in the Pacific.

All summer he'd lie on the couch and play the song "Court and Spark" by Joni Mitchell—that one song over and over. The song would end, he'd get up from the couch, he'd spin it again … was he trying to spark what he felt the first time he heard it?

"Just treat me normal," Marshall said when I first tried talking to him about it. I wanted to know how I should treat him. How should I be around this new brother of mine?

"Maybe I'll return to normal again," he said, "if everyone just treats me normal."

We tried treating him normal, he tried acting normal, but he never returned to what he once knew as normal.

New Age

We pulled off the freeway. We were almost at the Electric Fetus, and I kept saying "left here left here" because Stan got so involved in the conversation that he kept forgetting to take directions. He might have driven us back to California if I wasn't watching him.

Then he started in on a new theme: how all of us Minnesotans—Marshall, Marna, Jim, me, the ex-Bethel crowd—have apparently been swayed by New Age philosophy and religion. This turn startled me, and I wondered where it came from.

I knew that evangelical Christians passed out pamphlets, wrote books, held seminars, and grew increasingly worried about the dangers of encroaching "secular humanism," and that New Age spirituality got dumped into this mix. It was "spirituality" that wasn't Christian, and if it wasn't Christian it wasn't sacred, and if it wasn't sacred it was of the world, and if it was of the world it was of the secular realm. In other words, it was of the Devil. I'd been around fundamentalists enough to understand the logic, but I still wondered how Stan came to lump his fallen friends into this New Age scheme.

"New Age? You think we're New Agers?" I asked.

"Well, what was that Buddhist proverb at the wedding all about? Where did that come from?"

"You think we're all New Agers simply because Dave Batstone read a Buddhist proverb at the wedding?" I didn't mention the fact that Buddhism has been around for thousands of years, and I found it ridiculous and extremely disrespectful to call it a New Age religion. So much to say, so little time. The Electric Fetus was less than a mile away, so I had to choose my battles wisely.

"I don't know what you are," Stan said. "I don't know what to call you. All I know is that a Christ-centered wedding wouldn't include a Buddhist proverb. And I know that a lot of New Age spirituality is simply modern interpretations of ancient Eastern religions like Buddhism."

"But … New Age? What is that?" I said. "It's not one thing. It's just a marketing label. It doesn't mean anything to me. Except at the Electric Fetus."

More ammunition, I suppose, for the New Age conspiracy theory: I worked at a place called the Electric Fetus, established by certified hippies in 1968. The store even sells crystals and New Age books and a wide assortment of smoking paraphernalia.

"New Age is the section in the store," I went on, "where we put the grooveless lite-instrumental music. New Age is just grooveless music that isn't jazz and isn't classical."

At this point, Jon jumped in to defend Stan. "You use the term 'evangelical Christian,' as if that's just one thing. You categorize all of our beliefs under a marketing label, too. That's all 'evangelical Christianity' is. A marketing label. Just say 'Christians.' That's what I call myself. I don't call myself an 'evangelical Christian.'"

"Call yourself whatever you want to call yourself," I said. "Maybe 'evangelical Christian' has become mostly a marketing label. But I do have a very good idea of what evangelical Christianity is, beyond how it is marketed—because I grew up in it for twenty or so years of my life. I lived in it. New Age, on the other hand, is just some catchall term that means absolutely nothing to me. Take a left here, Stan."

He didn't respond. He looked like he was trying to think of what to say next.

"Stanley, you need to be in the left lane, because you're going to be turning left at the light up there."

Stan signaled and turned into the left lane.

"I should just say 'fundamentalist Christians' instead of 'evangelical Christians,'" I said. "That's what I'm really talking about."

Stan and Jon looked at each other, and smiled. I'd used the "f" word, which, to them, was way off the mark.

"You think that we're," Stan said, cringing at the word, "fundamentalists?"

"Yes, I do," I said. "I sure do."

"I'm not a fundamentalist," Stan said.

"I'm not a fundamentalist," Jon said.

"I'm not a New Ager," I said. "Stan, take a left here at Franklin Avenue."

We got to the Fetus, and we were still heavily into the conversation. I was five minutes late. They were denying that they were fundamentalists, I was denying that I was a New Ager, and we were getting nowhere. We decided to leave the conversation at that strange nowhere and walk into the store.

Their eyes got big. I'd forgotten to warn them about the pipes and bongs and varieties of *Test Pure.* I knew what they were thinking: head shop. Mark works in a head shop.

"What's that, Mark?" Stan asked. He smiled and pointed at a metal pipe.

"A tobacco pipe, Stan. That's a tobacco pipe," I said, and smiled back.

Stan laughed. Maybe that was, in his mind, one difference between fundamentalists and nonfundamentalists: fundamentalists don't, under any circumstances, laugh at sin. I remembered our old youth pastor Larry's favorite line: God has a sense of humor too.

Stan, Jon, Jim, Marshall, Mike, and I used to laugh a lot together. Some days, some nights, a long time back, that's about all we did. Goofy joke after goofy joke, and we didn't talk all the time about our Christian faith, because that was a given. That was, we believed, the tie that binds, but it wasn't the only thing we talked about.

Was that how Stan and Jon understood adult friendship? The adult believer saved the friend's soul first, got to the here-and-now laughter once that had been done. Assure Heaven first, and then get to the earthbound laughter. That was the ideal. If Heaven can't be won, if the unbeliever won't submit, go for the laughter and hope that the faith follows. If we had another day to spend together, maybe we'd be able to leave the heaviness of faith and lost faith and get back into the laughter that binds. Maybe they'd give up on saving my soul and settle for one thing that sustains it.

I have to remind myself: they were only trying to re-save my soul. It was an unhappy way to be together, but maybe there was some love in it. They only wanted us all to laugh together eternally in Heaven.

The means felt like hatred, but maybe the end had love in it. Who can say?

I guided them through the store, and they were genuinely impressed by its size and selection. They expected a much smaller shop. They wandered around as I slipped Al Green's *Truth N' Time* into the CD player.

They started going through the bins to see if we had any of their favorite obscure progressive rock bands like Ozric Tentacles. That's what gets me: most of those seventies progressive rock bands had lyrics that could be called New Age, lyrics that were heavily influenced by Eastern religion. And a lot of the seventies progressive rockers are now making New Age records. I believe, in fact, that I could (if I did the grueling musicological research) make a convincing argument that seventies progressive rock helped build the template and market for eighties and nineties New Age music.

Stan and Jon were impressed that we at least had a divider for Ozric Tentacles, but disappointed that we had none of their CDs in stock.

Jon wandered over to look at used CDs. When I walked up to Stan (in the "O" bins of Pop/Rock), he got right back into the car conversation.

"So, where are you with your faith right now?" he asked.

"Stan, that's too overwhelming and complex to get into here," I said.

I wanted to say, "Shut up! I'm at work. Don't keep up with this faith conversation while I'm at work. Do you understand that this is where I work?" Instead, I avoided eye contact and tried to redirect him to music.

"Check this out, Stan," I said as we walked over to the Pop/Rock "C" bins. "We have two copies of the Camel anthology in stock. That's something, huh?"

He nodded and smiled at this reference to one of our progressive rock favorites from way back when—way back when I still had faith.

He still wasn't ready to let go, so he made one last comment for me to ponder. "Just remember, Mark: a relationship with Jesus Christ is a very simple thing. Not everything has to be so complex."

At that point a customer walked up to my cash register, so I went behind the counter and rang up the sale.

Bubba Present

I might have said to Stan that the religious right, Jerry Falwell's Moral Majority, Ronald Reagan's embrace of born-again Christendom, born-again Christendom's embrace of Ronald Reagan, all played a huge part in why I began to question the faith I'd grown up with. But how would I say that to someone who was still of that world? How could I say that to a person standing there telling me that a relationship with Jesus Christ is a very simple thing?

At this point, you need to know about Bubba. Bubba, the music minister dad hired in 1980, kept me coming back to La Crescenta First Baptist Church in those confusing early eighties.

Twenty-two year old Bubba graduated from a Southern California Christian college after growing up in South Central Los Angeles. His real name was Sylvester, so he could have been a "Syl" or a "Sly," but he stood six-feet-two, weighed over 250 pounds, and sang in a voice like a fountain flowing deep and wide, so his family and friends donned him "Bubba." That's how he was introduced to La Crescenta First Baptist Church: "our new choir director, Bubba." Bubba was black. The La Crescenta First Baptist congregation was white.

I was away at Bethel College when Bubba first came to La Crescenta. When I came home for the summer, everyone wanted to tell me about this great new black choir director—wanted to tell me about him before anyone else had the chance. Bubba: a huge man with a booming (always "booming") baritone voice ("he shakes the pews without a mike"); an incredible pianist with a bluesy gospel style; a man who danced, a man who rocked back and forth when he sang and directed; a man with charisma, a wonderful sense of humor, that star quality. The Blessed Truth, the youth choir, doubled in size when Bubba became director. When he took over the adult sanctuary choir, so many new people wanted to join he had to hold auditions.

"Can you believe that?" people said. "Auditions for the sanctuary choir? Last year it was so bad, they had to beg the best singers not to quit."

La Crescenta First Baptist, all agreed, felt new and exciting—like a totally different place. Bubba: the overnight sensation, the most popular pastor, the undisputed King of Gospel Soul, the celebrity, the superstar. The pews filled. People came from far and wide to see La Crescenta's black music ambassador.

"We were sitting in that little prayer chapel down the hall from the church offices," Dad told me when I asked him how Bubba came to La Crescenta First Baptist. "Don Rainbow, the Christian Education Director, interviewed Bubba with me. We got done asking questions, and I asked, 'Would you mind doing a song for us?' So he sat down at the piano in the corner. The song he did was 'The Rock.' Remember that one? It became one of my favorite songs."

"In the middle of the chorus, Don and I just looked at each other in amazement. We couldn't believe what we were hearing. His booming baritone voice literally shook the room. He had so much passion—but he could also bring his voice down to that gentle falsetto tone when he needed to. And he was a virtuoso on the piano. He knew old gospel and he knew the classics and I'll bet he could play jazz too. He got to the middle of that first chorus of 'The Rock' and I remember thinking to myself, 'I'll bet this little chapel has never felt anything like this before.' It was like being in the upper room on the day of Pentecost, with the rushing mighty wind blowing through."

We wanted to believe that we were Bubba's second family, that our house was his home away from home. When he wasn't a guest elsewhere, he had Sunday dinner with us, and Mom regularly invited him over for postchurch Sunday evening pizza-chips-pie-socializing.

That's how I remember my late teens and early twenties in La

Crescenta: Bubba present. Church services, dinners, birthdays, holidays: Bubba's presence.

Bubba and Dad sometimes came home from work together. If they were still laughing as they walked in the front door, we knew that they'd probably have a silly new anecdote or two to share. As Mom got dinner ready, they told the latest stories of the two ministers getting goofy—being human, instead of playing pastor.

Mom would set another place at the table as Dad and Bubba switched into story mode. They'd spent the afternoon unintentionally gathering new material, and now it was time to show Barb and the kids what they'd found. There was no pretense of pastorly edification or moralizing: this was purely entertainment.

"Barb, you should have seen John today in downtown L.A.," Bubba said one evening.

Mom rolled her eyes and said, "I don't know if I want to hear this."

"Oh Barb," Bubba said, "of course you want to hear it. You love it when your hubby steps out of his preacher hat and lets loose. You do! You just have to play the pastor's wife every now and then to keep him in line."

We all laughed and admired, once again, Bubba's wonderful ability to read people.

"It's true, Barb. You get this pastor's wifey look on your face and you're all, 'Oh, John,' but you're loving it the whole time. Anyway, John and I were walking back to the car after the clergy luncheon, and we passed this street corner where there's usually some evangelist preaching and telling everyone how they're going to Hell: 'Repent from your evil ways, for the last days are at hand' and all that. I say, 'Look John, there's nobody preaching today.' And your dad gets this big grin on his face and says, 'Let's have a little church service. I'll preach and you do the special music.'"

Bubba made eye contact with the three of us—Marshall, Marna, Mark—to tell us about the Pastor John that he knew, the man in his whiling away.

"You kids don't get to see this side of your Dad. He started doing this sermon on God and country and Old Glory and financial success coming to those who serve the Lord. Talking about how much God has blessed America with material riches. All that nonsense."

"John!" Mom scolded, as she laughed. "What if someone from church saw you?"

Dad opened his mouth to answer, but Bubba beat him to it.

"Someone from La Crescenta in the city of L.A.? How often do La Crescenta people even come to the city? Besides, if anyone from church saw him, they would have been proud. He was preaching the gospel that most of them believe. They wouldn't have known it was a joke. It was like he'd rehearsed and memorized it. Totally impromptu, and the words just flowed from his mouth. He never stepped out of character. I'm telling you, this man is an improv actor!"

"Tell them what you did, Bubba," Dad said. "I wasn't the only one acting."

"Then," Bubba went on, "I start softly singing 'The Battle Hymn of the Republic' while he's preaching. A small crowd starts to gather—about five or six people. And John's totally in stride, never misses a beat. Somehow we time it so that he ends the sermon just as I'm ready to break into the chorus: 'Glory glory Hallelujah! Glory glory Hallelujah!' John's shouting, 'everybody sing along'—and everybody does! Even we're starting to feel a little patriotic."

"It's the type of thing," Dad said, "that makes you proud to be an American."

I think he meant it too. Away from La Crescenta, in downtown L.A., getting goofy with Bubba, preaching a false gospel, singing the "Battle Hymn of the Republic": in those brief moments, Dad felt free.

At first Bubba commuted to La Crescenta from South Central L.A., but he eventually moved into a little parsonage next to the church. He sometimes said that he felt like an exile in La Crescenta, a stranger in a very strange land. We Andersons said, "You're not alone. We don't belong here either." One major difference: we could conceal our sense of not belonging. We could walk anywhere without getting eyed suspiciously; we could drive anywhere without the fear of getting pulled over for no reason, slammed against the hood of a police car, frisked, and told, "Get out of our town and don't come back."

Bubba, on the other hand, couldn't.

The first time this happened, Dad took Bubba down to the Foothill Police Station and introduced him to officers, clerks, and administrators. "This man is the minister of music at La Crescenta First Baptist Church. His name is Sylvester, but we call him Bubba. Bubba lives here. Make a note of it."

I'm remembering the story of the black La Crescenta basketball coach and family, and that Lawrence Powell graduated from Crescenta Valley High School in 1980, the year that Ronald Reagan was elected president, the year that Bubba came to our church. And I'm remembering when Bubba played Jesus Christ in the summer 1981 church basement production of the musical *Godspell.* Twenty-three-year-old Bubba, the only black person in an all-white cast, played Jesus Christ dying on the cross for an all-white audience. It remains the most real and believable representation I've seen of Christ's crucifixion: a black Jesus lynched by a white mob in the church basement.

In the Joan Armatrading Section

When I got back to Stan, he shifted back into the music mode. The image of me taking cash registered in his mind: "Oh yeah, Mark is at work. He won't want to talk about a relationship with Jesus Christ being a very simple thing."

I found Stan thumbing through the Joan Armatrading section. It wasn't that he was interested in finding out which Joan Armatrading CDs we had in stock; instead, he wanted me to find him looking at Joan Armatrading CDs. That's how it looked to me.

"I still think of you whenever I see the name Joan Armatrading," he said.

"I haven't listened to her for a while. I should give her a listen again. I still love her. You know, Joan Armatrading is one of the coolest people in the history of pop music."

"Remember when Jon and I gave you so much grief for being into Joan Armatrading? We were like, 'Joan Armatrading? Who's that?' We'd never heard of her before you came to La Crescenta. We had to give you grief for liking someone we'd never even heard of."

"Of course you did. You had to give me grief for liking anything that wasn't progressive rock. Otherwise the committee would take your cards away."

"Yeah, and we absolutely couldn't allow you to like Springsteen."

"Man, don't even get me started on how cruel you guys were about Bruce."

He laughed. "Yeah, we were pretty mean about Bruce. I still feel bad about that sometimes."

Was Stan trying to indirectly apologize for the car argument? I'm not sure, but it seemed like a worthy tactic: apologize for present intolerance by atoning for past intolerances. It felt like an attempt at reconciliation.

Stan was acknowledging that even then—sixteen, seventeen, eighteen years earlier—I was the musical oddball. I was the one who strayed from the aesthetic commandments of our secular religion, progressive rock music. Try as they did, Jon and Stan couldn't keep me from liking Joan Armatrading, Bruce Springsteen, Jackson Browne, Neil Young, Tom Petty, Joni Mitchell, and others who wrote songs instead of epic suites. The singer-songwriters were the first ones to lead me off the straight and narrow progressive rock path. When I started listening to punk–new wave (Elvis Costello, The Clash, Patti Smith, X, Graham Parker, The Pretenders, The Sex Pistols ...) in my college years, my California friends knew that I was changing in ways that they couldn't control. I was a goner.

And there I was in 1995, clerking at a place named the Electric Fetus on a Sunday morning at eleven o'clock, as services were beginning in churches across the land. Maybe that's what Stan really meant when he mentioned Joan Armatrading: "We should have seen this coming. You were never really like us."

Or maybe he simply meant, "I still remember you."

A relationship with Jesus Christ is a very simple thing. Those words kept running through my head the rest of the day and most of the week. I know what he meant: you should have the faith of a child, so don't make this simple thing so complicated. It became a day of wishing I'd said what I thought of later. Among all of the other later-thoughts that occurred to me as I was ringing up CDs, I wished I'd had a chance to say, "Wait a minute, Stan. You claim that Jesus Christ is the Son of God. That Jesus Christ is God. And a relationship with the Son of God, a relationship with the person who you claim is the One Way to God, is a very simple thing? I would have thought the opposite."

If I am ever going to have a relationship with God, I want it to be the opposite: complex, mysterious, and confounding. I've chosen to remain in this world and of this world, so how could it be anything but that? And if you want to boil my lost faith down to one single thing, that's it. The problem is that it isn't and it never will be one single thing. As a matter of fact, I don't even know what the "it" in the last sentence refers to.

Reclining Picture

Years ago, somebody took a picture of Jim, Jon, Stan, Mike, Marshall, and me. They stood behind me in a row with arms outstretched—held me vertical as I reclined. We all laughed. Especially me. Fingers tickled my ribs, and I was beginning to fall. I had short hair and a beard then. I think it was a coming-home-from-college picture. Christmas or summer break. A beginning or an ending—a jacuzzi gathering or a last supper. '79, '80, '81, or '82?

Jon brought it with other old pictures from California. During the reception, we all looked at them together.

"Hey, let's do a repeat of that picture where we're holding Mark," Jon said.

We positioned ourselves: Jon, the brawny tan one; Jim, Malcolm X glasses and Monk cap; bearded Marshall; thin Mike, military-haircut; wiry short-blond Stan; longer-hair-unbearded reclining me.

Mom snapped the photo.

A repeat. For necessary reunion. If we posed like we did then and took a picture of it, shutter speed might capture missed magic.

We smiled, but no one laughed.

Stan, Jon, and Mike had traveled thousands of miles for a re-creation of that image.

returns and gatherings

Free Your Mind and Your Ass Will Follow

"Protest, frivolity generate conflict," proclaims a front page headline in the May 13, 1983, Bethel *Clarion*. A newly discovered truth, an encapsulation of an event, an equation: Protest + frivolity = conflict.

"Students gathered in Kresge Courtyard to watch and dance to the music of Rockamole" [pronounced Rock-ah-moleee], reads the caption below the accompanying photograph. It might have said, instead, "Students gathered in Kresge Courtyard to watch other students dance to the music of Rockamole." That's how it looks to me now. Students watching students dancing.

In the foreground of the picture, about 150 students sit in the bleachers (wood-beam retaining wall upon wood-beam retaining wall built into a small hill above a brick stage) and watch a circle of about 50 students dancing down below. The picture shows only the seated students' backsides as they crane to clearly see the spectacle to the left of the stage: students in a circle bobbing and clapping in time to the rock and roll, as two among them dance in the center, show their stuff, shake what they've got, testify.

I sometimes feel embarrassed when I tell the story of the short-lived dance revolt that took place at Bethel College in May 1983. To those unfamiliar with the school and its "Lifestyle Statement," the incident seems eerily out of time, absurd, trivial. As it should.

It is difficult to explain why I chose to go to Bethel in the first place, more difficult to explain why I stayed there despite my growing discontentment with evangelical Christianity, even more difficult to explain how, in 1983, college students dancing on campus to rock and roll could still be controversial somewhere in America.

"Are you kidding?" some have asked. "At the college that you graduated from, all dancing was illegal?"

It's true. All entering Bethel students and faculty had to sign the school "Lifestyle Statement" which said (and I paraphrase), While I am a student or staff member at Bethel College, I agree not to drink alcohol, use tobacco, dance on or off campus, gamble, indiscriminately attend movies, or engage in premarital sexual intercourse. I understand that participation in any of the aforementioned activities is grounds for expulsion or termination.

When the Dance Revolt of '83 happened, Bethel administrators sent the dean of men down to stop it from escalating into something bigger. And after listening to his pleading and mild threats ("This is, I'll remind you, a violation of the Bethel Lifestyle Statement"), the rebels stopped dancing.

Even at its peak, it wasn't a very big revolt: about fifty students who were dancing to Rockamole, the garage trio in which I was drumming. Still, it was a huge deal. A great crowd of onlookers gathered all around the dancing throng: shocked students gazed from the windows of their dorms, secretaries looked down from office windows, professors stepped out of the staff lounge to bear witness (and the more liberal ones secretly rejoiced). On that afternoon, on that secluded and self-contained suburban campus, the whole school was watching the dancers.

In all of Bethel's years of No Dancing (dating back into the nineteenth century), this had never happened before. The *Clarion*, the weekly campus newspaper, devoted much of its final 1983 issue to the incident: a front page feature, a two-page photo spread with an earnest editorial in the center, a point-counterpoint debate.

When I now think about my years at Bethel College, the dance revolt stands out more than anything else. It broke from the rhythmic pattern that I knew at Bethel, and I even felt like a celebrity for a few days. Countless students (and a few professors) stopped me in the hall to express thanks, support, and congratulations for pounding out the beat that spawned the rebellion.

All of this praise and attention for drumming a very simple backbeat that I knew long before college: it made my graduation a week later feel anticlimactic.

This is not the stuff of myth or legend. This is only one example of a great Minnesota tradition. One bitterly cold and bland February afternoon, a rock and roll trio formed in a Bethel College band room. There was no magic in the air.

There was no bliss, no ecstasy, no feeling of transcendence, no triumphant sense of escape from the here and now. We had no repertoire, and we had little knowledge of how to begin being a band. We knew only what we held in common: a disdain for "contemporary Christian rock" and a desire to be in a band that played songs by artists who we admired (all *men,* I'm now noticing): The Beatles, Chuck Berry, Buddy Holly, Ray Charles, the Rolling Stones, Little Richard, The Who, Jonathan Richman, Bruce Springsteen …

The only spoken goal was easy enough to accomplish: to meet and make noise in that band room on Saturday afternoons. The guitarist-singer named Jerry, the singer–bass player named Steve, and the drummer who was me, only wanted to blow off steam and shorten the long winter. We weren't going anywhere, and it was something to do. Better and worse worlds have begun with so little to work with.

It wasn't a jam session. We didn't know how to jam and we never really learned. If we weren't playing a song, we weren't playing anything. This wasn't a conscious choice, an articulated attempt to follow the less-is-more aesthetic. The three of us barely knew how to play together. We weren't competent enough to lose and find ourselves in our music. Steve later confessed that the first time he'd ever picked up a bass was the night before that February afternoon—and he only played bass because that's what we needed, not because he wanted to play bass.

Jerry, a missionary kid who grew up in Peru, knew enough riffs and leads to get us through the afternoon. A scruffy-haired guy who wore white T-shirts with bell-bottom jeans (years after bell-bottoms went out of style, years before they came back into style), Jerry was known at Bethel for walking around the halls barefoot in the dead of winter as he delivered audio-visual equipment from classroom to classroom. He grew up listening to Kiss, Yes, Seals and Crofts, Larry Norman, Led Zeppelin, The Eagles, The Beatles, Chuck Berry, Bachman Turner Overdrive, and whatever else found its way to his Peruvian boarding school.

After a lot of stumbling, fumbling, garbled lyrics, and false starts, we settled into the song that we all knew enough to sustain for more than two minutes: Chuck Berry's "Johnny B. Goode," the garage band pledge of allegiance about the country boy who "never ever learned to read or write so well / but he could play a guitar just like a-ringin'-a bell."

We played the song a first time (enough to know that we knew enough to get to the end). We played it a second time (a lot better, and a little worse). The third time was the train wreck rendition, the one that humbles all bands who begin to think that songs will get progressively better the more times they are played. Puffed-up with pride that I could pound out a steady beat two run-throughs in a row, I dropped the beat completely halfway through the third. I dropped the beat, lost the groove, dropped my sticks, and fell out of the song. Jerry and Steve did their best to keep things moving while I tried to find my way back in, but the rhythmic momentum of the big dead space was too much for us to overcome. The song went limp and tumbled onto the floor.

"Let's try it one more time," I suggested.

The fourth time, we played "Johnny B. Goode" straight and sloppy and true. From the four stick clicks to the accidental coda, we stayed together, and we called this good. It didn't matter that we were sloppy, loose, out of tune and time, embarrassingly inept: we could play one song.

Steve had an idea. We could rehearse and rehearse that one song and try out for Moods, the Bethel College spring talent show. If we felt up to it, we could learn another song for an encore, but we'd only need one song to get into the show. "Johnny B. Goode."

It didn't matter that we were playing a Chuck Berry song overplayed by garage bands since the dawn of the duckwalk, a song that has become both a rock and roll standard and a rock and roll cliché. We'd play it as if the world did, in fact, need another band to play "Johnny B. Goode." As that world did. That timewarp in-but-not-of-world removed from the world where Johnny could free his mind and his mindfollowing ass to be good. As if the world didn't need another smiling Christian waving a John 3:16 banner in front of the camera, another self-proclaimed believer resisting unto death belief in goodness, good things, good beings.

That afternoon we called our work good and decided to become a band.

It often happens this way: there is the band, and there is the tribe that adopts the band as their own. The band will forever be owned by and accountable to the tribe. No matter how far they go or what they sign or who they become, the band will never completely get over the tribe, and the tribe will never completely get over the band. At Bethel College in 1983, Rockamole was the band, and the Peace and Justice Committee was our tribe.

The Peace and Justice Committee (P&J) was a group of left-leaning Bethel College students who put recently digested liberation theology into practice and invited like-minded students to begin a forum for dissent. Weekly P&J meetings became a place to just say no to the rightward turn of the country and the rightward leadership of evangelical Christendom. P&Jers, stuck as they were between sixties hippie idealism and eighties punk cynicism, kept what they could of both. This split was best represented in their anointed musical heroes: The Clash, Bob Marley, Bob Dylan, Bruce Cockburn, and U2, all of whom combined adventurous music with lyrics that P&Jers could sing at parties and, if the spirit led, recite at meetings.

P&J members numbered from fifteen to fifty, depending on whether the count included only the people who attended the meetings and seminars, or if it also included all of the rebellious sons and daughters who skipped the meetings but frequented the parties. This follows a timeworn leftist tradition: there are the genuine activists, and there are those who sympathize enough to party with the genuine activists. Not even behind-the-times Bethel was immune to radical chic.

The more devoted P&J members (at the top of that list was brother Marshall) counted me as one who was in but not fully of the group. I religiously showed up at all of the parties but only intermittently attended the meetings and seminars. The devotees might have pressured me to get involved more, but I was a drummer in a rock-and-roll band, so they cut me some slack.

I attribute my half-assed commitment to lack of time, lack of knowledge, persistent cynicism, a need to distance myself from my brother (the former zealous evangelist who became, in his junior year, the zealous P&J leader), and a greater passion for music and literature. Because I studied literature compulsively, constantly, I viewed the actual study of peace and justice as an extracurricular activity that I just didn't have time for. I was the guy who half-listened to P&J discussions, and then asked, "Now, who are the Sandinistas and who are the Contras? And which side are we for?"

My former evangelical zealotry made matters more confusing. I told myself, "I don't want to replace my evangelical Christian soul-saving with peace and justice world-saving." It was, in other words, difficult for me to distinguish between what was real and what was rationalization. The result: instead of holding a "U.S. out of North America" sign on the steps of the state capitol in twenty-below

January weather, I preferred to work up a sweat drumming to The Clash's "I'm So Bored with the U.S.A."

At many colleges, P&J types would have gone largely unnoticed, but at Bethel (where the Young Republicans were thriving, where most students rejoiced that their President Reagan called himself "born again," where the Moral Majority was mostly viewed as a necessary and positive new American force), P&Jers quickly gained reputations as malcontents, rebels, dissidents, partiers, troublemakers with bad attitudes, and, in general, angry nincompoops. The rumors that the Young Republicans spread were true: Bethel students drank alcohol, smoked, and danced at P&J parties. Some parties would end with large coed groups falling asleep on someone's living room floor. Sometimes pairs indiscriminately made out. Some couples sneaked off into bedrooms.

The more straight and narrow Bethelites could, quite simply, read Bad Attitude in the way P&Jers looked. P&Jers tended to wear army surplus fatigues, second-hand store duds, long and shaggy hair (guys and gals alike), thick beards and mustaches (except for the gals and punkier guys), black work boots (in the winter), Birkenstock sandals (in the fall and spring), and amused grins (like they knew better than everyone else, like everything at Bethel was just too funny).

The straight-and-narrows would have gladly turned us in to the authorities for repeated violations of the Bethel Lifestyle Statement, but they didn't know how to find our parties. Even if they knew where to find us, though, most of them wouldn't have ventured into the Minneapolis city neighborhoods (fifteen or twenty freeway minutes from the suburban Bethel campus) where P&Jers tended to live.

A group of us guys lived in a big white house on the corner of Oakland and Franklin Avenues in the Phillips neighborhood of South Minneapolis. We named the house "Oakland House." We felt like a "we" in those years (1983 to 1985) that constellate in my memory, so I'll call us one. Some among us were done at Bethel, others had a year or two left to go; no one seemed to pay much attention to who had graduated and who was still doing time.

Oakland House became the Bethel misfit flophouse where the disinclined could stay if they absolutely could not fathom going back to the campus that night. Oakland House welcomed Bethel strays, Bethel backsliders. We were, after all, rebels with a fear of getting caught and kicked out, and Bethel was not a place anyone could return to while reeking of alcohol, cigarettes, sweaty-dance-stench, sex—Sin City. We didn't want to disgrace our parents, bring shame to the family name. We only wanted to have some fun and party like it was 1984, not 1954.

There were many many good reasons (most of them musical, the rest drugs-and-sex related) for wanting to get away from Bethel back in those early to mid-eighties. The Replacements, Hüsker Dü, and Soul Asylum were still playing at little clubs like Duffy's, Goofy's, The Cabooze, and 7th Street Entry. Prince (and affiliates such as The Time and Vanity 6) did the occasional cameo in the First Avenue Mainroom. The Meat Puppets, The Minutemen, R.E.M., The Dead Kennedys, U2, Black Flag, Minor Threat, Fishbone, Scratch Acid, Sonic Youth, The Swans, Big Black, and on and on: bands were coming to the twin towns, and a Bethel dorm was nowhere at all for a young music lover to end a weekend night. Oakland House became the place where Bethel punk wannabes (their numbers were few, but their presence was strong) could crash after a Hüsker Dü night of drinking, slam-dancing, and stage-diving at Duffy's.

There we found ourselves: Bethel guys living in a big old Minneapolis house, consolidating our record collections, sitting around and listening to more music than we had time for, drinking cheap beer, smoking cigarettes, feeling happy because we had friends like us. Friends who wanted to drop into the nearest alley dumpster the heavy burden of guilt that we'd pilgrimmed on our backs for twenty-plus years.

Most of us envisioned a nonevangelical Christian adulthood that involved full immersion in a world we were taught to be in but not of. But maybe it was too late for us to ever enter that world—maybe our past dictated that we'd remain outsiders in whatever world we tried to enter. Or maybe we could slip quietly into the city without anyone noticing that we didn't belong.

One of those odd paradoxes: we felt most threatened by our religious upbringing while at Bethel, yet we chose to remain there, despite what the institution came to represent. Bethel College was the higher-ed embodiment of all that our parents wanted for us to become: upstanding, college-educated believers in Jesus Christ who would be deeply committed to our churches and happily wedded to the accoutrements of the American Dream.

I never stopped hoping that Bethel would become to me what it was to my parents: the glory place of the glory years. Ever since I was a child, I'd heard about my parent's Bethel years. Bethel was that wonderful place in their past, the place where they met (no Bethel, no me), the place where they had the time of their life in the happy mid-fifties. Oh, the fun they had, the friends they made, the Christian love and joy they shared. Bethel was college, college was Bethel, and nearly every St. Paul hovel that had been around since the fifties (except for bars) fell within its nostalgia zone.

Sometimes it even seemed like Bethel was another parent that I didn't know how to leave behind.

It's time for a midwinter college talent show, the annual Moods that everyone who is anyone at Bethel attends. Some go to laugh and mock, some go to cheer friends, some go to sincerely enjoy, others go for the pure ironic value. It's pretty much a no-lose proposition for all spectators. Truly wretched performances still carry plenty of entertainment value, and who will argue with true talent?

The performers that night? Is this what I remember? A woman in a kilt dancing foursquare to recorded Scottish bagpipes; five campus thespians performing their original skit satirizing campus cliquishness and ending with a plea for oneness in Jesus Christ; a folk singer earnestly offering Larry Norman's standard about the Rapture, "I Wish We'd All Been Ready"; two sisters dressed like toddlers in bunny rabbit pajamas, singing in baby voices an old movie tune about sisters and misters and respecting boundaries, more or less; a pianist solemnly, perfectly playing "Jesu, Joy of Man's Desiring"; a big-haired Christian metal band in red and black spandex singing an original song about the Tribulation: "You can run but you can't hide / the Beast has got your number / he's right at your side"; a ventriloquist with a dummy that quotes favorite Bible verses; and a trio named Rockamole featuring a guitar-playing missionary kid, a bass-playing Paul McCartney worshiper, and a drumming son of a preacher man.

With a wiseass, cocksure, missionary-kid smirk, Jerry stepped on the pedal and screeched out the Chuck Berry invocation. The lead was greeted with whoops, applause, and half-guilty grins that Jerry refused to acknowledge with even a nod. This, he knew, was his time and this was his place. He had always been out of time and out of place, so what in the hell did he have to prove to the church geeks in the bleachers? They didn't know him.

As Steve sang the lines about the kid who "used to carry his guitar in a gunny sack / and sit beneath the trees down by the railroad track," Jerry became Johnny B. Goode, the barefoot kid in bell-bottoms finding his spot beneath the trees in that Peruvian rainforest, picking the Chuck Berry riffs that another missionary kid brought back from furlough in the States, dreaming of the longest furlough, a furlough of nothing but guitar, a furlough that would last and last like a prayer unceasing, forever and ever, world without end, amen.

As the rhythms of Jerry's thrashing arm dropped into place, the backbeat of my snare rocked into the standing audience. Within seconds, the place rolled into a steady backbeat clap, a clap that lifted me from above and below, and assured me that I wouldn't lose it. If I lost it for an instant, it wouldn't stay lost. It was out of me and into the crowd. Can I get a witness?

We earned a standing ovation and were cheered back for an encore. We played the other song we'd learned just in case the audience begged for more: Chuck Berry's "Rock and Roll Music." What else?

It was our night at the Apollo, the shining moment to build on, our heyday, the ten minutes of fame that we couldn't let slip by. People stopped us in the hall all week to confess that they almost danced: that it was painful for them not to dance when we played that night.

"Ever since Moods," Steve said to Jerry and me at our next Saturday session, "lots of people have been asking me when we're playing again. A lot of people really would love to see us do a whole show."

We had no good reason to question Steve. Of the three of us, he most understood the tenor of Bethel. While Jerry and I hung out with the P&J types, Steve walked among the more normal Bethel students. He was a well-groomed nice guy who did the best he knew to walk the straight and narrow path to salvation: he still attended the Baptist church that he grew up in, still adhered to Bethel's Lifestyle Statement, still dated women who went to church and read their Bibles daily (and would gladly give up their careers if Mr. Right thought it God's will for them to be housewives), and he still entertained the possibility of entering the ministry. He wore short brown hair, a brown simulated-leather jacket, and creased double-knit slacks. Yes, Steve was a creased slacks guy.

"You can't play rock and roll looking like that!" someone might protest.

At Bethel you could play rock and roll looking like anything because you weren't supposed to play it at all. If you played it just to play it, if you played it without the necessary Christianizing of it, if you played it without the motive of proselytization or edification, you could play it looking like anything. You could play it looking like any old lost soul in creased slacks.

Steve didn't care much for the P&J crowd. He laughed and shook his head at us, as if he'd been warned that there would be cynical rebels at Bethel for him to ignore. We were of a type. He came to some of our parties, but he didn't drink or smoke—and he didn't tattle on us. Outside of rehearsal, we didn't pal around or talk about much besides music. For all I know, he might have been a Young Republican.

If Jerry and I had been at a different school, a bigger college, a secular college, a college at which three guys playing in a band was as common as three guys playing intramural flag football, we would have looked for someone else to sing and play bass. It's best to avoid starting a band with a guy who might at any minute decide that it's God's will for him to give up the Devil's music, as Steve did in his time-to-get-serious senior year. He quit Rockamole and joined one of Bethel's "gospel teams," coed choral groups that roved from Baptist church to Baptist church and sang lite-contemporary gospel favorites accompanied by piano and acoustic guitar. Sid Vicious Steve wasn't.

The mysteriously redeeming side to Steve was his fondness and feel for old rock and roll: Chuck Berry, Buddy Holly, Elvis Presley, Little Richard, Carl Perkins, The Beatles ... I don't know where that love came from, and I never thought to ask. Maybe he was the guy who actually bought all those "Golden Hits from the '50s and '60s" three-record sets not available in any store—the guy who watched all the Ozzie and Harriet reruns, sat through all the commercials, ordered products as advertised on television to keep them from disappearing forever.

Another possibility: maybe his mother and father gave up rock and roll to follow Jesus Christ back in the fifties and couldn't resist one last nostalgia binge when the early-seventies back-to-the-fifties craze hit. Steve inherited the records when their guilt set in and, quite miraculously, made it through the seventies without buying a single Led Zeppelin, Aerosmith, or Ted Nugent record. Mother and father felt vindicated: their castoffs saved their son from a heavy metal adolescence.

"I don't know about you guys," Steve went on breathlessly, "but I'd really love to do an hour-long outdoor concert in May. We had the audience in the palm of our hands at Moods—we were far and away the most well-received act in the talent show."

Steve thought that it would be a shame not to follow up the buzz with one big hyped-up concert.

"But we only know three songs," I protested.

I thought of the time it would take to learn enough songs to fill an hour. My senior paper, a comparison of modernisms in Eliot's *The Waste Land* and Hemingway's *The Sun Also Rises,* was due in a few weeks, and I didn't know how I was ever going to pull it together. I didn't have room for one more thing.

"We only know," I said, "'Johnny B. Goode,' 'Roll Over Beethoven,' and 'Rock and Roll Music.'"

"That's where," Steve said, "you're wrong, Mark. You're a drummer, and you don't understand what guitarists take for granted. We actually know about five hundred songs. It's true. Jerry, how many songs could we play with the chord progression to 'Johnny B. Goode' alone?"

"Probably a couple million," Jerry said.

"How many rock and roll songs," Steve asked me, "could you play with the drum beat that you play in 'Johnny B. Goode'?"

"A couple million. At least."

"So what's the problem? I know the lyrics and chords to about fifty great rock and roll songs."

Steve wasn't bluffing. He knew song upon song after song that Jerry and I wouldn't have learned otherwise: "Brown Eyed Handsome Man," "I Saw Her Standing There," "Rave On," "Sweet Little Sixteen," "Good Golly Miss Molly," "Not Fade Away," "All Shook Up," "Oh Boy," "Hallelujah, I Love Her So," and on and on. He'd been singing these songs for years alone in his Brooklyn Park bedroom, and his time to perform them was, he knew, nigh.

At the time, I took for granted what's odd to me now: the catalyst, the one who knew the lyrics and chords to the covers, the kid who lined up the talent show audition, the gig hustler who set up and zealously promoted Rockamole's May concert in the courtyard—this huckster was also the band member who most looked and acted the part of Bethel student, who didn't object to signing and living the Bethel Lifestyle Statement, who would later join a singing gospel team (to atone for Rockamole?).

"How many songs do you know, Jerry?" Steve asked.

"Probably about fifty."

"See, Mark. We could learn twenty songs so quickly right now. Just bang out about five new songs at every rehearsal. Rehearse twice a week in April, tighten up in May. The songs are nothing. The hardest thing is finding a drummer. Right Jerry?"

Jerry nodded.

"Are you up for it, Jerry?"

"I'm game."

"Great, now we just need to find a drummer. Hey Mark, word has it that you play drums. Might you be up for a big concert in May?"

"It's looking that way."

"Whooh! Whoooh!" Steve yelled. "We've got songs. We've got a band. Man, I'm going to hype the heck out of this show!"

It just goes to show: behind every flavor-of-the-week rock and roll band there's a tent evangelist prepared to pull up the stakes and conquer the next town. After all, Jimmy Swaggart and Jerry Lee Lewis really are cousins.

We rehearsed twice a week and learned four or five new songs at each two-hour rehearsal. Bing bang bong. One, Four, Five. G, D, C. Nothing tough, nothing fancy. Guitar, bass, drums. Keep it rolling, keep it raw. Chuck Berry, Buddy Holly, Gene Vincent, Eddie Cochran, Ray Charles, Little Richard, Elvis, The Beatles: Steve's Top 20 of all time. We even had time to learn two Jerry originals, a Jerry and Mark collaboration, a favorite of Jerry's since childhood ("Little Red Riding Hood" by Sam the Sham and the Pharoahs), Bruce Springsteen's "State Trooper," Jonathan Richman's "Roadrunner" and "I'm a Little Airplane," and a song to be dedicated to the Peace and Justice Committee: The Who's "My Generation."

We were a garage band from evangelical Christian garageland playing, for the most part, typical covers. If Bethel had been a secular college, Rockamole would have been nowhere. But Bethel was Bethel, a place where members of a retro-hippie group like the Peace and Justice Committee could feel bohemian radical by wearing long hair and baggy army surplus clothes, skipping daily chapel, writing "U.S. Out of El Salvador" on bathroom stalls, drinking beer at the rented flophouse in the city, and smoking nonchalantly with the heavy smokers in the smoking room of the U of M's Wilson Library. When commonplace going-away-to-college rituals are forbidden, it doesn't take much to feel rebellious.

And how did our Bethel rock and roll band rebel? By playing only secular songs, mostly radio hits from the fifties and sixties—not songs by the Sex Pistols or Patti Smith or Black Flag or X or The Clash.

The Peace and Justice Committee needed Bethel for an antagonist as much as Rockamole needed Bethel for a performance venue.

Our big show happened on a sunny May Thursday, a late-spring day in which the temperature hovered in the eighties. It's likely that it was the warmest day we'd known that spring. It's likely that the last of the April snow melted a week or two earlier.

The dancing started how dancing always starts: at first it was only two dancers, then two more and two more and one more and three more and six more … There was nothing particularly outrageous or sensational about it. People felt like dancing, so they did.

As their numbers grew, the dancers formed a large circle. Two danced in the center for twelve bars of rhythm, danced back into the unbroken circle as two others prepared to take their place. Applause and whoops greeted each dancer who decided to publicly testify in the circle's center. That's when it looked most out of hand.

The dancing circle brought the administrative representative down to the scene. The dancing had taken a shape that could only grow bigger.

In another *Clarion* picture, brother Marshall, Bethel's P&J longhair guru in rainbow suspenders, raises his left hand to his forehead. Is he blocking out the sun, readjusting his bandana, asking a question, wiping sweat from his brow? He's got a sneer on his face, a look that doesn't hide his disdain for the dean of men, a thirtysomething white-shirt-and-tie man who stands a few feet away. The dean has come down to scatter the dancers in all directions, break the spirit of the protest-frivolity, then apologize for the administration. As he explains his presence to the dancers, Marshall would like to spit in his face.

This dean is what Marshall might have become. The dean is what I once expected Marshall to become: a toady for the Lord. A toady for Jesus.

The dean has been elected to tell the dancers, "Here at Bethel we're trying to create an alternative, distinctly Christian environment for our students and faculty. We're trying to model an alternative lifestyle. We are not Hamline University, we are not Macalester College, we are not the University of Minnesota. We are Bethel, a college that is attempting to be an example to the world of our Lord and Savior Jesus Christ."

Everything the dean is saying, Marshall knows he could say better. Marshall hears what the dean is going to say before he even speaks, and Marshall hears all that the dean should have said instead.

"I wonder," Marshall thinks, "if this guy has ever had an original idea. I wonder if he has had even one thought of his own."

Beside Marshall slumps a dejected-looking P&J woman. Only the left side of her face is visible. Her left eye is closed and her lips arch down. The dean of men is looking into her closed eyes, trying to make contact, but she won't look at him. She looks down and away instead of up and in.

She can't believe this. Minutes ago they were dancing together. Nearly fifty of them. The dean came down to stop the dancing, and he's succeeded. She can't believe it: they've all stopped dancing. The band is still playing "Little Red Riding Hood," the song they were playing when she shouted, "Uh-oh! Here comes the big bad wolf!"

She envisioned everyone dancing long after the big bad wolf walked onto the dance floor. She knew that they wouldn't quit, even as he shouted, "If the dancing doesn't stop *right now,* guys and gals, we will turn off the sound system." The administration would pull the plug on the music, but the dancers would continue dancing to the unmiked backbeat of the drums. That's how she imagined it.

The powers that be (would they call the local police?) would grab the drummer's sticks, grab his arms, handcuff them. Backbeat dead, they'd physically restrain the dancers. As they danced into the waiting paddy wagon, the dancers would chant "The whole school is watching the whole school is watching the whole school is watching the whole school is watching … "

That's how it would be: confrontation, showdown, clash, repression, reeepressshhhunnn. The whole school would be watching.

She looks down and away as the dean tries to make eye contact. She can't believe this. Everyone quit dancing when the dean walked onto the dance floor, as if they really believed all along that they were doing something wrong.

She hears herself repeating to the dean, "I can't believe you're going to make us stop dancing. I can't even fathom that. It's just so far from me. I can't believe you're going to make us stop dancing. There's something really sick about that." As if she's learning today, harder than ever, who she has spent her life among.

Rockamole's still playing "Little Red Riding Hood" as the dean defends the administration's position to the dancers: "It's not like I enjoy being Mr. Killjoy here. But put yourself in my shoes. It's not that dancing in and of itself is sinful—I'm not here to cast judgment and call you sinners. It's just that the Lifestyle Statement that you all signed upon entering Bethel specifically prohibits dancing on or off campus …"

He knows he's not being heard, so he speaks louder.

The dean needs more volume, a microphone, so he heads for the stage. Our stage. He needs to explain the administration's position to the whole school at once. He's still convinced that he can make himself understood to the majority, even if he fails with a handful of unyielding individuals.

I'm behind the drums thinking, "I hope this jerk doesn't think that he can come up here on our stage and use our mike to tell our audience that they need to quit dancing to our music."

He just keeps on coming, walking onto the stage as I yell, "Get off the stage!" As I think to myself, "Get the fuck off our stage!" I want to throw my drumsticks at his head.

He turns to face us, holds out his right hand in a "Peace be still," his imitation of Christ.

In the picture's foreground, the dean is standing behind the mike. He's out of focus, blurred, a watery presence more than a person. He stands and looks like a testimony-giver, but he's giving someone else's testimony, passing on the story that's been told to him of the world out there and the different we-in-here.

"Here at Bethel," he's saying, "we're trying to create a special and unique Christian community vis-à-vis an atmosphere that you won't find on most college campuses."

Whoever he is, whatever he really thinks or feels, is irrelevant. He has become the Bethel Lifestyle P.R. man. He's not standing there to theologize or philosophize. He's there to sell the school.

"That's why, while you're a student here, you don't drink, you don't smoke, you don't play cards and gamble, you don't have sexual intercourse if you aren't married. And you don't dance. If one component is compromised, it's all up for grabs."

The voice is blurred and indistinct, Charlie Brown's teacher underwater: "Bwaah bwah bwah bwah bwaaah. Bwah bwabwah bwahbwahbwah. Bwaaaaaah. Bwah bwahbwah bwah."

Jerry and I are focused in the picture's background. I'm wearing a black "Suburbs" T-shirt (a favorite local band), holding both of my drumsticks in my left hand. Only the right side of my face is visible: I've got a full mustache and beard, and my hair is cut above my ears. I'm turned toward Jerry, saying something sarcastic about the dean. Jerry's looking at the dean's feet with wide eyes and a full-toothed grin.

At that moment, I despise the dean. As he apologizes for the administration, as he tries to buddy-up to the angry dancers, as he longs to be the levelheaded young-at-heart man the kids can relate to, as he appears calm and approachable, as he uses what he's learned about "How to Minister to Today's Youth," as he eats up our time in the limelight, as he saps my rhythm adrenaline, I loathe him.

I can see it in my face: "When is he going to quit talking? He just keeps on talking. We should kick him off the stage. I just want to play. I was just starting to feel warmed up. Adrenaline was flowing, I was in the groove, people were dancing, and then this doorknob stops the dancers, marches up to the stage, puts out his 'Peace be still' Jesus hand, and starts talking."

"Did we invite him up here, Jerry?" I mutter. "No we didn't. Call security, I say. Have him hauled off. Know what I mean?"

Jerry nods and smiles, then says in his slow drawl: "How about if I just give him a good whack on the head with my guitar. Not a whack that would hurt him. Not a whack that would kill him or even knock him out. Just a stunner. Stun him and shut him up. He'd have a lump on his head in the morning, but that would go away."

"But here at Bethel," the dean continues, "we as Christians are called to bwah bwah bwah bwaaaah bwahbwah."

"I should sit down at my drums and start pounding out a beat. That's what I should do."

"You could do your Keith Moon impression and destroy your drum set. Go crazy and smash it all to pieces. Then blow it all up with a stick of dynamite like he did on *The Smothers Brothers*."

"But I love my drums. I could never do that to them. I hate him, though. I can't believe the jerk is still talking. What kind of a person is this? It baffles me. What kind of a man stops dancers from dancing, walks onto a stage in the middle of a performance, makes the performers quit, and then talks without ceasing?"

After about twenty minutes of institution-defense, the dean realized that he was only repeating himself, so he pronounced his edict: "The music can continue, but the dancing must stop. Our mistake was not stopping it as soon as it started. If the dancing continues, there will be consequences. At the very least, we will pull the plug on the music."

"I see," I thought. "We're just pawns. He thinks that he can dole Rockamole out, use us as his reward or punishment, depending on the behavior of our dedicated fans. I see."

I turned to Jerry and said two words: "My Generation."

"'My Generation'?"

"We've got to play it. What else can we play? Can you think of anything else?"

"Not really. That's the angriest song we know. We're not really an angry band, are we? Sure, I'll sing it. I'm ready for 'My Generation.'"

I'll admit: it wasn't a stunningly original idea. How many millions of garage bands before us had done that song in a spirit of righteous anger? But originality was not the point. We needed to invoke the spirit of that community, that throng of witnesses, that heavenly fold: all of those bands who'd played "My Generation" because they had, at one moment in time, a good reason to play it. As we did. As we didn't know what else to do. We wanted to voice dissent; we wanted to scream to the dancers, "Don't listen to him—this is our show, and we want you to keep on dancing"; we wanted to re-ignite the anger that the dean was trying to snuff out with unyielding words spoken in a reasonable, consoling, big-buddy-brother tone. We didn't know how else to respond to a man who strove to sell us community but couldn't allow us to create and know community, the real rhythm of our bodies-and-spirits in communion.

Most great rock anthems are sustained by one or two heady, fist-thrusting lines and a chorus that millions can sing together. "My Generation" feeds forever on the stuttered "cold" and the oft-quoted line about hoping to die before getting old.

As Pete Townshend has grown older, he has had the line thrown back in his face many times—but maybe "My Generation" has nothing to do with aging. Maybe it's more about dying, growing gravely cold. I hope I die before I'm dying. At that moment in 1983, we and our dancers felt forever young, and the dean looked like an old and cold and dying man. Maybe even dead. At the very least, he was unable to generate anything more than the sale of his institution, Bethel College.

As he left the stage, stood below, and waited to see what would happen next, I did something that I'd never done before and haven't done since. I grabbed one of my drum mikes and, with all of the drama and disdain of my undying inner-teen, I introduced the song.

"We were going to send this next song out to Ronald Reagan, but now we've got someone else who we'd like to dedicate it to." I looked straight at the dean, put the mike back in the holder, sat back, nodded to Jerry and Steve, and clicked **ONE TWO THREE *FOUR***.

As Jerry stepped on his distortion pedal, gnashed out the two big power chords, and shout-stuttered his way through the song with unbridled passion and conviction, I felt proud to be pounding out the beat for that missionary kid in his bell bottoms and bare feet, singing against hard-souled deans who knew not how to dance. I felt proud and grateful that we wound up in the same college, in the same trashy rock band, on the same stage playing "My Generation" and believing, on that sunny May afternoon, that it actually meant something.

The afternoon's stirring sense of importance pretty much faded away after we finished "My Generation," our statement of solidarity with the dancers, the only protest anthem that we knew. I looked at the set list posted on my bass drum and was disheartened to see mostly Little Richard, Buddy Holly, Chuck Berry, and early-Beatles tunes sung by Steve, our Paul McCartney. Don't get me wrong: I love these lighthearted, exhilarating party songs, and Steve had a great feel for them. But they were songs meant to be danced to, and there was to be no more dancing.

The once-aroused dancers looked limp and lethargic, dry and cooling, too weary to will a second wave of dance protest. As the bored and hungry lookers-on left to eat coffee shop hamburgers and french fries, as the depression that follows euphoria lulled the dancers into sleepy introspection, as the late-afternoon sun wore down, as we coasted through our final set, I kept hoping that one or two zealous souls would lead the weary ones onto the path of heightened confrontation. It didn't happen. No one danced again that afternoon.

But no one forgot.

And the image of the dancing circle remains. The two will dance in the center for twelve bars of rhythm, dance back into the unbroken circle, as two more prepare to take their place. Applause and whoops will greet each dancer who decides to publicly testify in the circle's center—each dancer who walks proudly to the altar and proclaims before the whole school watching: "I am a dancer in the place where there is no dancing."

One Good Day, One Good Place

It was a snow day in November 1983 or January 1984. Sometime around then. A blizzard the night before left us with over a foot of snow, dangerous road conditions. Schools were canceled, work was canceled, everything was canceled.

Day of mercy. Day of grace. Everything is canceled.

Eight relatively like-minded Bethel college women lived about a mile from the Oakland House guys in three different houses on Harriet Avenue in the Whittier neighborhood. Together, we formed the Oakland-Harriet-Bethel-Peace-and-Justice-Committee axis. We hung out a lot together.

It was a lot easier to gather impromptu back then. The guys on Oakland Avenue would get bored on a Friday night and call the women at the Harriet houses. The women at the Harriet houses would get bored on Saturday night and call the Oakland boys.

"We're going to have a party tonight. Spread the word."

Fifteen, twenty, thirty people would show up and dance. More people danced—danced hard—at those parties than at any I've been to since.

And on that snow day, the Harriet women called the Oakland guys in the morning and invited us over for a pancake breakfast. They asked us to bring music and, on our way there, stop at the SuperAmerica for bacon, milk, and juice. We dressed without showering, gathered our favorite records and tapes, bundled up, and trudged together through the calf-deep snow to spend a day in exile with the friends we loved.

One of the guys said, "When we stop at the SuperAmerica for the rest of the stuff, let's buy chocolate marshmallow ice cream and angel food cake. We'll pull the cake and ice cream out of the bag like that's what we thought they wanted us to buy." So we bought ice cream and bacon and coffee and orange juice and cigarettes and angel food cake, and asked the cashier to put the ice cream and cake in a separate bag.

It was a snow day: if we wanted to pour maple syrup on angel food cake and eat it with a serving spoon, we would.

We pushed cars out of the snow without grumbling, because we weren't in a hurry.

When we got to the park, across from the Art Institute, we made angels in the snow. We had nothing to prove, nothing to lose, nothing to be. Just guys in their twenties making angels in the snow.

When we walked into the kitchen where the pancakes sizzled, one guy pulled the angel food cake and ice cream out of the bag, and said, "See, we remembered!"

The women couldn't stop laughing, as if they'd wanted all along to invite us to a birthday party, and a snow day pancake breakfast was just a good excuse to have one.

One woman stood on a chair and found the paper plates on the top shelf, another opened the junk drawer and found the candles. Who did we sing "Happy Birthday" to? Who blew out the candles? Who was the surprise party for?

In the worthiest of all possible manners, we ate cake and ice cream, then we finished making breakfast.

I remember a big kitchen table at which we all sat. It was a long, rectangular kitchen table with wood four inches thick, like a cutting board for a butcher or a baker. All of us were seated at the table, we all fit there—all ten, twelve, fifteen, twenty of us.

Was there ever such a table? Was it really thick like a cutting board or made of plywood, cardboard, particle-board? Was it just a flimsy, fold-up church basement potluck table?

The pancakes kept coming for hours. Ashtrays filled and no one emptied them. Everyone smoked back then. Even the people who didn't smoke smoked. Coffee coffee coffee that somebody must have got up to make. Coffee and hippie music: Van Morrison, Bob Dylan, Bob Marley, U2, Rita Marley, Bruce Cockburn, Cris Williamson, Joni Mitchell, Janis Joplin, Creedence Clearwater Revival ... Hippie music all morning, and all good.

Then one woman said, "I just had this vision in my mind. We were all twenty years older living on a farm together. All of us. No one was married. No one ever wanted to get married because our friendship to this group of friends was too important to break up by any one person leaving or any two of us coupling. We were just one big, happy community."

"That would be so cool," a bunch of people agreed. "Building log cabins, living off the land, just caring for each other."

I remember thinking, "That would be cool. But what if two people fell in love? And would there be sex? If there was sex, would it be on the sly? Would sex with another community member be considered incest? Or would it be shared and natural, just what everyone did together? What if someone who no one liked wanted to be in the community? And what does it mean that I have a huge crush on the woman who had the vision of the community?"

Someone looked at the clock and said, "Oh my God! It's past three o'clock already! How did it get to be past three o'clock?"

By then, we'd all had too many pancakes. That last dozen or so just sat in the middle of the table on a big plate until the next morning.

The Gathering

Mom and Dad told me in the spring of 1998 that Carol and Ron had gotten worse and either of them could die at any time. I didn't and I still don't know what to do with how death came upon them, two people who had been together for nearly forty years, two people who'd formed a partnership in life and in ministry, two people dying of cancer at the same time. I wrote them a farewell card, something that I've never done before and something that I hope I'll never have to do again. The card said, more or less, "I know you are dying, you've meant more to me than you can possibly imagine, you've influenced who I've become more than you can possibly imagine, I love you dearly, I will always love you, good-bye."

It was a strange note to write for a few reasons. I'd never told them in writing or in person how much they meant to me (as people, as artists, as musicians), I didn't know what to say in the face of death (as no one ever does), and I didn't know for certain that they would be dying soon. A miracle might have happened, something that I couldn't imagine or entirely dismiss. They both might have lived for another thirty years and there would be this note from me that said, "You're dying, I love you, good-bye." Would the note be perceived as presumptuous? Would it become a part of the dying? Would it make dying soon more likely? I shuddered as I dropped it in the mail.

Carol died that June, and Ron thanked me for the card at the memorial gathering held for her at Central Baptist Church. I don't remember much about the service itself other than a beautiful slide show of Carol's life, put together by her eldest son, David. My father gave the main message, and I remember overhearing a man say, "Good old John."

"Yes, good old Dad," I said to myself as he said good-bye to Carol for all of the gathered. I wish I remember what he said. I can still picture his graceful gesturing, his lovingly arched eyebrows that invited all present into the terrifying beauty of the life transported from our here and now into the eternal gathering.

Sometimes I believe in that eternal gathering place. Other times I believe that I'll never come closer than memory.

One evening, in my sophomore year at Cal Poly State University in San Luis Obispo (my one college year away from Bethel), a neighbor stopped my three roommates and me as we walked back to our apartment. He looked into my eyes, said that he recognized me from somewhere. Then he remembered where.

"I know you," he said to me. "We did time together. Paso Robles prison, man. Yeah, that's where—Paso Robles prison. How you doing, man?"

I didn't recognize him, and I told him that I didn't. I told him that I had never done time in Paso Robles prison, or for that matter, any prison.

He insisted: "Oh c'mon. I know you. I recognize your face. You can't fool me. We did time together. Paso Robles prison. I've been thinking about you. How you doing, man?"

"No. It wasn't me. I've never done time in Paso Robles prison."

"Don't tell me that. It was you. I know that face. I never forget a face. We did time together. Paso Robles prison, man. Don't you remember? Oh yeah, I remember you."

"No, I've never done time in Paso Robles prison," I said one more time. I wasn't the man who he remembered.

"Oh man," he said, disappointed. "You can say it. You don't have to hide it. It's okay, man. Paso Robles prison."

My roommates were trying hard not to laugh. It became a running joke for the year, a tension breaker if one of us was upset: "I know you. We did time together. Paso Robles prison, man."

One odd thing about this was that I *had* been in Paso Robles prison for an afternoon, two years before this man stopped me. But I didn't tell him that. If he did see my face in Paso Robles prison, I didn't want him to know why and how and when. I didn't want him to mark me as the man he knew and remembered from Paso Robles prison.

The Sure Foundation stopped at Paso Robles prison on the trip from La Crescenta to Fresno, from Southern California to Northern California, in that 1978 summer when Marshall, Marna, and I joined the Central Baptist choir for a leg of their California tour. We'd been living in California for a year, and it was another one of those past-meets-present moments: my new California friends got to meet my Minnesota friends and my Minnesota friends got to meet my California friends. One of those things that looks better in anticipation and sounds meaningful in past reflection but is almost always disappointing when it happens. The past remains the past, the present remains the present, the old friends remain old friends, the new friends remain new friends, and nobody is any better or worse for the wear.

Not that it was a bad week. We had a fun time, it felt like a reunion, and I believed that it was a time of spiritual growth and renewal for me. I still thought like that back then. In fact, that summer before my senior year of high school, that summer of the camp-inspired plan to lead my whole high school to Jesus, found me in my most hyperevangelical frame of mind. I was in it deeper than ever, and I was convinced that I was in for life, and then eternity.

In the middle of that week, we found ourselves singing within the walls of California State Prison in Paso Robles. It was the first and only time that I have ever been inside a state prison, a place where men were doing serious time for serious crimes. I remember eating lunch in the prison cafeteria. Hot dogs and beans, food that you couldn't get right or wrong, food that would be how you expected it to be anywhere you went. Everything was what I'd expected of a prison cafeteria: long steel tables and chairs bolted to the floor, aluminum cups and plates. Everything looked metallic.

After lunch we went to a big room that reminded me of a small high school theater, a theater that seated about five hundred prisoners. We stood on the stage, on risers, and the prisoners sat below us on velvet-cushioned chairs. We were performing a musical titled *The Gathering* by a popular Christian composer named Ken Medema. It was a weekday afternoon, and the room was packed.

I remember how conscious I felt of singing for prisoners in a theater inside a prison. I noticed everything differently, and nothing seemed obvious. We were the choir and they were the audience and this was a place. This was a different place than a church and this was an audience of prisoners, not a congregation, and that changed the words of the songs we were singing. That changed what it meant to sing passionately as a choir, together, thinking about the words that we were singing. That changed Carol Eckert's arpeggios, and that changed drummer Dan's beats and fills, and that changed the guitarist's strums, and that changed Ron Eckert's red face and arms shaping the waves of us, the choir, and that changed who we all became on that stage on that day in that place.

Only the prison itself accounted for this audience, these prisoners, in that theater, seated and watching us. Who were they and why were they there? Maybe it didn't matter so much what we were doing or singing about: we were other humans to watch in a theater. We were humans of the world who'd decided to visit their world, and they came to wonder why. Why would we visit their world?

I don't remember any individuals, any faces. I don't even remember if they were mostly black or mostly white or mostly Latino or mostly young or mostly old. Who were they and why were they there? Some may have been believers who'd stumbled, backslid, fallen and fallen until they found themselves in that place, watching us. Some may have been newly converted cons who for the very first time muttered the sinner's prayer printed on the back of the *Four Spiritual Laws* pamphlet found on the floor of the cell that week. Some knew that there would be girls, young teenage girls, and it didn't matter what they were singing about: the girls would be on the stage and in full view. Some knew that there would be boys. Some came for the drums, bass, and guitar, for live music, because they knew that it was probably the closest they'd come to hearing and seeing a rock show that particular week or month or year. Some were there to scoff, for material to parody later around the dinner table. Some were there because it was, simply, a place to be, a place where people would become a gathering—a gathering that would, for an hour, feel different, maybe even better, than the lonely cell.

Maybe, just maybe, the man from San Luis Obispo saw me on that stage and remembered me later as a prisoner.

Ron and Carol lived for the gathering, for that which refuses to be alone. The groove inside that longs for the groove outside. Ron and Carol brought songs they loved into that place, Paso Robles Prison, and they knew how the songs would change when they entered that place. They knew how music shapes worship. They knew that music enters a room more fully and completely than anything else, that it fills a room differently every time, and that every person in the gathering changes the shape of the music. That is what Ron and Carol lived.

Ron whispered to us before each song, "Think about what you are singing. Think about the words. Concentrate. Remember who you are singing to today. Remember who you are singing to today."

As Ron whispered, Carol nodded behind the piano: "Listen. Listen. Listen to us all. Listen to the melody and harmony that I am rolling out for you." Ron had the whispers and the arm motions and the mouthed words and the red face and the waves of us to shape—but Carol had the melody. Carol was playing the shape of the song. Carol knew the song as it existed apart from the words: she knew what the melody meant.

In the gathering, people and songs come together in one place. The people become different people and the place becomes a different place and the songs become different songs. Ron and Carol knew this. They called it the working of the Holy Spirit. What do I call it? The Groove?

After Carol Eckert's June 1998 memorial service at Central Baptist, I was looking all around the orange-carpeted narthex for Marna and Jim. They were giving me a ride home, and I was ready to go.

For the first time since the wedding of Doug Eckert in the late eighties, all five of us Andersons were at Central together. Our return seemed like a much bigger deal to the Central members than it was to any of us. We came only to remember Carol, but the postservice reception felt like an impromptu reunion.

I felt very strange as people surrounded me, wanting to shake my hand and give me a big hug, and said things like, "You probably don't remember me—I was only seven years old when your family left Central. But I just want to meet you again and tell you how good it is to see you all here tonight."

So I was looking again for Marna. I'd seen her earlier, in the midst of the postservice greeting, and she whispered, "This is really weird, isn't it? I want to get out of here really soon."

"I'm ready when you are," I said.

But every time she said, "Okay now—let's go! Let's go!" someone else would corner me, I'd feel obliged, and another five minutes would pass. I could tell that she was getting annoyed. This time, though, I was searching for her, worried that maybe she and Jim decided to leave me there with the throng.

I found Marna in the coatroom, behind the narthex, talking to a white-haired man and woman.

"Look who is here," she said to me. "Remember Wally Johnson?"

"Of course," I said to Marna, to Wally, to Wally's second wife, Vi. His first wife, Alice, died fifteen years earlier.

"Wally was," Marna said, "the best Sunday school teacher ever, wasn't he?"

"Absolutely," I agreed. "You were the best Sunday school teacher any of us ever had."

Wally grinned and turned red in the face. Vi smiled, squeezed his hand, and looked him in the eyes.

After a few minutes of small talk and catching up, I decided to mention Wally's bike ride.

"I think I saw you riding your bike one day," I said. "I thought it was you."

No, I knew it was him.

"It was a couple of years ago," I went on, "when I used to live on Lafond."

"Where on Lafond do you live?" Wally asked.

"1639 Lafond," I said. "I don't live there anymore, though."

"1639? Oh, you're right down the street. We live on 1612 Lafond."

This startled me a lot more than it startled him. In fact, he seemed rather unimpressed. Two people living down the street from each other. No big deal. But I kept thinking, "I lived down the street from Wally Johnson all that time without even knowing it. I could have used Wally Johnson in my life back then." Not that he would have made any difference. Not that he could have kept me in that life. And when I did see him that one time, I let him ride by and didn't say a word.

"He can't ride his bike anymore," Vi said. "It was stolen. About a year ago."

Well, couldn't he buy another?

I kept the question to myself. When you get to a certain age, I suppose, things get lost or stolen and instead of replacing them, you give them up.

Ron Eckert died in June 1999, a little over a year after Carol died, and Central Baptist held a memorial service in August. People called it a blessing when Ron died. That's what people like to say about those who have been dying for a long time: it was a blessing when he or she went. People will say that they are together now, Ron and Carol—"together with the Lord." I want to believe that, but I don't know how or what to think about death anymore.

When I called myself a Christian, I had ways of thinking and speaking about death. I had a place for it. Jesus Christ died on the cross for our sins so that, after death, we could live eternally in Heaven instead of Hell. What strikes me most now is the weight of the fear of not living eternally that lies behind it all. Death becomes the thing most feared; all of life becomes preparation for avoiding it. My ways of thinking about death were really ways of denying it. Death was at the center of everything, it was the thing to live for, the thing to avoid above all else, but nobody ever tried to understand what death was.

Some will say it is a blessing. Some will say they are together with the Lord now. I do believe that Ron and Carol are together somewhere, but they died much too young. That is not a blessing.

I have a hard time concentrating at memorial services, because no matter how much is said it is not enough, and no matter what is said it is always a little bit wrong. Or a lot wrong.

One moment at Ron's service stood out, though. The choir sang a song that I remembered from way way back: "My God, I Love Thee." It's a song that Ron used to lead the choir through in the Central Baptist glory years: 1975, 1976, 1977. The song brought me into that timeless time that only music can bring me into—back to long-ago

Sundays, when I sat reverently in the sanctuary and believed every word that the choir sang. The song had remained all of those years, and something of me remained and still remains in the song, though I no longer remain in that life.

The voices sang these words written in Latin in the seventeenth century, translated into English in the nineteenth century: "My God, I love thee, not because I hope for Heaven thereby, nor yet because who love thee not are lost eternally."

I heard the words that night. They said something I don't remember hearing often enough as I was growing up in the church: God is worthy of love because God is God. Eternal love exists eternally and is not merely a reward for belief. It does not exist to gain Heaven or to avoid Hell. Eternal love exists, and it cannot be won or lost. When I believe, I believe that.

I know that such divine love is not always sustainable or even possible in this human realm of human hearts that place conditions on love. Even the love expressed in "My God, I Love Thee" has its conditions: "Thou, O my Jesus, thou didst me / upon the cross embrace; / For me thou didst bear the nails and spear / And manifold disgrace / And griefs and torments numberless, / And sweat of agony; / E'en death itself; and all for one / who was thine enemy." Would the writer of these words love Jesus Christ if Jesus hadn't born "the nails and spear / and manifold disgrace" to pay for the sins of humanity?

No small problem: the cross. What do I do with it?

Cross or no cross, the next verses moved me to tears when the choir sang them that night: "Then why, O blessed Jesu Christ, / should I not love thee well, / not for the sake of winning Heaven, / or of escaping Hell; / not with the hope of gaining aught / nor seeking a reward; / but as thyself hast loved me / O ever-loving Lord!" There's so much humility and love in those words. They make me think of Ron Eckert's pride, Ron's red-faced intensity that would feel affronted by a choir that sang words without meaning them, without thinking about them, without feeling them deep in their heart of hearts. The paradox of the demanding director: he wants so much for the words to be sung out of sheer devotion and praise and humility and all to the glory of the Lord, that anything less than excellence will not suffice.

That's where I imagine Carol flowing in to remind Ron that the reward does not need to be fought for and the punishment does not need to be feared. That love exists eternally. That's how Carol flowed: at peace with herself, as though she didn't fear ever losing love.

The choir sounded like Carol and Ron's choir: not a voice out of place, not a voice louder than any other voice, not a voice sounding alone in the crowd, not a voice going solo, but one voice together, as though Ron and Carol's love would always live in that song. And I felt old love of mine, love I'd known from the years when I still believed in that eternal love.

I wonder where all of that love goes. Where will it all go?

After the service I milled about in the narthex, saying hello to those who said hello to me and hugging those who hugged me. I didn't feel as strange as last time. This time I was prepared. I even looked forward to seeing many of them again. It was weird to think that some of those people had prayed for me, maybe even loved me, all of those years. Twenty-two years since we left Central Baptist, I still met eyes that recognized mine.

I thought I'd run into Wally Johnson again. I found him sitting down in the narthex, eating cake and peanuts, drinking coffee. I sat down next to him and asked if he remembered me, Mark Anderson, John Anderson's son.

"John Anderson? You're John Anderson's boy. I don't think I'll ever forget John Anderson. John Anderson will never be forgotten here."

He didn't remember me. I told Wally that he was my sixth-grade Sunday school teacher, that he was a great Sunday school teacher, the best I ever had. He smiled, blushed.

"The kids you never forget. I always love to see the kids. Yessir, the kids still come back to see me."

His responses were impersonal, not directly to me or the immediate situation, as if he was speaking to another presence who was making sense of it all. This was his running commentary on how things are. The kids you don't forget, the kids don't forget you. A lot has been forgotten, more will be forgotten, but the kids you don't forget and the kids don't forget you. If nothing else, you will remember that you taught Sunday school, and the kids who made it good to be alive will keep returning.

I asked him how he was doing.

"I'm walking with a cane now, but I'm pretty good. I'm not bad. My second wife, Vi, died this year. She was ninety. Well, that's been hard. I'm living alone now. I miss her. But she's with the Lord now."

He'd spent a few weeks, he said, in the hospital and just got out last week. One very hot July night he went to bed, forgot to turn on the air conditioner, and didn't wake up until one-thirty the next afternoon. His son found him there dehydrating, woke him up, and rushed him to the hospital.

"Then at the hospital I caught pneumonia, so I had to stay there a few weeks to get better. I'm feeling much better now. I'm glad that I could be at the service tonight. It sure is sad about Ron. And about Carol too, of course."

"It is really sad," I said.

"But," Wally added, "they are together with the Lord now."

I didn't know what to say to that. I couldn't have said it at that moment, but I was glad that Wally did.

Then came the awkward moment in our conversation, the moment when we had nothing more to say about death, but it felt irreverent to segue back into talk of life. I opted for a place in between life and death: memory. I wanted to play "remember when?"

"Remember when you used to take us ice skating at Aldrich Arena?"

"You remember skating at Aldrich Arena? Oh yes, I used to take my Sunday school kids skating at Aldrich Arena."

"You and Alice used to go there every week, didn't you?"

"We sure did. We sure did. Alice and I. Alice, you know, died fifteen years ago."

"Yes. I heard that."

Again, talk of death stopped the conversation for a moment.

"I remember," I said, "you taking us all into your grocery store after we went ice skating."

"Remember what I used to do when I brought my kids in the grocery store?" He smiled.

"You used to give us brown bags and let us fill them up with whatever we wanted."

He nodded and giggled nervously. I remembered his gracious gift.

"Oh, the kids," Wally said, "used to love that. Not all of the parents loved it when they came home with all of that candy and pop, but the kids never forgot it."

"I sure didn't forget it. I hope I remembered to thank you. If I didn't, thank you. That was very generous of you."

"Well, it didn't cost me much. When you own a grocery store, you get everything wholesale."

I looked up and saw the Eckert boys and the lines of people waiting to greet, hug, and express sympathy. As much as I wanted to remain there talking to Wally, I wanted spend more time with the old friends I hadn't seen since their mother's memorial service.

"It's been great talking to you, Wally," I said. "It's been very nice. But I need to talk to the Eckert boys before I go."

"So you're going now. Okay. Well, it sure has been good talking to you," Wally said. "Yes. It's always good to see the kids. You never forget the kids."

He was talking again to his confidant. The kids return and the kids you don't forget.

We shook hands and said good-bye.

As I walked by Wally fifteen minutes later, I saw a guy about my age sitting and talking to him. One of the Thomas boys, I thought, but I'd forgotten his first name. I'd seen that Thomas boy at both of the Central Baptist memorial services, and I was pretty sure he'd remained at Central Baptist for all of those twenty-two years since we'd moved to California. He never left, and so he didn't have to return. He wasn't reuniting with Wally: their conversation was ongoing.

Some of the kids leave, some return; some of the kids remain.

polyrhythms
an epilogue in five parts

Abundant Life

I found a second copy of *Jesus Sound Explosion* a few years ago in the used vinyl section of Cheapo Records, a place I visit nearly every day. This copy of the record was in better shape than the last. I never realized until then that it was a mail-order-only item, and this one was addressed to Mr. and Mrs. William Elftman. I probably shouldn't give their address to you, but I'm thinking I should drive by the south Minneapolis house sometime soon.

This copy of *Jesus Sound Explosion* even has the original inner sleeve. On one side, the sleeve says "The Medium Is Music for the 70s" (true) and advertises albums by The Great Commission Company, Born Yesterday, The Forerunners, The New Folk, and The Armageddon Experience. Printed on the other side of the sleeve is an LP-sized copy of *The Four Spiritual Laws.* I no longer believe Laws Two, Three, and Four, but if the record *Jesus Sound Explosion* is ever reissued, "The Medium Is Music" could be included as Law Five. Or it could be an addendum to Law One, the one about God's love and "wonderful plan" for my life. It complements the verse included to explain God's plan, John 10:10, "I came that they might have life and might have it abundantly."

On my best days, even on my better days, my life feels abundant. There are other days when I wish I could see and fully know the wonderful plan. But what would I do with that anyway?

More Returns

I meant to tell you about Paris, but I couldn't see a way to include the story. I saw Stephanie again, over twenty years ago, in Paris. After running away in 1976 and spending a year or so in a drugged-out haze, she returned home, finished high school, and enrolled in St. Catherine, a Catholic-affiliated liberal arts college for women in St. Paul. She called me, or maybe she wrote—I can't remember exactly—in California the summer before I was heading for a Bethel-sponsored England study tour in 1981. At the time, she was heading to Paris for the year, but I don't remember why. Let's just say she was going to study language at Sorbonne.

My Bethel College England tour included a week in Paris, and when Stephanie and I realized that we'd be there at the same time, we knew we had to meet again. In Paris, we spent a few friendly, platonic days together, but the tension of potential romance hung in the air until, finally, at the very end, just before I boarded Le Metro, we kissed once on the lips. That's the last I saw of her. A year or so later, I received a letter from her that said she'd met and married a man from France, they were having a baby, and they were living in Virginia or Maryland or maybe one of the Carolinas—or one of the original thirteen colonies.

Now that we've got the U.S.A. road atlas on the table, I want to direct your attention to St. Paul, Minnesota, where my parents returned in August 2000, after Dad retired from his church in St. Louis. Dad and Mom left California in 1985, came back to St. Paul from 1985 to 1990, the years Dad served as executive minister of the Minnesota Baptist Conference, and then Dad became, in 1990, the pastor of Third Baptist Church in St. Louis.

While we're in St. Louis with Mom and Dad, I need to mention that our old friend, Bubba, became the pastor of an African Methodist Episcopal (A.M.E.) church there in 1995. Dad and Bubba served on boards and committees together and reinitiated their friendship in a big city where they both seemed to belong. I saw Bubba in St. Louis at my mother's sixtieth birthday party, where he performed the song that Mom requested, his signature, "The Rock." I saw Bubba again in 1998 when he was the keynote preacher at a Minneapolis interfaith celebration of Martin Luther King's birthday.

We should probably stop by and say hi to Marna and Marshall in Minneapolis, who, with their spouses, Jim and Betty, bought houses less than three blocks from each other. Marna does fundraising for The Nature Conservancy, Jim is a Spanish interpreter at Hennepin County Medical Center, and they have a two-year-old daughter, Evelyn Rose. Marshall teaches kindergarten at Friends School in St. Paul, Betty is a nurse; Betty has a nineteen-year-old daughter named Ashly, and Marshall and Betty have a five-year-old son, Arlen Cloud, who is a kindergartner in Marshall's class.

I also need to mention that, a year after he retired, Dad took a job as part-time associate minister at, yes, Central Baptist Church in St. Paul. Mom runs an after-school neighborhood tutor program there, and they're as busy as ever in their semiretirement.

And me? I teach writing to college freshkids, live in St. Paul, buy too many records, and drum on most Sunday evenings in a band that plays at St. Paul's House of Mercy church and, now and then, gigs at local clubs such as Lee's Liquor Lounge and The Turf Club. No, the House of Mercy Band isn't one of those annoying Christian rock bands that sing backbeat-driven Jesus jingles to transmit the old message of shame, guilt, and End Times. We play country-gospel, in the tradition of The Louvin Brothers, The Carter Family, Johnny Cash, and Hank Williams, as well as countrified punk covers such as "I'm So Bored with the U.S.A." The local weekly, *City Pages,* named House of Mercy "Best Church for the Non-churchgoing" in its 2000 *Best of the Twin Cities* issue. It is a church that emphasizes grace, mercy, social justice, and the mystery of faith, not certainty of belief and theological correctness. I met my wonderful fiancée, a painter named Patricia, at House of Mercy.

The Electric Fetus has been a constant in my adulthood, though I've left and returned many times. I started in 1984, quit in '86, returned a few months later, stayed until '88, returned again in '89, left in '90, returned in '94, and stayed until '99. The Fetus has remained a source of stability for the past eighteen years: as I've moved from apartment to apartment to apartment to house to apartment to apartment; as Mom and Dad have moved from La Crescenta to St. Paul to St. Louis and then back to St. Paul; as I've married, divorced, fallen in love, broken up, fallen in love, gotten engaged again. From The Replacements and Hüsker Dü to John Coltrane and Sun Ra, and back to The Replacements and Hüsker Dü ... I'm thinking now of the song "To Sir with Love." I suppose the Electric Fetus has been a sort of "Sir" in my life, the music teacher that helped me find the world that I've most wanted to be in and of. The rendition of "To Sir" that I'm playing in my head is the one by Al Green. Yes, I love Lulu's original—who doesn't?—but Reverend Green's is the one that I've returned to more often, mainly because it ends the first side of his wonderful album *Truth N' Time*.

This might be presumptuous, but I like to think that I can always go back to the Fetus. Maybe it'll be my postretirement job.

Smiley's Clinic

There's an odd Electric Fetus–*Jesus Sound Explosion*–related incident I need to tell you about. I was working there at the beginning of a major depression, and on that fall afternoon I was having what I can now call a panic attack, but what I knew then as "Oh my God, I'm dying!" I can't explain why I thought that. I remember a dizziness, a feverishness, a lightheadedness, and a deep sadness, but nothing that added up to dying. I told my boss that I was feeling sick and needed to see a doctor right away, and he said, "Go!"

So I hopped into the red Toyota and drove east on Franklin Avenue to where I remembered seeing Smiley's Clinic. I was convinced that I was dying and that I wasn't going to make it there in time. If only I could make it there, I'd get another chance.

"Not yet not yet not yet not yet not yet ..." I kept screaming to God or Death or Whoever or Whatever was riding with me.

When I arrived at Smiley's sweating, breathing hard, the receptionist asked me what was wrong. I told her that it was serious, that

I wasn't sure why, but I thought I was dying. She gave me the forms to fill out, told me to wait right there until my name was called.

"Mark Anderson," a nurse called minutes later. She led me to a doctor's office, did the routine checks, and told me to wait right there.

As I sat there waiting, I looked around me, thought about where I was, thought about where I used to be, thought about the location of Smiley's Clinic and how well I knew that neighborhood: Franklin Avenue, Seward Co-op, Tracy's Saloon, Big Olaf's, Norwest Bank, Zipp's Liquors, the Goodwill Store. Wait. Where was the Goodwill Store, the place where I found that first copy of *Jesus Sound Explosion*? It was no longer there. Then I made the connection: it was this building where I was waiting for the doctor to arrive. When they remodeled the Goodwill it became Smiley's Clinic.

That's How I Got to Memphis

The depression of 1999 was the worst I've ever been through. It sometimes seems like I picked up where Marshall left off, around the years of his last big depression in the early nineties. I certainly don't mean to imply that my depressions are his fault, or that he's gotten over depression completely. Just that I am the Prozac-taker now, not Marshall, and the prescriptions started on that afternoon at Smiley's.

The holiday season was looking long and joyless. Instead of relishing the month that I'd be off from the teaching job I'd taken at the University of Minnesota's General College, I was dreading all of the empty hours ahead. I left The Fetus again at the beginning of the school year, and I thought about calling retail manager Bob to see if he'd take me back for the Christmas season.

I decided instead to go to St. Louis. I'd spent a lot of time talking to my parents on the phone about the depression. They were concerned and supportive and sympathetic and scared—and they didn't want me to be alone on Christmas Day. A few days before I flew there, they called with an idea, something they'd been talking about. What if we drove to Memphis? What did I think of that? We could walk Beale Street, visit Graceland, maybe even stop by Reverend Al Green's Full Gospel Tabernacle. Would I like that?

How times change. My parents were suggesting a trip down to the jazzy music mecca—a pilgrimage to the holy city where, they thought, I might just be healed. They didn't put it that way, but I wanted to believe that it occurred to them.

"You want to drive me to Memphis? Yeah, let's go," I said.

My depression was becoming my license to be indulged. On Thanksgiving Day, up at their cabin near Duluth, I'd confessed to them that I'd been smoking a lot. I'd always kept that hidden from them. I anticipated mild chastisement, expressions of disappointment, but they said that my smoking was the least of their concerns. They told me to go ahead and light up if it made me feel better, so I stepped outside for a smoke.

I could lie and say that we had, on the way to Memphis, some great highway conversations about life and love and rock and roll, but the truth is that I hardly said a word. I couldn't make conversation. I could respond briefly and succinctly to questions, but I couldn't sustain a topic. If I talked too much, I started to cry.

"Why were you so depressed?" friends have asked.

Circumstances: breakups that reminded me of the divorce, the divorce that reminded me of the breakups, stress from a new job, isolation, transition, et cetera. Chemical imbalances. Loss of faith in everything. I didn't know what my life was, I couldn't see any signs of hope around the corner, and it all seemed so long and lonely. I wanted to believe, but I couldn't. Why that depression came is as much a mystery to me as how it left.

I kept apologizing to Dad and Mom: "I'm sorry I'm such a drag to be around. I'm sorry I'm not much of a conversationalist."

"That's fine, Mark," they said. "You don't have to apologize. You don't have to say anything. We're glad just to be with you."

"Maybe you can pick out some good tapes for us to listen to," Mom said. "We can just listen to music on the way to Memphis."

That's how I'd pay my way to Memphis: I'd choose the music.

Over the years, I've given my parents a lot of tapes filled with my favorite music. I've taken it upon myself to expose them to some of the music that they missed in their striving to please the Gladys Snows. They might have listened to more of that jazzy music if they'd known a different cultural reality. I picked out the Simon and Garfunkel "Greatest Hits" tape that I gave to them for Christmas three years earlier. They would have listened to Simon and Garfunkel if they hadn't spent the sixties in Baptist churches.

A few songs into Simon and Garfunkel and I'd had enough.

"I'm sorry," I said. "Can we change the tape? This is making me too sad."

I wanted something more upbeat and soulful, so I put on an Al Green gospel tape that I made for them.

"Al Green," Dad said. "Good choice."

Years earlier, in 1985, I took Mom and Dad to see the documentary *The Gospel According to Al Green.* It was really important to me at the time, but it's hard to explain why. Or maybe I'm embarrassed by my motive: I wanted them to love some of the music that I loved so that they'd understand me better. So that they'd understand why I bought so many records, went to so many shows, played in bands, and worked at a record store with a name that they didn't like to repeat to church people. Al Green moved from the secular realm to the sacred realm, from pop star to gospel star, so I thought he'd be a good bridge between my world and theirs.

"See! This is what I love about music, this is what moves me," I wanted to say as my favorite singer lit up that arty little theater. The movie really climaxes—and I mean that in a sexual and spiritual sense—with Reverend Green singing, preaching, dancing, and dripping with sweat in his Memphis church.

When Mom, Dad, and I went out for dessert afterwards, I wanted to talk about the music, but they wanted to talk more about his dramatic conversion, his moving testimony of faith—grits and all. Sure, they talked about his music too, but it was the whole sin-to-salvation arc of the story that made a greater impression on them. I realized later that I was trying to convert them to my music, and they were hoping that Reverend Green would re-convert me to their Christian faith. I wanted to say, "See! Here is what I love!" I sensed that they wanted to say, "See! This is what faith in Jesus is all about: mercy, forgiveness, grace, redemption. Admit it: you still believe. Your faith is still there. It still moves you like before. Just reach out and take it!"

On the way to Memphis I needed to hear soulful songs of faith. I wanted to hear Al Green sing "Jesus Is Waiting"—even though I didn't believe. Maybe that was what the depression was about: wanting so much to believe, but knowing that that was impossible.

We arrived in Memphis and didn't know where to go, so we stopped at a visitor information building. Dad found a Graceland brochure.

"It looks like we still have time to catch a tour of Graceland," he said. "It's closed tomorrow." It was three o'clock and the last tour began at four. "Want to go to Graceland, Mark?"

I said sure.

"You have to go," Dad said, "to Graceland if you're in Memphis, don't you?"

He was asking me. He didn't want to assume. Did you have to go to Graceland if you were in Memphis?

"Pretty much," I said. "I don't know if it's a law, but it is strongly advised."

Dad laughed harder than he might have if I wasn't depressed. It had been a long time since I'd tried using humor.

We got on the freeway again and—because there was so much construction going on and the freeway wasn't clearly marked—we missed the Graceland exit. We got off at the next exit, turned around, got off at the next exit, turned around, and we kept missing the Graceland exit. Dad started to get ornery, and Mom read aloud every freeway sign along the way. Graceland would be closing soon and we were so very close to it.

I started to worry that we wouldn't make it in time—and that would mean something in the weight of how things felt. That's how it had been with me for months: everything felt too weighted.

Everything meant far more than it should have. What would it mean if we kept missing the exit to Graceland and didn't make it there in time? What would happen after that?

"You'd think they'd make it easier," Mom said, "to get to Graceland from the freeway."

After about twenty minutes of circling, Dad got off the freeway, stopped at a gas station, and asked for directions.

We arrived at Graceland just in time for the final tour of the day.

A woman in a uniform handed us our tour guide, a walkman and headphones, as we boarded the bus that took us across Elvis Presley Boulevard and through the Graceland gates. The voice of Priscilla Presley told us where to look and where to turn and when to move on. There was no way to know if the voice on our tapes was anywhere near synchronized, so we wandered into room after room, smiling and nodding at each other now and then.

I'd describe the rooms for you, but I really don't remember much. I couldn't concentrate. I drifted through the living room, the dining room, the kitchen, the jungle room, the basement and bar, the office, the barn, and then the tour was almost done. I didn't expect to feel anything.

We wandered into a building out back with plaques and gold records and outfits worn and guns collected and picture after picture of Elvis at all stages in his life. The room was dark and there was a lot to look at. The artifacts were organized in chronological order, from Elvis's humble beginnings to his triumphant rise to his tragic end.

Mom, Dad, and I got separated in the crowd.

Somewhere near the '68 NBC Special paraphernalia, I turned around and saw Mom again.

"Are you enjoying the tour?" she asked.

"I am. There's too much to look at in here. I wish I was—in a state of mind to appreciate it more."

"Well, you can come back someday when you're feeling better."

She was right. I could. I'd eventually feel better, and Graceland would, more than likely, still be there.

"Where's Dad?" I asked.

"I don't know. He was taking a long time looking at everything and I got ahead of him. He's going slow. He's reading everything. I don't think he's in any hurry."

I looked behind and saw a crowd of people wandering around the corner that led to the tour's final stretch. There was Dad. He didn't see us. He had his headphones on and he was listening to every word. He stopped at every featured item, read all of the words on the plaques and artifacts, then moved on to the next item, as Priscilla's voice told him to. He was taking the tour very seriously, determined to get his money's worth.

"This is something else, isn't it?" he said when he saw us looking at him.

Mom and I nodded.

"He really did a lot, didn't he? He recorded and sold so many records—in so many different styles. And he was quite a performer. I didn't realize at the time what a great singer he was. He really could sing."

He'd missed something big. Dad knew now. So he listened intently to Priscilla, read all of the words on all of the plaques, read the captions under all of the photos. As if he wanted to live in that Elvis world for as long as possible, as if he wanted to remain in that dark hallway of awards and gold records and jeweled jumpers and karate chops, as if he was nearing the end of Elvis's life and wanted to postpone the tragedy, as if he'd only started getting to know the man. As if to say, "I had no idea. Forgive me."

My Favorite Things: When in Doubt, Play John Coltrane

I came back to Minneapolis, still depressed, in cold January 2000. I remember lying on my bed one day in deep despair, numb, not moving at all, convinced that I couldn't be moved, believing that I'd remain there on my bed, and I'd lose nearly everything: my job, money, health insurance, my apartment, my friends ... I'd have to sell all of my music and move back to St. Louis with Mom and Dad. When they moved back to St. Paul, I'd move on to the psych ward.

I'd loaded up the six CD player with Coltrane. *My Favorite Things* was playing. Even in the worst of my depression, John Coltrane sounded right. I sometimes had pathetic images of myself in the psych ward, while Coltrane, one of the handful of favorite things that I hadn't lost, played on a boom box. All of my friends and loved ones would be standing around the bed, crying, feeling sorry for me, telling me they loved me, saying things like, "The only thing he ever wants to do is listen to John Coltrane." When I died of heartbreak, they'd say at my funeral, "How he loved Coltrane."

John Coltrane, I've discovered, fits with however I'm feeling, whatever I'm going through. I usually play jazz when I write, and he's playing as I'm writing this.

As I was lying on my bed in utter despondence, I started drumming on my legs, moving only the muscles of my four limbs—muscle drumming soundlessly with my favorite jazz drummer, Elvin Jones.

The first thing that changed me: I started hearing the swirl of polyrhythms. The 6/8 circling around the 4/4 and the 4/4 blowing long lines through the 6/8 and all of the infinite combinations that lie in between. Before long, I realized that I couldn't drum lying down, so I got up, walked into the living room, and sat in my faded pink, dirty, threadbare writing chair. I tried my best to imitate Elvin as I drummed on my legs. This time, my body needed to move differently before my mind would follow. My left foot found the hi-hat backbeat, my right foot dropped the kick drum bombs, my right arm rode the dotted sixteenths, and my left hand found the snare accents between. That's how the polyrhythms found their way into my body.

Of course, if I was drumming on real drums, making noise, I would have been the usual sloppy and imprecise drum hack that I am. Still, drumming on my legs to Coltrane was making me feel better. Maybe that's a step beyond playing air guitar, maybe it's a step below, but oh well. I knew that I was going to make it back into the polyrhythm of my life as I found my way back into the polyrhythm of *My Favorite Things*.